Inside Terrorism

For you, D.

Inside Terrorism

Bruce Hoffman

Columbia University Press
New York

Columbia University Press

Publishers Since 1893
New York
Copyright © 1998 Bruce Hoffman
First published in Great Britain in 1998 by Victor Gollancz Ltd, London

Library of Congress Cataloging-in-Publication Data
Hoffman, Bruce, 1954–
 Inside terrorism / Bruce Hoffman.
  p. cm.
 Includes bibliographical references (p.   ) and index.
 ISBN 0–231–11468–0 (cloth : alk. paper) — ISBN 0–231–11469–9
 (pbk.)
 1. Terrorism. I. Title.

                                                        98–23789

Casebound editions of Columbia University Press books are printed on
permanent and durable acid-free paper.

Printed in the United States of America

c 10 9 8 7 6 5 4 3
p 10 9 8 7 6

Contents

Preface

I have been studying terrorists and terrorism for more than twenty years. Yet I am still always struck by how disturbingly 'normal' most terrorists seem when one actually sits down and talks to them. Rather than the wild-eyed fanatics or crazed killers that we have been conditioned to expect, many are in fact highly articulate and extremely thoughtful individuals for whom terrorism is (or was) an entirely rational choice, often reluctantly embraced and then only after considerable reflection and debate. It is precisely this paradox, whereby otherwise apparently 'normal' persons have nonetheless deliberately chosen a path of bloodshed and destruction, that has long intrigued me and indeed prompted me to write this book.

My aim, however, is not to offer some new theoretical treatise or conceptual reinterpretation of the subject. Instead, I have focused on what I believe to be the most salient and important trends in terrorism – both past and present – as a means to explain why terrorists 'do what they do' as well as to shed light on likely future patterns and potentialities. This somewhat selective – and thus perhaps idiosyncratic – approach deliberately emphasizes key historical themes over abstract theory and relies on empirical evidence rather than explanatory models to illustrate and support its main arguments. As such, this book is also intended to address a conspicuous gap in the literature by providing a work that is as accessible to students as it is relevant to scholars and which may therefore appeal equally to general as well as more specialized audiences.

The extensive bibliography of published and unpublished sources that I consulted in the course of this project is alone evidence of my indebtedness to the many other persons who have thought and written about terrorism. Their efforts have long shaped and influenced my own thinking and I would be remiss not to acknowledge the seminal contributions to this field of study made by Martha Crenshaw, Brian Jenkins, Walter Laqueur, David Rapoport, Grant Wardlaw and Paul Wilkinson. I have also benefited greatly from the work of – and not infrequently the helpful advice and trenchant criticism offered by – Konrad Kellen, Ariel Merari and Dennis Pluchinsky. I am of course solely responsible for any errors, solecisms or deficiencies that follow.

Over the years various people in various places who would prefer not to be identified have enhanced immeasurably my understanding of both terrorists and terrorism by granting me access to facilities not usually open to the public, introducing me to or arranging meetings with important personages or themselves by agreeing to discuss with me any number of sensitive matters. Even while I have respected their wish for anonymity, their impact is reflected – however obliquely – throughout this work and I remain eternally grateful for their assistance.

This book was researched and written during a period of time when I was afforded no respite from my teaching, administrative and fundraising responsibilities at the University of St Andrews. That I was able to find the time and mental space to complete the work is in no small way due to the assistance, support and friendship offered by my colleagues there. I should especially like to thank John Anderson, Rick Fawn, Ali Watson and particularly Gina Wilson in the Department of International Relations; David Claridge, Donna Hoffman, Suzanne Neilson, Magnus Ranstorp and Paul Wilkinson at the Centre for the Study of Terrorism and Political Violence; and Colin Vincent and John Beath as well. The many students I have had the privilege to teach or supervise since coming to St Andrews nearly four years ago have also contributed in often less perceptible ways to this book. In particular, I would also like to thank Gavin Cameron, Rohan Gunaratna, Melissa McPherson and the successive classes of IR 3008 – more colloquially known as 'Honours International Terrorism'.

I am grateful to the Center for Nonproliferation Studies, Frank Cass & Co., Jane's Information Group Ltd. and Taylor and Francis, the publishers respectively of *The Nonproliferation Review*, *Terrorism and*

Political Violence, Jane's Intelligence Review and *Studies in Conflict and Terrorism* for permission to use some material from articles I had previously written for those journals.

This undertaking could not have been realized without my family's unstinting love and encouragement. My gratitude to my parents and brother and most especially to my wife and children is as incalculable as it is immutable. No less critical has been the support and friendship provided by Karen Gardela, Ben and Tina Schwarz, Anders Stephanson, and Jennifer Taw.

It remains for me to thank the people at Gollancz who made publication of this book possible. Kate Hordern said the right things at a critical time that unbeknownst to her propelled the book to completion. Hugo Cox and Viv Redman were unfailingly helpful and Gillian Bromley's superlative editorial skills rescued yet another author from solecistic ignominy. My greatest debt though is to Sean Magee, who commissioned and helped develop this project – and never lost faith.

Bruce Hoffman
St Andrews, January 1998

Abbreviations

AD	Action Directe (Direct Action)
AIIB	Anti-Imperialist International Brigades =JRA
ANO	Abu Nidal Organization
ASALA	Armenian Army for the Secret Liberation of Armenia
BATF	(US) Bureau of Alcohol, Tobacco and Firearms
BSO	Black September Organization
CCC	Communist Combatant Cells (Belgium)
EOKA	Ethniki Organosis Kyprion Agoniston (National Organization of Cypriot Fighters)
FLQ	Front de Libération du Québec (Front for the Liberation of Quebec)
ETA	Euskadi ta Askatasuna (Freedom for the Basque Homeland)
FLN	Front de Libération Nationale (National Liberation Front)
GIA	(Algerian) Armed Islamic Group
IMRO	Inner Macedonian Revolutionary Organization
IRA	Irish Republican Army
IRS	(US) Internal Revenue Service
Irgun	Irgun Zvai Le'umi (National Military Organization)
Lehi	Lohamei Herut Yisrael (Freedom Fighters for Israel) = Stern Gang
JCAG	Justice Commandos of the Armenian Genocide
JRA	Japanese Red Army

MOM	Militia of Montana
NA	National Alternative (Berlin)
PFLP	Popular Front for the Liberation of Palestine
PIF	Palestine Islamic Jihad
PKK	Kurdish Workers Party
PLF	Palestine Liberation Front
PLO	Palestine Liberation Organization
RAF	Rote Armee Fraktion (Red Army Faction) = Baader–Meinhof Group
RB	Red Brigades (Italy)
RUC	Royal Ulster Constabulary
UNSCOP	United Nations Special Committee on Palestine
WAD	Afghan secret intelligence service
WMD	weapons of mass destruction

1

Defining Terrorism

What is terrorism? Few words have so insidiously worked their way into our everyday vocabulary. Like 'Internet' – another grossly over-used term that has similarly become an indispensable part of the argot of the late twentieth century – most people have a vague idea or impression of what terrorism is, but lack a more precise, concrete and truly explanatory definition of the word. This imprecision has been abetted partly by the modern media, whose efforts to communicate an often complex and convoluted message in the briefest amount of air-time or print space possible have led to the promiscuous labelling of a range of violent acts as 'terrorism'. Pick up a newspaper or turn on the television and – even within the same broadcast or on the same page – one can find such disparate acts as the bombing of a building, the assassination of a head of state, the massacre of civilians by a military unit, the poisoning of produce on supermarket shelves or the deliberate contamination of over-the-counter medication in a chemist's shop all described as incidents of terrorism. Indeed, virtually any especially abhorrent act of violence that is perceived as directed against society – whether it involves the activities of anti-government dissidents or governments themselves, organized crime syndicates or common criminals, rioting mobs or persons engaged in militant protest, individual psychotics or lone extortionists – is often labelled 'terrorism'.

Dictionary definitions are of little help. The pre-eminent authority on the English language, the much-venerated *Oxford English Dictionary*, is disappointingly unobliging when it comes to providing edification on this subject, its interpretation at once too literal and too historical to be of much contemporary use:

> **Terrorism**: A system of terror. 1. Government by intimidation as directed and carried out by the party in power in France during the revolution of 1789–94; the system of 'Terror'. 2. *gen.* A policy intended to strike with terror those against whom it is adopted; the employment of methods of intimidation; the fact of terrorizing or condition of being terrorized.[1]

These definitions are wholly unsatisfying. Rather than learning what terrorism is, one instead finds, in the first instance, a somewhat potted historical – and, in respect of the modern accepted usage of the term, a uselessly anachronistic – description. The second definition offered is only slightly more helpful. While accurately communicating the fear-inducing quality of terrorism, the definition is still so broad as to apply to almost any action that scares ('terrorizes') us. Though an integral part of 'terrorism', this definition is still insufficient for the purpose of accurately defining the phenomenon that is today called 'terrorism'.

A slightly more satisfying elucidation may be found in the *OED*'s definition of the perpetrator of the act than in its efforts to come to grips with the act itself. In this respect, a 'terrorist' is defined thus:

> 1. As a political term: a. Applied to the Jacobins and their agents and partisans in the French Revolution, esp. to those connected with the Revolutionary tribunals during the 'Reign of Terror'. b. Any one who attempts to further his views by a system of coercive intimidation; *spec.* applied to members of one of the extreme revolutionary societies in Russia.[2]

This is appreciably more helpful. First, it immediately introduces the reader to the notion of terrorism as a *political* concept. As will be seen, this key characteristic of terrorism is absolutely paramount to understanding its aims, motivations and purposes and critical in distinguishing it from other types of violence.

Terrorism, in the most widely accepted contemporary usage of the term, is fundamentally and inherently political. It is also ineluctably about power: the pursuit of power, the acquisition of power, and the use of power to achieve political change. Terrorism is thus violence – or, equally important, the threat of violence – used and directed in pursuit of, or in service of, a political aim. With this vital point clearly illuminated, one can appreciate the significance of the additional definition of 'terrorist' provided by the *OED*: 'Any one who attempts to further his views by a system of coercive intimidation'. This definition underscores clearly the other fundamental characteristic of terrorism: that it is a planned, calculated, and indeed systematic act.

Given this relatively straightforward elucidation, why, then, is terrorism so difficult to define? The most compelling reason perhaps is because the meaning of the term has changed so frequently over the past two hundred years.[3]

The Changing Meaning of Terrorism

The word 'terrorism' was first popularized during the French Revolution. In contrast to its contemporary usage, at that time terrorism had a decidedly *positive* connotation. The system or *régime de la terreur* of 1793–4 – from which the English word came – was adopted as a means to establish order during the transient anarchical period of turmoil and upheaval that followed the uprisings of 1789, as it has followed in the wake of many other revolutions. Hence, unlike terrorism as it is commonly understood today, to mean a *revolutionary* or anti-government activity undertaken by non-state or subnational entities, the *régime de la terreur* was an instrument of governance wielded by the recently established revolutionary *state*. It was designed to consolidate the new government's power by intimidating counter-revolutionaries, subversives and all other dissidents whom the new regime regarded as 'enemies of the people'. The Committee of General Security and the Revolutionary Tribunal ('People's Court' in the modern vernacular) were thus accorded wide powers of arrest and judgement, publicly putting to death by guillotine persons convicted of treasonous (i.e. reactionary) crimes. In this manner, a powerful lesson was conveyed to any and all who might oppose the revolution or grow nostalgic for the *ancien régime*.

Ironically, perhaps, terrorism in its original context was also closely associated with the ideals of virtue and democracy. The revolutionary leader Maximilien Robespierre firmly believed that virtue was the mainspring of a popular government at peace, but that during the time of revolution must be allied with terror in order for democracy to triumph. He appealed famously to 'virtue, without which terror is evil; terror, without which virtue is helpless', and proclaimed: 'Terror is nothing but justice, prompt, severe and inflexible; it is therefore an emanation of virtue.'[4]

Despite this divergence from its subsequent meaning, the French Revolution's 'terrorism' still shared at least two key characteristics in common with its modern-day variant. First, the *régime de la terreur* was neither random nor indiscriminate, as terrorism is often portrayed today, but was organized, deliberate and systematic. Second, its goal and its very justification – like that of contemporary terrorism – was the creation of a 'new and better society' in place of a fundamentally corrupt and undemocratic political system. Indeed, Robespierre's vague and utopian exegeses of the revolution's central goals are remarkably similar in tone and content to the equally turgid, millenarian manifestos issued by many contemporary revolutionary – primarily left-wing, Marxist-oriented – terrorist organizations. For example, in 1794 Robespierre declared, in language eerily presaging the communiqués issued by groups such as Germany's Red Army Faction and Italy's Red Brigades nearly two centuries later:

> We want an order of things . . . in which the arts are an adornment to the liberty that ennobles them, and commerce the source of wealth for the public and not of monstrous opulence for a few families . . . In our country we desire morality instead of selfishness, honesty and not mere 'honor', principle and not mere custom, duty and not mere propriety, the sway of reason rather than the tyranny of fashion, a scorn for vice and not a contempt for the unfortunate . . .[5]

Like many other revolutions, the French Revolution eventually began to consume itself. On 8 Thermidor, year two of the new calendar adopted by the revolutionaries (26 July 1794), Robespierre announced to the National Convention that he had in his possession a new list of traitors. Fearing that their own names might be on that list, extremists joined forces with moderates to repudiate both Robespierre and his *régime de la terreur*. Robespierre and his closest followers themselves met the same fate that had befallen some 40,000 others: execution by guillotine. The Terror was at an end; thereafter terrorism became a term associated with the abuse of office and power – with overt 'criminal' implications.[6] Within a year of Robespierre's demise, the word had been popularized in English by Edmund Burke who, in his famous polemic against the French Revolution, described the 'Thousands of those Hell hounds called Terrorists . . . let loose on the people'.[7]

One of the French Revolution's more enduring repercussions was the impetus it gave to anti-monarchical sentiment elsewhere in Europe. Popular subservience to rulers who derived their authority from God through 'divine right of rule', not from their subjects, was increasingly questioned by a politically awakened continent. The advent of nationalism, and with it notions of statehood and citizenship based on the common identity of a people rather than the lineage of a royal family, were resulting in the unification and creation of new nation-states such as Germany and Italy. Meanwhile, the massive socio-economic changes engendered by the industrial revolution were creating new 'universalist' ideologies (such as communism/Marxism), born of the alienation and exploitative conditions of nineteenth-century capitalism. From this milieu a new era of terrorism emerged, in which the concept had gained many of the familiar revolutionary, anti-state connotations of today. Its chief progenitor was arguably the Italian republican extremist, Carlo Pisacane, who had forsaken his birthright as duke of San Giovanni only to perish in 1857 during an ill-fated revolt against Bourbon rule. A passionate advocate of federalism and mutualism, Pisacane is remembered less on this account than for the theory of 'propaganda by deed',[8] which he is credited with defining – an idea that has exerted a compelling influence on rebels and terrorists alike ever since. 'The propaganda of the idea is a chimera,' Pisacane wrote. 'Ideas result from deeds, not the latter from the former, and the people will not be free when they are educated, but educated when they are free.'[9] Violence, he argued, was necessary not only to draw attention to, or generate publicity for, a cause, but to inform, educate and ultimately rally the masses behind the revolution. The didactic purpose of violence, Pisacane argued, could never be effectively replaced by pamphlets, wall posters or assemblies.

Perhaps the first organization to put into practice Pisacane's dictum was the Narodnaya Volya, or People's Will (sometimes translated as People's Freedom), a small group of Russian constitutionalists that had been founded in 1878 to challenge tsarist rule. For the Narodnaya Volya, the apathy and alienation of the Russian masses afforded few alternatives to the resort to daring and dramatic acts of violence designed to attract attention to the group and its cause. However, unlike the many late twentieth-century terrorist organizations who have cited the principle of 'propaganda by deed' to justify the wanton targeting of civilians in order to assure them publicity through the shock and horror produced by wholesale bloodshed, the Narodnaya Volya displayed an almost quixotic attitude to the violence they wrought. To them, 'propaganda by deed' meant the selective targeting of specific individuals whom the group considered the embodiment of the autocratic, oppressive state.[10] Hence their victims – the tsar, leading members of the royal family, senior government officials – were deliberately chosen for their 'symbolic' value as the dynastic heads and subservient agents of a corrupt and tyrannical regime. An intrinsic element in the group's collective beliefs was that 'not one drop of superfluous blood' should be shed in pursuit of aims, however noble or utilitarian they might be.[11] Even having selected their targets with great care and the utmost deliberation, group members still harboured profound regrets about taking the life of a fellow human being. Their unswerving adherence to this principle is perhaps best illustrated by the failed attempt on the life of the Grand Duke Serge Alexandrovich made by a successor organization to the Narodnaya Volya in 1905. As the royal carriage came into view, the terrorist tasked with the assassination saw that the duke was unexpectedly accompanied by his children and therefore aborted his mission rather than risk harming the intended victim's family (the duke was killed in a subsequent attack). By comparison, the mid-air explosion caused by a terrorist bomb on Pan Am flight 103 over Lockerbie, Scotland, in December 1988 indiscriminately claimed the lives of all 259 persons on board – innocent men, women and children alike – plus eleven inhabitants of the village where the plane crashed.

Ironically, the Narodnaya Volya's most dramatic accomplishment also led directly to its demise. On 1 March 1881 the group assassinated Tsar Alexander II. The failure of eight previous plots had led the conspirators to take extraordinary measures to ensure the success of this attempt. Four volunteers were given four bombs each and deployed along the alternative routes followed by the tsar's cortege. As two of the bomber-assassins stood in wait on the same street, the sleighs carrying the tsar and his Cossack escort approached the first terrorist, who hurled his bomb at the passing sleigh, missing it by inches. The whole entourage came to a halt as soldiers seized the hapless culprit and the tsar descended from his sleigh to check on a bystander wounded by the explosion. 'Thank God, I am safe,' the tsar reportedly declared – just as the second bomber emerged from the crowd and detonated his weapon, killing both himself and his target. The full weight of the tsarist state now fell on the heads of the Narodnaya Volya. Acting on information provided by the arrested member, the secret police swept down on the group's safe houses and hide-outs, rounding up most of the plotters, who were quickly tried, convicted and hanged. Further information from this group led to subsequent arrests, so that within a year of the assassination only one member of the original executive committee was still at large. She too was finally apprehended in 1883, at which point the first generation of Narodnaya Volya terrorists ceased to exist, although various successor organizations subsequently emerged to carry on the struggle.[12]

At the time, the repercussions of the tsar's assassination could not have been known or appreciated by either the condemned or their comrades languishing in prison or exiled to Siberia. But in addition to precipitating the beginning of the end of tsarist rule, the group also deeply influenced individual revolutionaries and subversive organizations elsewhere. To the nascent anarchist movement, the 'propaganda by deed' strategy championed by the Narodnaya Volya provided a model to be emulated.[13] Within four months of the tsar's murder, a group of radicals in London convened an 'anarchist conference' which publicly applauded the assassination and extolled tyrannicide as a means to achieve revolutionary change. In hopes of encouraging and coordinating worldwide anarchist activities, the conferees decided to establish an 'Anarchist International' (or 'Black International'). Although this idea, like most of their ambitious plans, came to nought, the publicity generated by even a putative 'Anarchist International' was sufficient to create a myth of global revolutionary pretensions and thereby stimulate fears and suspicions disproportionate to its actual impact or political achievements. Disparate and uncoordinated though the anarchists' violence was, the movement's emphasis on individual action or operations carried out by small cells of like-minded radicals made detection and prevention by the police particularly difficult, thus further heightening public fears. For example, following the assassination of US President William McKinley in 1901 (by a young Hungarian refugee, Leon Czolgocz, who, while not a regular member of any anarchist organization, was nonetheless influenced by the philosophy), Congress swiftly enacted legislation barring known anarchists or anyone 'who disbelieves in or is opposed to all organized government' from entering the United States.[14] However, while anarchists were responsible for an impressive string of assassinations of heads of state and a number of particularly notorious bombings from about 1878 until the second decade of the twentieth century,[15] in the final analysis, other than stimulating often exaggerated fears, anarchism made little tangible impact on either the domestic or the international politics of the countries affected. It does, however, offer an interesting historical footnote: much as the 'information revolution' of the late twentieth century is alleged to have made the means and methods of bomb-making and other types of terrorist activity more readily available via the Internet, on CD-ROM, and through ordinary libraries and bookstores, one of anarchism's flourishing 'cottage industries' more than a century earlier was the widespread distribution of similar 'how-to' or DIY-type manuals and publications of violence and mayhem.[16]

On the eve of the First World War, terrorism still retained its revolutionary connotations. By this time, growing unrest and irredentist ferment had already welled up within the decaying Ottoman and Habsburg Empires. In the 1880s and 1890s, for example, militant Armenian nationalist movements in eastern Turkey pursued a terrorist strategy against continued Ottoman rule of a kind that would later be adopted by most of the post-Second World War ethno-nationalist/separatist movements. The Armenians' objective was simultaneously to strike a blow against the despotic 'alien' regime through repeated attacks on its colonial administration and security forces, in order to rally indigenous support, as well as to attract international attention, sympathy and support.[17] Around the same time, the Inner Macedonian Revolutionary Organization (IMRO) was active in the region overlapping present-day Greece, Bulgaria and Serbia.[18] Although the Macedonians did not go on to suffer the catastrophic fate that befell the Armenians during the First World War (when an estimated one million persons perished in what is considered to be the first officially implemented genocide of the twentieth century),[19] IMRO never came close to achieving its aim of an independent Macedonia and thereafter degenerated into a mostly criminal organization of hired thugs and political assassins.

The events immediately preceding the First World War in Bosnia are of course more familiar because of their subsequent cataclysmic impact on world affairs. There, similar groups of disaffected nationalists – Bosnian Serb intellectuals, university students and even schoolchildren, collectively known as Mlada Bosna, or Young Bosnians – arose against continued Habsburg suzerainty. While it is perhaps easy to dismiss the movement, as some historians have, as comprised of 'frustrated, poor, dreary and maladjusted'[20] adolescents – much as many contemporary observers similarly denigrate modern-day terrorists as mindless, obsessive and maladjusted – it was a member of Young Bosnia, Gavrilo Princip, who is widely credited with having set in motion the chain of events that began on 28 June 1914, when he assassinated the Habsburg Archduke Franz Ferdinand in Sarajevo, and culminated in the First World War. Whatever its superficially juvenile characteristics, the group was nonetheless passionately dedicated to the attainment of a federal South Slav political entity – uniting Slovenes, Croats and Serbs – and resolutely committed to assassination as the vehicle with which to achieve that aim. In this respect, the Young Bosnians perhaps had more in common with the radical republicanism of Giuseppe Mazzini, one of the most ardent exponents of Italian unification in the nineteenth century, than with groups such as the Narodnaya Volya – despite a shared conviction in the efficacy of tyrannicide. An even more significant difference, however, was the degree of involvement in, and external support provided to, Young Bosnian activities by various shadowy Serbian nationalist groups. Principal among these was the pan-Serb secret society, the Narodna Obrana ('The People's Defence' or 'National Defence').

The Narodna Obrana had been established in 1908 originally to promote Serb cultural and national activities. It subsequently assumed a more subversive orientation as the movement became increasingly involved with anti-Austrian activities – including terrorism – mostly in neighbouring Bosnia and Hercegovina. Although the Narodna Obrana's exclusionist pan-Serbian aims clashed with the Young Bosnians' less parochial South Slav ideals, its leadership was quite happy to manipulate and exploit the Bosnians' emotive nationalism and youthful zeal for their own purposes. To this end, the Narodna Obrana actively recruited, trained and armed young Bosnians and Hercegovinians from movements such as the Young Bosnians who were then deployed in various seditious activities against the Habsburgs. As early as four years before the archduke's assassination, a Hercegovinian youth, trained by a Serb army officer with close ties to the Narodna Obrana, had attempted to kill the governor of Bosnia. But, while the Narodna Obrana included among its members senior Serbian government officials, it was not an explicitly government-controlled or directly state-supported entity. Whatever hazy government links it maintained were further and deliberately obscured when a radical faction left the Narodna Obrana in 1911 and established the Ujedinjenje ili Smrt, 'The Union of Death' or 'Death or Unification' – more popularly known as the Crna Ruka, or the 'Black Hand'. This more militant and appreciably more clandestine splinter has been described by one historian as combining

> the more unattractive features of the anarchist cells of earlier years – which had been responsible for quite a number of assassinations in Europe and whose methods had a good deal of influence via the writings of Russian anarchists upon Serbian youth – and of the [American] Ku Klux Klan. There were gory rituals and oaths of loyalty, there were murders of backsliding members, there was identification of members by number, there were distributions of guns and bombs. And there was a steady traffic between Bosnia and Serbia.[21]

This group, which continued to maintain close links with its parent body, was largely composed of serving Serbian military officers. It was led by Lieutenant-Colonel Dragutin Dmitrievich (known by his pseudonym, Apis), himself the chief of the Intelligence Department of the Serbian general staff. With this key additional advantage of direct access to military armaments, intelligence and training facilities, the Black Hand effectively took charge of all Serb-backed clandestine operations in Bosnia.[22]

Although there were obviously close links between the Serbian military, the Black Hand and the Young Bosnians, it would be a mistake to regard the relationship as one of direct control, much less outright manipulation. Clearly, the Serbian government was well aware of the

Black Hand's objectives and the violent means the group employed in pursuit of them; indeed, the Serbian Crown Prince Alexander was one of the group's benefactors. But this does not mean that the Serbian government was necessarily as committed to war with Austria as the Black Hand's leaders were, or that it was prepared to countenance the group's more extreme plans for fomenting cross-border, anti-Habsburg terrorism. There is some evidence to suggest that the Black Hand may have been trying to force Austria's hand against Serbia and thereby plunge both countries into war by actively abetting the Young Bosnians' plot to assassinate the archduke. Indeed, according to one revisionist account of the events leading up to the murder,[23] even though the pistol used by Princip had been supplied by the Black Hand from a Serb military armoury in Kragujevac, and even though Princip had been trained by the Black Hand in Serbia before being smuggled back across the border for the assassination, at the eleventh hour Dmitrievich had apparently bowed to intense government pressure and tried to stop the assassination. According to this version, Princip and his fellow conspirators would hear nothing of it and stubbornly went ahead with their plans. Contrary to popular assumption, therefore, the archduke's assassination may not have been specifically ordered or even directly sanctioned by the Serbian government.[24] However, the obscure links between high government officials and their senior military commanders and ostensibly independent, transnational terrorist movements, and the tangled web of intrigue, plots, clandestine arms provision and training, intelligence agents and cross-border sanctuary these relationships inevitably involved, provide a pertinent historical parallel to the contemporary phenomenon known as 'state-sponsored' terrorism (that is, the active and often clandestine support, encouragement and assistance provided by a foreign government to a terrorist group), which is discussed below.

By the 1930s, the meaning of 'terrorism' had changed again. It was now used less to refer to revolutionary movements and violence directed against governments and their leaders, and more to describe the practices of mass repression employed by totalitarian states and their dictatorial leaders against their own citizens. Thus the term regained its former connotations of abuse of power by governments, and was applied specifically to the authoritarian regimes that had come to power in Fascist Italy, Nazi Germany and Stalinist Russia. In Germany and Italy respectively, the accession to office of Hitler and Mussolini had depended in large measure on the 'street' – the mobilization and deployment of gangs of brown- or black-shirted thugs to harass and intimidate political opponents and root out other scapegoats for public vilification and further victimization. 'Terror? Never,' Mussolini insisted, demurely dismissing such intimidation as 'simply . . . social hygiene, taking those individuals out of circulation like a doctor would take out a bacillus'.[25] The most sinister dimension of this form of 'terror' was that it became an intrinsic component of Fascist and Nazi governance, executed at the behest of, and in complete subservience to, the ruling political party of the land – which had arrogated to itself complete, total control of the country and its people. A system of government-sanctioned fear and coercion was thus created whereby political brawls, street fights and widespread persecution of Jews, communists and other declared 'enemies of the state' became the means through which complete and submissive compliance was ensured. The totality of party control over, and perversion of, government was perhaps most clearly evinced by a speech given by Hermann Goering, the newly appointed Prussian minister of the interior, in 1933. 'Fellow Germans,' he declared,

> My measures will not be crippled by any judicial thinking. My measures will not be crippled by any bureaucracy. Here I don't have to worry about Justice; my mission is only to destroy and exterminate, nothing more. This struggle will be a struggle against chaos, and such a struggle I shall not conduct with the power of the police. A bourgeois State might have done that. Certainly, I shall use the power of the State and the police to the utmost, my dear Communists, so don't draw any false conclusions; but the struggle to the death, in which my fist will grasp your necks, I shall lead with those there – the Brown Shirts.[26]

The 'Great Terror' that Stalin was shortly to unleash in Russia both resembled and differed from that of the Nazis. On the one hand, drawing inspiration from Hitler's ruthless elimination of his own political opponents, the Russian dictator similarly transformed the political party he led into a servile instrument responsive directly to his personal will, and the state's police and security apparatus into slavish organs of coercion, enforcement and repression. But conditions in the Soviet Union of the 1930s bore little resemblance to the turbulent political, social and economic upheaval afflicting Germany and Italy during that decade and the previous one. On the other hand, therefore, unlike either the Nazis or the Fascists, who had emerged from the political free-for-alls in their own countries to seize power and then had to struggle to consolidate their rule and retain their unchallenged authority, the Russian Communist Party had by the mid-1930s been firmly entrenched in power for more than a decade. Stalin's purges, in contrast to those of the French Revolution, and even to Russia's own recent experience, were not 'launched in time of crisis, or revolution and war . . . [but] in the coldest of cold blood, when Russia had at last reached a comparatively calm and even moderately prosperous condition'.[27] Thus the political purges ordered by Stalin became, in the words of one of his biographers, a 'conspiracy to seize total power by terrorist action',[28] resulting in the death, exile, imprisonment or forcible impressment of millions.

Certainly, similar forms of state-imposed or state-directed violence and terror against a government's own citizens continue today. The use of so-called 'death squads' (often off-duty or plain-clothes security or police officers) in conjunction with blatant intimidation of political opponents, human rights and aid workers, student groups, labour organizers, journalists and others has been a prominent feature of the right-wing military dictatorships that took power in Argentina, Chile and Greece during the 1970s and even of elected governments in El Salvador, Guatemala, Colombia and Peru since the mid-1980s. But these state-sanctioned or explicitly ordered acts of *internal* political violence directed mostly against domestic populations – that is, rule by violence and intimidation by those *already* in power against their own citizenry – are generally termed 'terror' in order to distinguish that phenomenon from 'terrorism', which is understood to be violence committed by non-state entities.

Following the Second World War, in another swing of the pendulum of meaning, 'terrorism' regained the revolutionary connotations with which is it most commonly associated today. At that time, the term was used primarily in reference to the violent revolts then being prosecuted by the various indigenous nationalist/anti-colonialist groups that emerged in Asia, Africa and the Middle East during the late 1940s and 1950s to oppose continued European rule. Countries as diverse as Israel,

Kenya, Cyprus and Algeria, for example, owe their independence at least in part to nationalist political movements that employed terrorism against colonial powers. It was also during this period that the 'politically correct' appellation of 'freedom fighters' came into fashion as a result of the political legitimacy that the international community (whose sympathy and support was actively courted by many of these movements) accorded to struggles for national liberation and self-determination. Many newly independent Third World countries and communist bloc states in particular adopted this vernacular, arguing that anyone or any movement that fought against 'colonial' oppression and/or Western domination should not be described as 'terrorists', but were properly deemed to be 'freedom fighters'. This position was perhaps most famously explained by the Palestine Liberation Organization (PLO) chairman Yassir Arafat, when he addressed the United Nations General Assembly in November 1974. 'The difference between the revolutionary and the terrorist,' Arafat stated, 'lies in the reason for which each fights. For whoever stands by a just cause and fights for the freedom and liberation of his land from the invaders, the settlers and the colonialists, cannot possibly be called terrorist...'[29]

During the late 1960s and 1970s, terrorism continued to be viewed within a revolutionary context. However, this usage now expanded to include nationalist and ethnic separatist groups outside a colonial or neo-colonial framework as well as radical, entirely ideologically motivated organizations. Disenfranchised or exiled nationalist minorities – such as the PLO, the Quebecois separatist group FLQ (Front de Libération du Québec), the Basque ETA (Euskadi ta Askatasuna, or Freedom for the Basque Homeland) and even a hitherto unknown South Moluccan irredentist group seeking independence from Indonesia – adopted terrorism as a means to draw attention to themselves and their respective causes, in many instances with the specific aim, like their anti-colonial predecessors, of attracting international sympathy and support. Around the same time, various left-wing political extremists – drawn mostly from the radical student organizations and Marxist/Leninist/Maoist movements in Western Europe, Latin America and the United States – began to form terrorist groups opposing American intervention in Vietnam and what they claimed were the irredeemable social and economic inequities of the modern capitalist liberal-democratic state.

Although the revolutionary cum ethno-nationalist/separatist and ideological exemplars continue to shape our most basic understanding of the term, in recent years 'terrorism' has been used to denote broader, less distinct phenomena. In the early 1980s, for example, terrorism came to be regarded as a calculated means to destabilize the West as part of a vast global conspiracy. Books like *The Terror Network* by Claire Sterling propagated the notion to a receptive American presidential administration and similarly susceptible governments elsewhere that the seemingly isolated terrorist incidents perpetrated by disparate groups scattered across the globe were in fact linked elements of a massive clandestine plot, orchestrated by the Kremlin and implemented by its Warsaw Pact client states, to destroy the Free World.[30] By the middle of the decade, however, a series of suicide bombings directed mostly against American diplomatic and military targets in the Middle East was focusing attention on the rising threat of state-sponsored terrorism. Consequently, this phenomenon – whereby various renegade foreign governments such as the regimes in Iran, Iraq, Libya and Syria became actively involved in sponsoring or commissioning terrorist acts – replaced communist conspiracy theories as the main context within which terrorism was viewed. Terrorism thus became associated with a type of covert or surrogate warfare whereby weaker states could confront larger, more powerful rivals without the risk of retribution.[31]

In the early 1990s the meaning and usage of the term 'terrorism' were further blurred by the emergence of two new buzzwords: 'narco-terrorism' and the so-called 'gray area phenomenon'.[32] The former term revived the Moscow-orchestrated terrorism conspiracy theories of previous years while introducing the critical new dimension of narcotics trafficking. Thus 'narco-terrorism' was defined by one of the concept's foremost propagators as the 'use of drug trafficking to advance the objectives of certain governments and terrorist organizations' – identified as the 'Marxist-Leninist regimes' of the Soviet Union, Cuba, Bulgaria and Nicaragua, among others.[33] The emphasis on 'narco-terrorism' as the latest manifestation of the communist plot to undermine Western society,[34] however, had the unfortunate effect of diverting official attention away from a bona fide emerging trend. To a greater extent than ever in the past, entirely criminal (that is, violent, *economically* motivated) organizations were now forging strategic alliances with terrorist and guerrilla organizations or themselves employing violence for specifically political ends. The growing power of the Colombian cocaine cartels, their close ties with left-wing terrorist groups in Colombia and Peru, and their repeated attempts to subvert Colombia's electoral process and undermine successive governments constitute perhaps the best-known example of this continuing trend.

Those who drew attention to this 'gray area phenomenon' were concerned less with grand conspiracies than with highlighting the increasingly fluid and variable nature of subnational conflict in the post-Cold War era. Accordingly, in the 1990s terrorism began to be subsumed by some analysts within the 'gray area phenomenon'. Thus the latter term came to be used to denote 'threats to the stability of nation states by non-state actors and non-governmental processes and organizations';[35] to describe violence affecting 'immense regions or urban areas where control has shifted from legitimate governments to new half-political, half-criminal powers';[36] or simply to group together in one category the range of conflicts across the world that no longer conformed to traditionally accepted notions of war as fighting between the armed forces of two or more established states, but instead involved irregular forces as one or more of the combatants.[37] Terrorism had shifted its meaning again from an individual phenomenon of subnational violence to one of several elements, or part of a wider pattern, of non-state conflict.

Why is Terrorism so Difficult to Define?

Not surprisingly, as the meaning and usage of the word have changed over time to accommodate the political vernacular and discourse of each successive era, terrorism has proved increasingly elusive in the face of attempts to construct one consistent definition. At one time, the terrorists themselves were far more cooperative in this endeavour than they are today. The early practitioners didn't mince their words or hide behind the semantic camouflage of more anodyne labels such as 'freedom fighter' or 'urban guerrilla'. The nineteenth-century anarchists, for example, unabashedly proclaimed themselves to be terrorists and frankly proclaimed their tactics to be terrorism.[38] The members of Narodnaya Volya similarly displayed no qualms in using these same words to describe themselves and their deeds.[39] However, such frankness did not last. The Jewish terrorist group of the 1940s known as Lehi (the Hebrew acronym for Lohamei Herut Yisrael, the Freedom Fighters for Israel, more popularly known simply as the Stern Gang after their founder and first leader, Abraham Stern) is thought to be one of the last terrorist groups actually to describe itself publicly as such.[40] It is significant, however, that even Lehi, while it may have been far more candid than its latter-day counterparts, chose as the name of the organization not 'Terrorist Fighters for Israel', but the far less pejorative 'Freedom Fighters for Israel'. Similarly, although more than twenty years later the Brazilian revolutionary Carlos Marighela displayed few compunctions about openly advocating the use of 'terrorist' tactics,[41] he still insisted on depicting himself and his disciples as 'urban guerrillas' rather than 'urban terrorists'. Indeed, it is clear from Marighela's writings that he was well aware of the word's undesirable connotations, and strove to displace them with positive resonances. 'The words "aggressor" and "terrorist"', Marighela wrote in his famous *Handbook of Urban Guerrilla War* (also known as the 'Mini-Manual'), 'no longer mean what they did. Instead of arousing fear or censure, they are a call to action. To be called an aggressor or a terrorist in Brazil is now an honour to any citizen, for it means that he is fighting, with a gun in his hand, against the monstrosity of the present dictatorship and the suffering it causes.'[42]

This trend towards ever more convoluted semantic obfuscations to side-step terrorism's pejorative overtones has, if anything, become more entrenched in recent decades. Terrorist organizations almost without exception now regularly select names for themselves that consciously eschew the word 'terrorism' in any of its forms. Instead these groups actively seek to evoke images of:

- freedom and liberation (e.g. the National Liberation Front, the Popular Front for the Liberation of Palestine, Freedom for the Basque Homeland, etc.);
- armies or other military organizational structures (e.g. the National Military Organization, the Popular Liberation Army, the Fifth Battalion of the Liberation Army, etc.);
- actual self-defence movements (e.g. the Afrikaner Resistance Movement, the Shankhill Defence Association, the Organization for the Defence of the Free People, the Jewish Defense Organization, etc.);
- righteous vengeance (the Organization for the Oppressed on Earth, the Justice Commandos of the Armenian Genocide, the Palestinian Revenge Organization, etc.);

– or else deliberately choose names that are decidedly neutral and therefore bereft of all but the most innocuous suggestions or associations (e.g. the Shining Path, Front Line, al-Dawa ('The Call'), Alfaro Lives – Damn It!, Kach ('Thus'), al-Gamat al-Islamiya ('The Islamic Organization'), the Lantero Youth Movement, etc.).

What all these examples suggest is that terrorists clearly do not see or regard themselves as others do. 'Above all I am a family man,' the arch-terrorist Carlos, 'The Jackal', described himself to a French newspaper following his capture in 1994.[43] Cast perpetually on the defensive and forced to take up arms to protect themselves and their real or imagined constituents only, terrorists perceive themselves as reluctant warriors, driven by desperation – and lacking any viable alternative – to violence against a repressive state, a predatory rival ethnic or nationalist group, or an unresponsive international order. This perceived characteristic of self-denial also distinguishes the terrorist from other types of political extremists as well as from persons similarly involved in illegal, violent avocations. A communist or a revolutionary, for example, would likely readily accept and admit that he is in fact a communist or a revolutionary. Indeed, many would doubtless take particular pride in claiming either of those appellations for themselves. Similarly, even a person engaged in illegal, wholly disreputable or entirely selfish violent activities, such as robbing banks or carrying out contract killings, would probably admit to being a bank robber or a murderer for hire. The terrorist, by contrast, will *never* acknowledge that he is a terrorist and moreover will go to great lengths to evade and obscure any such inference or connection. Terry Anderson, the American journalist who was held hostage for almost seven years by the Lebanese terrorist organization Hezbollah, relates a telling conversation he had with one of his guards. The guard had objected to a newspaper article that referred to Hezbollah as terrorists. 'We are not terrorists,' he indignantly stated, 'we are fighters.' Anderson replied, 'Hajj, you are a terrorist, look it up in the dictionary. You are a terrorist, you may not like the word and if you do not like the word, do not do it.'[44] The terrorist will always argue that it is society or the government or the socio-economic 'system' and its laws that are the *real* 'terrorists', and moreover that if it were not for this oppression, he would not have felt the need to defend either himself or the population he claims to represent.[45] Another revealing example of this process of obfuscation-projection may be found in the book *Invisible*

Armies, written by Sheikh Muhammad Hussein Fadlallah, the spiritual leader of the Lebanese terrorist group responsible for Anderson's kidnapping. 'We don't see ourselves as terrorists,' Fadlallah explains, 'because we don't believe in terrorism. We don't see resisting the occupier as a terrorist action. We see ourselves as *mujihadeen* [holy warriors] who fight a Holy War for the people.'[46]

On one point, at least, everyone agrees: terrorism is a pejorative term.[47] It is a word with intrinsically negative connotations that is generally applied to one's enemies and opponents, or to those with whom one disagrees and would otherwise prefer to ignore. 'What is called terrorism', Brian Jenkins has written, 'thus seems to depend on one's point of view. Use of the term implies a moral judgement; and if one party can successfully attach the label *terrorist* to its opponent, then it has indirectly persuaded others to adopt its moral viewpoint.'[48] Hence the decision to call someone or label some organization 'terrorist' becomes almost unavoidably subjective, depending largely on whether one sympathizes with or opposes the person/group/cause concerned. If one identifies with the victim of the violence, for example, then the act is terrorism. If, however, one identifies with the perpetrator, the violent act is regarded in a more sympathetic, if not positive (or, at the worst, an ambivalent) light; and it is not terrorism.

The implications of this associational logic were perhaps most clearly demonstrated in the exchanges between Western and non-Western member states of the United Nations following the 1972 Munich Olympics massacre, in which eleven Israeli athletes were killed. The debate began with the proposal by the then UN Secretary-General, Kurt Waldheim, that the UN should not remain a 'mute spectator' to the acts of terrorist violence then occurring throughout the world but should take practical steps that might prevent further bloodshed.[49] While a majority of the UN member states supported the Secretary-General, a disputatious minority – including many Arab states and various African and Asian countries – derailed the discussion, arguing (much as Arafat would do two years later in his own address to the General Assembly) that 'people who struggle to liberate themselves from foreign oppression and exploitation have the right to use all methods at their disposal, including force'.[50]

The Third World delegates justified their position with two arguments. First, they claimed that all bona fide liberation movements are invariably decried as 'terrorists' by the regimes against which their struggles for freedom are directed. The Nazis, for example, labelled as terrorists the resistance groups opposing Germany's occupation of their lands, Moulaye el-Hassen, the Mauritanian ambassador, pointed out, just as 'all liberation movements are described as terrorists by those who have reduced them to slavery'. Therefore, by condemning 'terrorism' the UN was endorsing the power of the strong over the weak and of the established entity over its non-established challenger – in effect, acting as the defender of the status quo. According to Chen Chu, the deputy representative of the People's Republic of China, the UN thus was proposing to deprive 'oppressed nations and peoples' of the only effective weapon they had with which to oppose 'imperialism, colonialism, neo-colonialism, racism and Israeli Zionism'.[51] Second, the Third World delegates argued forcefully that it is not the violence itself that is germane, but its 'underlying causes': that is, the 'misery, frustration, grievance and despair' that produce the violent acts.[52] As the Mauritanian representative again explained, the term 'terrorist' could 'hardly be held to apply to persons who were denied the most elementary human rights, dignity, freedom and independence, and whose countries objected to foreign occupation'.[53] When the issue was again raised the following year, Syria objected on the grounds that 'the international community is under legal and moral obligation to promote the struggle for liberation and to resist any attempt to depict this struggle as synonymous with terrorism and illegitimate violence'.[54] The resultant definitional paralysis subsequently throttled UN efforts to make any substantive progress on international cooperation against terrorism beyond very specific agreements on individual aspects of the problem (concerning, for example, diplomats and civil aviation).

The opposite approach, where identification with the victim determines the classification of a violent act as terrorism, is evident in the conclusions of a parliamentary working group of NATO (an organization comprised of long-established, status quo Western states). The final report of the 1989 North Atlantic Assembly's Subcommittee on Terrorism states: 'Murder, kidnapping, arson and other felonious acts constitute criminal behavior, but many non-Western nations have proved reluctant to condemn as terrorist acts what they consider to be struggles of national liberation.'[55] In this reasoning, the defining characteristic of terrorism is the act of violence itself, not the motivations or justification for or reasons behind it. This approach has long been espoused by analysts such as Jenkins who argue that terrorism should be defined 'by the nature of the act, not by the identity of the perpetrators or the nature of their cause'.[56] But this is not an entirely satisfactory solution either, since it fails to differentiate clearly between violence perpetrated by states and by non-state entities, such as terrorists. Accordingly, it plays into the hands of terrorists and their apologists who would argue that there is no difference between the 'low-tech' terrorist pipe-bomb placed in the rubbish bin at a crowded market that wantonly and indiscriminately kills or maims everyone within a radius measured in tens of feet and the 'high-tech' precision-guided ordnance dropped by air force fighter-bombers from a height of 20,000 feet or more that achieves the same wanton and indiscriminate effects on the crowded marketplace far below. This rationale thus equates the random violence inflicted on enemy population centres by military forces – such as the Luftwaffe's raids on Warsaw and Coventry, the Allied fire-bombings of Dresden and Tokyo, and the atomic bombs dropped by the United States on Hiroshima and Nagasaki during the Second World War, and indeed the countervalue strategy of the post-war superpowers' strategic nuclear policy, which deliberately targeted the enemy's civilian population – with the violence committed by substate entities labelled 'terrorists', since both involve the infliction of death and injury on non-combatants.[57] Indeed, this was precisely the point made during the above-mentioned UN debates by the Cuban representative, who argued that 'the methods of combat used by national liberation movements could not be declared illegal while the policy of terrorism unleashed against certain peoples [by the armed forces of established states] was declared legitimate'.[58]

It is a familiar argument. Terrorists, as we have seen, deliberately cloak themselves in the terminology of military jargon. They consciously portray themselves as bona fide (freedom) fighters, if not soldiers, who – though they wear no identifying uniform or insignia – are entitled to treatment as prisoners of war (POWs) if captured and therefore should not be prosecuted as common criminals in ordinary courts of law. Terrorists further argue that, because of their numerical inferiority, far more limited firepower and paucity of resources compared with an established nation-state's massive defence and national security apparatus, they have no choice but to operate clandestinely, emerging from the shadows to carry out dramatic (in other words, bloody and destructive) acts of hit-and-run violence in order to attract attention to, and ensure publicity for, themselves and their cause. The bomb-in-the-rubbish-bin, in their view, is merely a circumstantially imposed 'poor man's air force':[59] the only means with which the terrorist can challenge – and get the attention of – the more powerful state. 'How else can we bring pressure to bear on the world?' one of Arafat's political aides once enquired. 'The deaths are regrettable, but they are a fact of war in which innocents have become involved. They are no more innocent than the Palestinian women and children killed by the Israelis and we are ready to carry the war all over the world.'[60]

But rationalizations such as these ignore the fact that, even while national armed forces have been responsible for far more death and destruction than terrorists might ever aspire to bring about, there nonetheless is a fundamental qualitative difference between the two types of violence. Even in war there are rules and accepted norms of behaviour that prohibit the use of certain types of weapons (for example, hollow-point or 'dum-dum' bullets, CS 'tear' gas, chemical and biological warfare agents), proscribe various tactics and outlaw attacks on specific categories of targets. Accordingly, in theory, if not always in practice, the rules of war – as observed from the early seventeenth century when they were first proposed by the Dutch jurist Hugo Grotius and subsequently codified in the famous Geneva and Hague Conventions on Warfare of the 1860s, 1899, 1907 and 1949 – not only grant civilian non-combatants immunity from attack, but also

- prohibit taking civilians as hostages;
- impose regulations governing the treatment of captured or surrendered soldiers (POWs);
- outlaw reprisals against either civilians or POWs;
- recognize neutral territory and the rights of citizens of neutral states; and
- uphold the inviolability of diplomats and other accredited representatives.

Even the most cursory review of terrorist tactics and targets over the past quarter-century reveals that terrorists have violated all these rules. They not infrequently have

- taken hostage civilians, whom in some instances they have then brutally executed (e.g. the former Italian prime minister Aldo Moro and the German industrialist Hans Martin Schleyer, who were respectively taken captive and later murdered by the Red Brigades and the Red Army Faction);
- similarly abused and murdered kidnapped military officers – even when they were serving on UN-sponsored peacekeeping or truce supervisory missions (e.g. the American Marine Lieutenant-Colonel William Higgins, the commander of a UN truce monitoring detachment, who was abducted by Lebanese Shi'a terrorists in 1989 and subsequently hanged);
- undertaken reprisals against wholly innocent civilians, often in countries far removed from the terrorists' ostensible 'theatre of operation', thus disdaining any concept of neutral states or the rights of citizens of neutral countries (e.g. the brutal 1986 machine-gun and hand-grenade attack on Turkish Jewish worshippers at an Istanbul synagogue carried out by the Palestinian Abu Nidal Organization in retaliation for a recent Israeli raid on a guerrilla base in southern Lebanon); and
- repeatedly attacked embassies and other diplomatic installations (e.g. the bombings of the US embassies in Beirut and Kuwait City in 1983 and 1984, and the mass hostage-taking at the Japanese ambassador's residence in Lima, Peru, in 1996–7), as well as deliberately targeting diplomats and other accredited representatives (e.g. the British ambassador to Uruguay, Sir Geoffrey Jackson, who was kidnapped by leftist terrorists in that country in 1971, and the fifty-two American diplomats taken hostage at the Tehran legation in 1979).

Admittedly, the armed forces of established states have also been guilty of violating some of the same rules of war. However, when these transgressions do occur – when civilians are deliberately and wantonly attacked in war or taken hostage and killed by military forces – the term 'war crime' is used to describe such acts and, imperfect and flawed as both international and national judicial remedies may be, steps nonetheless are often taken to hold the perpetrators accountable for these crimes. By comparison, one of the fundamental *raisons d'être* of international terrorism is a refusal to be bound by such rules of warfare and codes of conduct. International terrorism disdains any concept of delimited areas of combat or demarcated battlefields, much less respect of neutral territory. Accordingly, terrorists have repeatedly taken their often parochial struggles to other, sometimes geographically distant, third party countries and there deliberately enmeshed persons completely unconnected with the terrorists' cause or grievances in violent incidents designed to generate attention and publicity.

The reporting of terrorism by the news media, which have been drawn into the semantic debates that divided the UN in the 1970s and continue to influence all discourse on terrorism, has further contributed to the obfuscation of the terrorist/'freedom fighter' debate, enshrining imprecision and implication as the lingua franca of political violence in the name of objectivity and neutrality. In striving to avoid appearing either partisan or judgemental, the American media, for example, resorted to describing terrorists – often in the same report – as variously guerrillas, gunmen, raiders, commandos and even soldiers. A random sample of American newspaper reports of Palestinian terrorist activities between June and December 1973, found in the terrorism archives and database maintained at the University of St Andrews in Scotland, provided striking illustrations of this practice. Out of eight headlines of articles describing the same incident, six used the word 'guerrillas' and only two 'terrorists' to describe the perpetrators. An interesting pattern was also observed whereby those accounts that immediately followed a particularly horrific or tragic incident – that is, involving the death and injury of innocent persons (in this instance, the attack on a Pan Am airliner at Rome airport, in which thirty-two passengers were killed) – tended to describe the perpetrators as 'terrorists' and their act as 'terrorism' (albeit in one case only in the headline, before reverting to the more neutral terminology of 'commando', 'militants', and 'guerrilla attack' in the text) more frequently than did reports of less serious or non-lethal incidents.[61] One *New York Times* leading article, however, was far less restrained than the stories describing the actual incident, describing it as 'bloody' and 'mindless' and using the words 'terrorists' and 'terrorism' interchangeably with 'guerrillas' and 'extremists'.[62] Only six months previously, however, the same newspaper had run a story about another terrorist attack that completely eschewed the terms 'terrorism' and 'terrorist', preferring 'guerrillas' and 'resistance' (as in 'resistance movement') instead.[63] The *Christian Science Monitor*'s reports of the Rome Pan Am attack similarly avoided 'terrorist' and 'terrorism' in favour of 'guerrillas' and 'extremists';[64] an Associated Press story in the next day's *Los Angeles Times* also stuck with 'guerrillas',[65] while the two *Washington Post* articles on the same incident opted for the terms 'commandos' and 'guerrillas'.[66]

This slavish devotion to terminological neutrality, which David Rapoport first observed over twenty years ago,[67] is still in evidence today. A recent article appearing in the *International Herald Tribune* (a Paris-based newspaper published in conjunction with the *New York Times* and *Washington Post*) reported an incident in Algeria where thirty persons had been killed by perpetrators who were variously described as 'terrorists' in the article's headline, less judgementally as 'extremists' in the lead paragraph and as the still more ambiguous 'Islamic fundamentalists' in the article's third paragraph.[68] In a country that since 1992 has been afflicted with an unrelenting wave of terrorist violence and bloodshed that has claimed the lives of an estimated 75,000 persons, one might think that the distinctions between 'terrorists', mere 'extremists' and ordinary 'fundamentalists' would be clearer. Equally interesting was the article that appeared on the opposite side of the same page of the newspaper that described the 'decades of sporadic *guerrilla* [my emphasis] warfare by the IRA' in Northern Ireland.[69] Yet fifty years ago the same newspaper apparently had fewer qualms about using the word 'terrorists' to describe the two young Jewish men in pre-independence Israel who, while awaiting execution after having been convicted of attacking British military targets, committed suicide.[70] Other press accounts of the same period in *The Times* of London and the *Palestine Post* similarly had no difficulties, for example, in describing the 1946 bombing by Jewish terrorists of the British military headquarters and government secretariat located in Jerusalem's King David Hotel as a 'terrorist' act perpetrated by 'terrorists'.[71] Similarly, in perhaps the most specific application of the term, the communist terrorists against whom the British fought in Malaya throughout the late 1940s and 1950s were routinely referred to as 'CTs' – for 'Communist terrorists'. As Rapoport warned in the 1970s, 'In attempting to correct the abuse of language for political purposes, our journalists may succeed in making language altogether worthless.'[72]

The cumulative effect of this proclivity towards equivocation is that today there is no one widely accepted or agreed definition for terrorism. Different departments or agencies of even the same government will themselves often have very different definitions for terrorism. The US State Department, for example, uses the definition of terrorism contained in Title 22 of the United States Code, Section 2656f(d):

> premeditated, politically motivated violence perpetrated against noncombatant targets by subnational groups or clandestine agents, usually intended to influence an audience,[73]

while the US Federal Bureau of Investigation (FBI) defines terrorism as

> the unlawful use of force or violence against persons or property to intimidate or coerce a Government, the civilian population, or any segment thereof, in furtherance of political or social objectives,[74]

and the US Department of Defense defines it as

> the unlawful use of – or threatened use of – force or violence against individuals or property to coerce or intimidate governments or societies, often to achieve political, religious, or ideological objectives.[75]

Not surprisingly, each of the above definitions reflects the priorities and particular interests of the specific agency involved. The State Department's emphasis is on the premeditated and planned or calculated nature of terrorism in contrast to more spontaneous acts of political violence. Its definition is also the only one of the three to emphasize both the ineluctably political nature of terrorism and the perpetrators' fundamental 'subnational' characteristic. The State Department definition, however, is conspicuously deficient in failing to consider the psychological dimension of terrorism. Terrorism is as much about the threat of violence as the violent act itself and, accordingly, is deliberately conceived to have far-reaching psychological repercussions beyond the actual target of the act among a wider, watching, 'target' audience. As Jenkins succinctly observed two decades ago, 'Terrorism is theatre.'[76]

Given the FBI's mission of investigating and solving crimes – both political (e.g. terrorism) and other – it is not surprising that its definition focuses on different elements. Unlike the State Department, this definition does address the psychological dimensions of the terrorist act described above, laying stress on terrorism's intimidatory and coercive aspects. The FBI definition also identifies a much broader category of terrorist targets than only 'noncombatants', specifying not only governments and their citizens, but also inanimate objects, such as private and public property. The FBI definition further recognizes social alongside political objectives as fundamental terrorist aims – though it offers no clearer elucidation of either.

The Department of Defense definition of terrorism is arguably the most complete of the three. It highlights the terrorist threat as much as the actual act of violence and focuses on terrorism's targeting of whole societies as well as governments. The Defense Department definition further cites the religious and ideological aims of terrorism alongside its fundamental political objectives – but curiously omits the social dimension found in the FBI's definition.

It is not only individual agencies within the same governmental apparatus that cannot agree on a single definition of terrorism. Experts and other long-established scholars in the field are equally incapable of reaching a consensus. In the first edition of his magisterial survey, *Political Terrorism: A Research Guide*,[77] Alex Schmid devoted more than a hundred pages to examining more than a hundred different definitions of terrorism in an effort to discover a broadly acceptable, reasonably comprehensive explication of the word. Four years and a second edition later, Schmid was no closer to the goal of his quest, conceding in the first sentence of the revised volume that the 'search for an adequate definition is still on'.[78] Walter Laqueur despaired of defining terrorism in both editions of his monumental work on the subject, maintaining that it is neither possible to do so nor worthwhile to make the attempt.[79] 'Ten years of debates on typologies and definitions', he responded to a survey on definitions conducted by Schmid, 'have not enhanced our knowledge of the subject to a significant degree.'[80] Laqueur's contention is supported by the twenty-two different word categories occurring in the 109 different definitions that Schmid identified in his survey (see Table 1 overleaf).

At the end of this exhaustive exercise, Schmid asks 'whether the above list contains all the elements necessary for a good definition. The answer', he suggests, 'is probably "no".'[81] If it is impossible to define terrorism, as Laqueur argues, and fruitless to attempt to cobble together a truly comprehensive definition, as Schmid admits, are we to conclude that terrorism is impervious to precise, much less accurate definition? Not entirely. If we cannot define terrorism, then we can at least usefully distinguish it from other types of violence and identify the characteristics that make terrorism the distinct phenomenon of political violence that it is.

Table 1.1 Frequencies of definitional elements in 109 definitions of 'terrorism'

Element	Frequency (%)
1 Violence, force	83.5
2 Political	65
3 Fear, terror emphasized	51
4 Threat	47
5 (Psychological) effects and (anticipated) reactions	41.5
6 Victim–target differentiation	37.5
7 Purposive, planned, systematic, organized action	32
8 Method of combat, strategy, tactic	30.5
9 Extranormality, in breach of accepted rules, without humanitarian constraints	30
10 Coercion, extortion, induction of compliance	28
11 Publicity aspect	21.5
12 Arbitrariness; impersonal, random character; indiscrimination	21
13 Civilians, noncombatants, neutrals, outsiders as victims	17.5
14 Intimidation	17
15 Innocence of victims emphasized	15.5
16 Group, movement, organization as perpetrator	14
17 Symbolic aspect, demonstration to others	13.5
18 Incalculability, unpredictability, unexpectedness of occurrence of violence	9
19 Clandestine, covert nature	9
20 Repetitiveness; serial or campaign character of violence	7
21 Criminal	6
22 Demands made on third parties	4

Source: Alex P. Schmid, Albert J. Jongman et al., *Political Terrorism: A New Guide to Actors, Authors, Concepts, Data Bases, Theories, and Literature*. New Brunswick, Transaction Books, 1988, pp. 5–6.

Distinctions as a Path to Definition

Guerrilla warfare is a good place to start. Terrorism is often confused or equated with, or treated as synonymous with, guerrilla warfare. This is not entirely surprising, since guerrillas often employ the same tactics (assassination, kidnapping, bombings of public gathering-places, hostage-taking, etc.) for the same purposes (to intimidate or coerce, thereby affecting behaviour through the arousal of fear) as terrorists. In addition, both terrorists and guerrillas wear neither uniform nor identifying insignia and thus are often indistinguishable from non-combatants. However, despite the inclination to lump both terrorists and guerrillas into the same catch-all category of 'irregulars', there are nonetheless fundamental differences between the two. 'Guerrilla', for example, in its most widely accepted usage, is taken to refer to a numerically larger group of armed individuals,[82] who operate as a military unit, attack enemy military forces, and seize and hold territory (even if only ephemerally during daylight hours), while also exercising some form of sovereignty or control over a defined geographical area and its population. Terrorists, however, do not function in the open as armed units, generally do not attempt to seize or hold territory, deliberately avoid engaging enemy military forces in combat and rarely exercise any direct control or sovereignty either over territory or population.[83]

It is also useful to distinguish terrorists from ordinary criminals. Like terrorists, criminals use violence as a means to attaining a specific end. However, while the violent act itself may be similar – kidnapping, shooting, arson, for example – the purpose or motivation clearly is not. Whether the criminal employs violence as a means to obtain money, to acquire material goods, or to kill or injure a specific victim for pay, he is acting primarily for selfish, personal motivations (usually material gain). Moreover, unlike terrorism, the ordinary criminal's violent act is not designed or intended to have consequences or create psychological repercussions beyond the act itself. The criminal may of course use some short-term act of violence to 'terrorize' his victim, such as waving a gun in the face of a bank clerk during a robbery in order to ensure the clerk's expeditious compliance. In these instances, however, the bank robber is conveying no 'message' (political or otherwise) through his act of violence beyond facilitating the rapid handing over of his 'loot'. The criminal's act therefore is not meant to have any effect reaching beyond either the incident itself or the immediate victim. Further, the violence is neither conceived nor intended to convey any message to anyone other than the bank clerk himself, whose rapid cooperation is the robber's only objective. Perhaps most fundamentally, the criminal is not concerned with influencing or affecting public opinion: he simply wants to abscond with his money or accomplish his mercenary task in the quickest and easiest way possible so that he may reap his reward and enjoy the fruits of his labours. By contrast, the fundamental aim of the terrorist's violence is ultimately to change 'the system' – about which the ordinary criminal, of course, couldn't care less.[84]

The terrorist is also very different from the lunatic assassin, who may use identical tactics (e.g. shooting, bombing) and perhaps even seeks the same objective (e.g. the death of a political figure). However, while the tactics and targets of terrorists and lone assassins are often identical, their purpose is not. Whereas the terrorist's goal is again ineluctably political (to change or fundamentally alter a political system through his violent act), the lunatic assassin's goal is more often intrinsically idiosyncratic, completely egocentric and deeply personal. John Hinckley, who tried to kill President Reagan in 1981 to impress the actress Jodie Foster, is a case in point. He acted not from political motivation or ideological conviction but to fulfil some profound personal quest (killing the president to impress his screen idol). Such entirely *apolitical* motivations can in no way be compared to the rationalizations used by the Narodnaya Volya to justify its campaign of tyrannicide against the tsar and his minions, nor even to the Irish Republican Army's efforts to assassinate Prime Minister Margaret Thatcher or her successor, John Major, in hopes of dramatically changing British policy towards Northern Ireland. Further, just as one person cannot credibly claim to be a political party, so a lone individual cannot be considered to constitute a terrorist group. In this respect, even though Sirhan Sirhan's assassination of presidential candidate and US Senator Robert Kennedy in 1968 had a political motive (to protest against US support for Israel), it is debatable whether the murder should be defined as a terrorist act since Sirhan belonged to no organized political group and acted entirely on his own, out of deep personal frustration and a profound animus that few others shared. To qualify as terrorism, violence must be perpetrated by some organizational entity with at least some conspiratorial structure and identifiable chain of command beyond a single individual acting on his or her own.

Finally, the point should be emphasized that, unlike the ordinary criminal or the lunatic assassin, the terrorist is not pursuing purely egocentric goals – he is not driven by the wish to line his own pocket or satisfy some personal need or grievance. The terrorist is fundamentally an *altruist*: he believes that he is serving a 'good' cause designed to achieve a greater good for a wider constituency – whether real or imagined – which the terrorist and his organization purport to represent. The criminal, by comparison, serves no cause at all, just his own personal aggrandizement and material satiation. Indeed, a 'terrorist without a cause (at least in his own mind)', Konrad Kellen has argued, 'is not a terrorist'.[85] Yet the possession or identification of a cause is not a sufficient criterion for labelling someone a terrorist. In this key respect, the difference between terrorists and political extremists is clear. Many persons, of course, harbour all sorts of radical and extreme beliefs and opinions, and many of them belong to radical or even illegal or proscribed political organizations. However, if they do not use violence in the pursuance of their beliefs, they cannot be considered terrorists. The terrorist is fundamentally a *violent intellectual*, prepared to use and indeed committed to using force in the attainment of his goals.

By distinguishing terrorists from other types of criminals and terrorism from other forms of crime, we come to appreciate that terrorism is

- ineluctably political in aims and motives;
- violent – or, equally important, threatens violence;
- designed to have far-reaching psychological repercussions beyond the immediate victim or target;
- conducted by an organization with an identifiable chain of command or conspiratorial cell structure (whose members wear no uniform or identifying insignia); and
- perpetrated by a subnational group or non-state entity.

We may therefore now attempt to define terrorism as the deliberate creation and exploitation of fear through violence or the threat of violence in the pursuit of political change. All terrorist acts involve violence or the threat of violence. Terrorism is specifically designed to have far-reaching psychological effects beyond the immediate victim(s) or object of the terrorist attack. It is meant to instil fear within, and thereby intimidate, a wider 'target audience' that might include a rival ethnic or religious group, an entire country, a national government or political party, or public opinion in general. Terrorism is designed to create power where there is none or to consolidate power where there is very little. Through the publicity generated by their violence, terrorists seek to obtain the leverage, influence and power they otherwise lack to effect political change on either a local or an international scale.

2

The Post-colonial Era: Ethno-nationalist/Separatist Terrorism

Although terrorism motivated by ethno-nationalist/separatist aspirations had emerged from within the moribund Ottoman and Habsburg Empires during the three decades immediately preceding the First World War, it was only after 1945 that this phenomenon became a more pervasive global force. Two separate, highly symbolic events that had occurred early in the Second World War abetted its subsequent development. At the time, the repercussions for post-war anti-colonial struggles of the fall of Singapore and the proclamation of the Atlantic Charter could not possibly have been anticipated. Yet both, in different ways, exerted a strong influence on indigenous nationalist movements, demonstrating as they did the vulnerability of once-mighty empires and the hypocrisy of wartime pledges of support for self-determination.

On 15 February 1942 the British Empire suffered the worst defeat in its history when Singapore fell to the invading Japanese forces. Whatever its strategic value, Singapore's real significance – according to the foremost military strategist of his day, Basil Liddell Hart – was as the

outstanding symbol of Western Power in the Far East . . . Its easy capture in February 1942 was shattering to British, and European, prestige in Asia. No belated re-entry could efface the impression. The white man had lost his ascendancy with the disproof of his magic. The realisation of his vulnerability fostered and encouraged the post-war spread of Asiatic revolt against European domination or intrusion.[1]

Indeed, within weeks Japan had also conquered the Dutch East Indies (Indonesia) and Burma. Hong Kong had already capitulated the previous Christmas, and more than a year earlier Japan had imposed its rule over French Indochina. Thus, when the American garrison holding out on Corregidor in the Philippines finally surrendered in May 1942, Japan's conquest of Southeast Asia – and the destruction of the British, French, Dutch and American empires there – was complete.

The long-term impact of these events was profound. Native peoples who had previously believed in the invincibility of their European colonial overlords hereafter saw their former masters in a starkly different light. Not only had the vast British Empire been dealt a crushing blow, but American pledges of peace and security to its Pacific possessions had been similarly shattered. France's complete impotence in the face of Japanese bullying over Indochina had greatly undermined its imperial stature among the Vietnamese; while in Indonesia, Japanese promises of independence effectively negated any lingering feelings of loyalty to the Dutch. In the blink of an eye, the European powers' pre-war arguments that their variegated Asian subjects were incapable of governing themselves were swept aside by Japan's policy of devolving self-government to local administrations and nominal independence to the countries they now occupied. Paradoxically, in many places it was the natives who now ruled the interned Europeans – many of whom found themselves relegated to the most menial and back-breaking tasks. It is not surprising, therefore, that even as the tide of war shifted in the Allies' favour over the following years, almost all these peoples resolved never again to come under European imperial rule.

It was not only these declining colonial powers' Asian subjects who clamoured for independence and self-determination. This litany of humiliating defeats had struck responsive chords in other ears, everywhere challenging the myth of European – indeed, Western – power and military superiority, if not omnipotence. In the Middle East as well as in Africa, India, the Mediterranean and North Africa, indigenous peoples chafed at the prospect of returning to their pre-war colonial status quo. They were encouraged, however unintentionally, by promises of independence and self-determination made by the Allies early in the Second World War.[2] Even before the United States had entered the war in 1941, President Franklin D. Roosevelt had met with Britain's Prime Minister Winston Churchill on a warship off the coast of

Newfoundland to formulate both countries' post-war aims. The result was an eight-point document known as the Atlantic Charter, whose main purpose, one historian has observed, was to 'impress enemy opinion with the justice of the western cause'.[3] Its effects, however, went far beyond that lofty aim.

The Charter's first point innocuously affirmed that both countries sought no 'aggrandisement, territorial or other' from the war; it was the second and third points that would be the source of future difficulties for the European powers. Point two declared unequivocally that neither Britain nor the United States desired to 'see . . . territorial changes that do not accord with the freely expressed wishes of the peoples concerned', while point three further pledged both countries to 'respect the right of all peoples to choose the form of government under which they will live'.[4] These principles were embodied in the 'Declaration of the United Nations', agreed to by Britain and the United States on 1 January 1942, which all the governments at war with Germany subsequently signed, thus committing their countries to respect promises that in some instances they had no intention of keeping. Although on the first anniversary of the Charter's signing Churchill attempted to qualify and restrict the terms of the original agreement – arguing that it was not intended that these principles should apply either to Asia or Africa, and especially not to India and Palestine, but only to those peoples in hitherto sovereign countries conquered by Germany, Italy and Japan[5] – the damage had already been done. Indeed, all subsequent efforts by the European colonial powers to redefine or re-interpret the Charter in ways favourable to the prolongation of their imperial rule fell for the most part on deaf ears.

The situation in post-war Algeria was perhaps typical of the bitterness, engendered by broken promises and misplaced hopes, that nurtured intractable conflict. In 1943, shortly after the Allied landings had liberated North Africa from Vichy rule, a delegation of Algerian Muslims sought an audience with the newly installed Free French commander, General Henri Giraud. Their request amounted to nothing more than recognition of the rights and freedoms that had been so loftily proclaimed in the Atlantic Charter, of which, of course, the French government-in-exile was a signatory. Giraud's reply was dismissively brusque. 'I don't care about reforms,' he thundered, 'I want soldiers first.'[6] The ever-compliant Algerians obligingly provided these volunteers – much as they had some thirty years before; but they did so now in the expectation – shared by other European powers' colonial subjects elsewhere – that their loyalty would be rewarded appropriately at the war's end. As was the case in at least a dozen other colonial settings, however, their antici-pation was to be disappointed. Indeed, by 1947 the future leader of the anti-British guerrilla campaign in Cyprus, General George Grivas (a Greek Cypriot who had fought beside the Allies), had already despaired in the face of repeated prevarications concerning Britain's own wartime promises of self-determination. 'More and more,' he recalled, 'it seemed to me that only a revolution would liberate my homeland.'[7] The Algerians were rapidly coming to the same conclusion. They were further encouraged by the catastrophic defeat inflicted on the French at Dien Bien Phu in 1954 and by France's subsequent ignominious withdrawal from Indochina. Meanwhile, a revolt against British rule had broken out in Palestine, waged by two small Jewish terrorist organi-zations – the Irgun Zvai Le'umi (National Military Organization, or Irgun) and the Lohamei Herut Yisrael (Freedom Fighters for Israel, known to Jews by its Hebrew acronym, Lehi, and to the British as the Stern Gang). The Irgun's campaign was the more significant of the two, in that it established a revolutionary model which thereafter was emulated and embraced by both anti-colonial and post-colonial era terrorist groups around the world.

Post-war Palestine

Palestine had, of course, long been the scene of numerous riots and other manifestations of intercommunal violence that between 1936 and 1939 had culminated in a full-scale rebellion by its Arab inhabitants. In 1937, a new element was added to the country's incendiary landscape when the Irgun commenced retaliatory terrorist attacks on the Arabs. The group expanded its operations to include British targets in 1939 following the government's promulgation of a White Paper in May that imposed severe restrictions on Jewish immigration to Palestine, thereby closing one of the few remaining avenues of escape available to European Jews fleeing Hitler. But the Irgun's inchoate revolt against British rule was short-lived. Less than three months after it began, Britain was at war with Germany. Confronted by the prospect of the greater menace of a victorious Nazi Germany, the Irgun declared a truce and announced the suspension of all anti-British operations for the war's duration. Like the rest of the Jewish community in Palestine, who had also pledged to support the British war effort, the Irgun hoped that this loyalty would later result in the recognition of Zionist claims to statehood.

In May 1942, a young private attached to General Anders' Polish army-in-exile arrived in Palestine. Menachem Begin's journey had been a circuitous one. Born in 1913 in Brest Litovsk, Poland, the future prime minister of Israel (1977–83) had first become involved in Zionist politics as a teenager when he joined Betar, a right-wing nationalist Jewish youth group. By the time he had received his law degree from Warsaw University in 1935, Begin was head of the group's Organization Department for Poland. Three years later he was appointed its national commander. However, when Germany invaded Poland in September 1939, Begin was forced to flee to Lithuania. A year later, Russian secret police arrested him on the ironic charge of being 'an agent of British imperialism'. After spending nine months in a local gaol, Begin was sentenced to eight years' 'correctional labour'. In June 1941, when Germany invaded Russia, he was on a Russian ship carrying political prisoners to a Stalinist labour camp in Siberia. A reprieve came in the form of an offer to join the Polish army or continue his journey. Begin chose the former and found himself in a unit ordered to Palestine. Shortly after his arrival, he established contact with the Irgun high command.

Since the suspension of its revolt, the Irgun had fallen into disarray. The deaths of its ideological mentor, Vladimir Jabotinsky, in August 1940 and its military commander, David Raziel, nine months later had deprived the group of leadership and direction at a time when its self-imposed dormancy required someone at the top with the vision and organizational skills necessary to hold it together. Throughout 1943, Begin met with the Irgun's surviving senior commanders to discuss the group's future. As the war against Germany moved decisively in the Allies' favour, they became convinced that the Irgun should resume its revolt. Four dominant considerations influenced this decision. First and foremost was news of the terrible fate that had befallen European Jewry under Nazi domination. Second, the expiration in March 1944 of the White Paper's rigidly enforced five-year immigration quota would be likely to choke off all future Jewish immigration to Palestine. Third, the Irgun's leaders agreed that the reasoning behind the self-imposed truce they had declared four years before – that harming Britain might help

Germany – was no longer tenable since the course of the Second World War had now virtually assured an Allied victory. Finally, by renewing the revolt, the Irgun's revamped high command sought to position themselves and their organization at the vanguard of the active realization of the Jews' political and nationalist aspirations.

On 1 December 1943 Begin formally assumed command of the group and finalized plans for the resumption of anti-British operations. As a lowly enlisted man in an exile army with only the bare minimum of formal military training, Begin was an unlikely strategist. But he possessed an uncanny analytical ability to cut right to the heart of an issue and an intuitive sense about the interplay between violence, politics and propaganda that ideally qualified him to lead a terrorist organization. Begin's strategy was simple. The handful of men and few weapons that in 1943 comprised the Irgun could never hope to challenge the British army on the battlefield and win. Instead, the group would function in the setting and operate in the manner that best afforded the terrorist with means of concealment and escape. Based in the city, its members would bury themselves within the surrounding community, indistinguishable from ordinary, law-abiding citizens. Then, at the appropriate moment, they would emerge from the shadows to strike before disappearing back into the anonymity of Palestine's urban neighbourhoods, remaining safely beyond the reach of the authorities. The Irgun's plan, therefore, was not to defeat Britain militarily, but to use terrorist violence to undermine the government's prestige and control of Palestine by striking at symbols of British rule. 'History and our observation', Begin later recalled, 'persuaded us that if we could succeed in destroying the government's prestige in Eretz Israel [literally 'the land of Israel'], the removal of its rule would follow automatically. Thenceforward, we gave no peace to this weak spot. Throughout all the years of our uprising, we hit at the British Government's prestige, deliberately, tirelessly, unceasingly.'[8]

In contrast to other colonial rebellions that either had sought decisive military victories in actual battle or had relied on a prolonged strategy of attrition, the Irgun adopted a strategy that involved the relentless targeting of those institutions of government that unmistakably represented Britain's oppressive rule of Palestine. Thus the Irgun recommenced operations in February 1944 with the simultaneous bombings of the immigration department's offices in Palestine's three major cities – Jerusalem, Tel Aviv and Haifa. Subsequent attacks were mounted against the government land registry offices, from which the White Paper's provisions restricting Jewish land purchase were administered; the department of taxation and finance, responsible for collecting the revenue used to fund the government's repressive policies; and of course the security forces – the police and army – which were charged with the White Paper's enforcement.

The Irgun's most spectacular operation was without doubt its bombing in July 1946 of Jerusalem's King David Hotel. Although much has been written about this controversial incident, it is worth recalling that the King David was no ordinary hostelry. On two floors of its southern wing (beneath which the explosives were placed), the hotel housed the nerve centre of British rule in Palestine: the government secretariat and headquarters of British military forces in Palestine and Transjordan. The attack's target, therefore, was neither the hotel itself nor the persons working or staying in it, but the government and military offices located there. Nor was its purpose random, indiscriminate carnage. Unlike many terrorist groups today, the Irgun's strategy was not deliberately to target or wantonly harm civilians. At the same time, though, the claim of Begin and other apologists that warnings were issued to evacuate the hotel before the blast cannot absolve either the group or its commander from responsibility for the ninety-one persons killed and forty-five others injured: men and women, Arabs, Jews and Britons alike. Indeed, whatever non-lethal intentions the Irgun may or may not have had, the fact remains that a tragedy of almost unparalleled magnitude was inflicted at the King David Hotel, so that to this day the bombing still holds an infamous distinction as one of the world's single most lethal terrorist incidents of the twentieth century.

Despite – or perhaps because of – the tragic loss of life, so far as the Irgun was concerned the bombing achieved its objective: attracting worldwide attention to the group's struggle and the worsening situation in Palestine. Leading articles in all the British newspapers focused on the nugatory results of recent military operations against the terrorists that had been previously trumpeted as great successes. Typical of these was the *Manchester Guardian*'s observation that the bombing 'will be a shock to those who imagined that the Government's firmness had put a stop to Jewish terrorism and had brought about an easier situation in Palestine. In fact, the opposite is the truth.'[9] These reactions accorded perfectly with Begin's plan to foster a climate of fear and alarm in Palestine so pervasive as to undermine confidence both there and in Britain in the government's ability to maintain order. Indeed, in these circumstances, the government could only respond by imposing on Palestine a harsh regimen of security measures encompassing a daily routine of curfews, road blocks, snap checks, cordon-and-search operations and, for a time, even martial law. The failure of these measures to stop the Irgun's unrelenting terrorist campaign would, Begin hoped, have the effect of further underscoring the government's weakness. He also banked on the fact that the massive disruptions caused to daily life and commerce by the harsh and repressive countermeasures that the British were forced to take would further alienate the community from the government, thwart its efforts to obtain the community's cooperation against the terrorists, and create in the minds of the Jews an image of the army and the police as oppressors rather than protectors. Moreover, the more conspicuous the security forces seemed, the stronger the terrorists appeared.

At the foundation of this strategy was Begin's belief that the British, unlike the Germans who during the war had carried out wholesale reprisals against civilians, were incapable of such barbarity.[10] 'We knew', he explained, 'that Eretz Israel, in consequence of the revolt, resembled a glass house. The world was looking into it with ever-increasing interest and could see most of what was happening inside . . . Arms were our weapons of attack; the transparency of the "glass" was our shield of defence.'[11] By compelling a liberal democracy like Britain to take increasingly repressive measures against the public, the terrorists sought to push Britain to the limit of its endurance. In this respect, the Irgun did not have to defeat Britain militarily; they only had to avoid losing. Accordingly, British tactical 'successes' did nothing to change the balance of forces or bring the security forces any closer to victory. Rather, measures such as massive cordon-and-search operations and the imposition of martial law proved to bring only ephemeral benefits, bought at the cost of estranging the population from the government. Nearly a quarter of a century later, the Brazilian revolutionary theorist Carlos Marighela would advocate the same strategy in his famous 'Mini-Manual', the *Handbook of Urban Guerrilla War*.[12]

In sum, this was not a war of 'numbers'. Success was measured not in terms of casualties inflicted (between 1945 and 1947, the worst years of the conflict, just under 150 British soldiers were killed) or assets destroyed, but – precisely as Begin had wanted – by psychological impact. In place of a conventional military strategy of confrontation in battle, Begin and his lieutenants conceived operations that were designed less to kill than to tarnish the government's prestige, demoralize its security forces and undermine Britain's resolve to remain in Palestine. Explaining his strategy, Begin argued that 'The very existence of an underground must, in the end, undermine the prestige of a colonial regime that lives by the legend of its omnipotence. Every attack which it fails to prevent is a blow at its standing. Even if the attack does not succeed, it makes a dent in that prestige, and that dent widens into a crack which is extended with every succeeding attack.'[13] Thus, even though the British forces outnumbered the terrorists by twenty to one – so that there was, according to one account, 'one armed soldier to each adult male Jew in Palestine'[14] – even with this overwhelming numerical superiority, the British were still unable to destroy the Irgun and maintain order in Palestine.

Finally, an integral and innovative part of the Irgun's strategy was Begin's use of daring and dramatic acts of violence to attract international attention to Palestine and thereby publicize simultaneously the Zionists' grievances against Britain and their claims for statehood. In an era long before the advent of CNN and instantaneous satellite-transmitted news broadcasts, the Irgun deliberately attempted to appeal to a worldwide audience far beyond the immediate confines of the local struggle, beyond even the ruling regime's own homeland. In particular, the Irgun – like its non-violent and less violent Zionist counterparts – sought to generate sympathy and marshal support among powerful allies such as the Jewish community in the United States and its elected representatives in Congress and the White House, as well as among the delegates to the fledgling United Nations Organization, to bring pressure to bear on Britain to grant Jewish statehood. The success of this strategy, Begin claims, may be seen in the paucity of global coverage afforded to the civil war that had erupted in Greece after the Second World War, compared to that devoted to events in Palestine. Palestine, he wrote, had undeniably become a 'centre of world interest. The revolt had made it so. It is a fact', Begin maintains,

that no partisan struggle had been so publicized throughout the world as was ours . . . The reports on our operations, under

screaming headlines, covered the front pages of newspapers everywhere, particularly in the United States . . . The interest of the
newspapers is the measure of the interest of the public. And the
public – not only Jews but non-Jews too – were manifestly interested
in the blows we were striking in Eretz Israel.[15]

In this respect, pro-Irgun Jewish-American lobbyists were noticeably
successful in obtaining the passage of resolutions by the US Congress
condemning 'British oppression' and re-affirming American support
for the establishment of a Jewish state in Palestine.[16] These activities,
which presaged the efforts undertaken more recently by Irish-American
activists on behalf of Sinn Fein and the IRA, had similarly corrosive
effects on Anglo-American relations more than half a century ago.

By 1947 the Irgun had in fact achieved its objectives. Reporting on the
situation to Washington, the American consul-general in Jerusalem
observed that

with [British] officials attempting to administrate from behind
masses of barbed wire, in heavily defended buildings, and with the
same officials (minus wives and children evacuated some time ago)
living in pathetic seclusion in 'security zones', one cannot escape the
conclusion that the Government of Palestine is a hunted organization with little hope of ever being able to cope with conditions in this
country as they exist today.[17]

Indeed, each successive terrorist outrage illuminated the government's
inability to curb, much less defeat the terrorists. Already sapped by the
Second World War, Britain's limited economic resources were further
strained by the cost of deploying so large a military force to Palestine to
cope with the tide of violence submerging the country. Public opinion in
Britain, already ill-disposed to the continued loss of life and expenditure
of effort in an unwinnable situation, was further inflamed by incidents
such as the King David Hotel bombing and the Irgun's hanging in July
1947 of two sergeants in retaliation for the government's execution of
three convicted Irgun terrorists. As the renowned British historian of
the Middle East, Elizabeth Monroe, has noted in respect of the
hangings: 'The British public had taken Palestine in its stride . . . and
had looked upon "disturbances" and "violence" there much as it viewed

"the troubles" in Ireland – as an unpleasant experience that was part of the white man's burden.' All this changed, however, with the cold-blooded murder of the sergeants. Photographs of the grim death scene – depicting the two corpses just inches above the ground, the sergeants' hooded faces and bloodied shirts – were emblazoned across the front pages of British newspapers under headlines decrying their execution as an act of 'medieval barbarity'. As inured to the almost daily reports of the death and deprivation suffered by the army in Palestine as the British public was, the brutal execution of the two sergeants made a deep and unalterable impression on the national psyche. 'All home comment on that deed', Monroe continued, was 'different in tone from that on earlier terrorist acts, many of which caused greater loss of life – for instance, the blowing up of the officers' club or of the King David Hotel.'[18] For both the British public and the press, the murders seemed to demonstrate the futility of the situation in Palestine and the pointlessness of remaining there any longer than was absolutely necessary.

At the time, Britain was also of course coming under intense pressure from the United States and other quarters regarding the admission to Palestine of tens of thousands of Jewish displaced persons still languishing throughout liberated Europe and was itself trying to stem the flood of illegal Jewish immigrants attempting to enter Palestine. In addition, throughout the summer of 1947 the Special Committee on Palestine (UNSCOP) appointed by the UN General Assembly was completing its investigations regarding the country's future.[19] It is a measure of the Irgun's success that Begin was twice granted audiences with the committee to explain the group's aims, motivations and vision of a Jewish state in Palestine. The committee's unanimous recommendation calling for the immediate termination of British rule and granting of independence to Palestine finally forced the government's hand.[20] In September the colonial secretary, Arthur Creech-Jones, announced that Britain would no longer be responsible for governing Palestine and that all civilian and military personnel would be evacuated as soon as was practicable.

A decade and a half after the event, Creech-Jones cited four pivotal considerations that influenced the government's decision. First, there were the irreconcilable differences between Palestine's Arab and Jewish communities; second, the drain on Britain's shrinking financial resources imposed by the country's heavy military commitment in

Palestine; third, the force of international, American and parliamentary opinion; and finally – and, he believed, most significant – the public outcry in Britain that followed the Irgun's hanging of the two sergeants. Describing the confluence of events that compelled the government to surrender the mandate, the former colonial secretary recalled specifically that 'Terrorism was at its worst and the British public seemed unable to stand much more.' Hence, with 'accelerating speed', Creech-Jones explained, 'the Cabinet was pushed to the conclusion that they could [no] longer support the Mandate'.[21] On 15 May 1948 Britain's rule over Palestine formally ended and the establishment of the State of Israel was proclaimed. In a communiqué issued that same day by the Irgun, Begin declared:

> After many years of underground warfare, years of persecution and suffering . . . [the] Hebrew revolt of 1944–48 has been crowned with success . . . The rule of enslavement of Britain in our country has been beaten, uprooted, has crumbled and been dispersed . . . The State of Israel has arisen. And it has arisen 'Only Thus': through blood, fire, a strong hand and a mighty arm, with suffering and sacrifices.[22]

The Anti-colonial Struggles of the 1950s: Cyprus and Algeria

The Irgun's revolt provided a template for subsequent anti-colonial uprisings elsewhere. Indeed, the most effective irredentist struggles of the immediate post-war era were those that emulated Begin's strategy and deliberately sought to appeal to – and thereby attract the attention and sympathy of – an international audience. 'Our intention', explained General George Grivas, the founder and commander of EOKA (Ethniki Organosis Kyprion Agoniston, or National Organization of Cypriot Fighters), in his memoirs, 'was to focus the eyes of the world on Cyprus and force the British to fulfil their promises.'[23] Similarly, the 1954 proclamation of revolt against French rule of Algeria by the FLN (Front de Libération Nationale, or National Liberation Front) prominently cited the 'internationalism of the Algerian problem' as among its principal goals.[24]

In pursuit of this end, both groups also made a conscious effort to appeal directly to the United Nations for help. EOKA's own proclamation of revolt, for example, was specifically addressed to 'Diplomats of the World'. It called upon them to 'Look to your duty. It is shameful that, in the twentieth century, people should have to shed blood for freedom, that divine gift for which we too fought at your side and for which you, at least, claim that you fought against Nazism.'[25] In Algeria, FLN offensives, general strikes and other demonstrations were timed to occur when the UN General Assembly reconvened or was already scheduled to discuss the conflict. In January 1957 the fabled 'Battle of Algiers', immortalized by the 1966 Gillo Pontecorvo film of the same name, when the FLN unleashed its campaign of mass urban terrorism, was deliberately choreographed to coincide with the General Assembly's annual opening session. The FLN communiqué announcing the strike that accompanied the new terrorist offensive candidly admitted to this timing, announcing its desire to 'bestow an incontestable authority upon our delegates at the United Nations in order to convince those rare diplomats still hesitant or possessing illusions about France's liberal policy'.[26] To a large extent, therefore, the success of both EOKA and the FLN in ending foreign rule of their respective countries was predicated upon their ability to attract external attention to their respective struggles much as the Irgun had a decade before.

In Cyprus, from the very start, Grivas appreciated the necessity of reaching out to an audience beyond the immediate geographical boundaries of his group's struggle. 'The enlightenment of international public opinion', he recognized, 'was bound to play an important part in bringing home to all concerned the Cypriot people's demand for self-determination. It is a fact that there were many foreigners and even United Nations representatives who were completely ignorant of why we were demanding our freedom.'[27] Accordingly, Grivas enshrined this principle in the 'Preparatory General Plan' that he had formulated in 1953 – two years before the campaign actually began – whose opening paragraph clearly states the fundamental objective 'to arouse international public opinion . . . by deeds of heroism and self-sacrifice which will focus attention on Cyprus until our aims are achieved'.[28] Although there is no evidence that Grivas ever read Begin's book (an English-language translation of *The Revolt* had been published in London and New York in 1951) or had studied the Irgun's campaign, the parallels between the two struggles are unmistakable. Grivas's strategy, like

Begin's, was not to win an outright military victory against the numerically superior British forces, but to rely on dramatic, well-orchestrated
and appropriately timed acts of violence to focus international attention
on the situation in Cyprus and the Greek Cypriots' demand for *enosis* –
unification with Greece.

'My small force was outnumbered by more than a hundred to one,'
Grivas later recalled, 'but, as I have said, this made no difference to the
type of subversive warfare I was planning.'[29] His plan was to deploy the
majority of EOKA forces in the island's urban centres, where they were
organized into individual terrorist cells numbering no more than eight
to ten men each. Their mission was to tie up as many British troops as
possible on static guard duties in the cities, thereby allowing EOKA to
consolidate its control over the rest of the island. In words reminiscent
of Begin's, Grivas explained in his treatise on guerrilla warfare that

> our strategy consisted in turning the whole island into a single field
> of battle in which there was no distinction between front and rear, so
> that the enemy should at no time and in no place feel himself secure.
> The enemy never knew where and when we might strike . . . This
> strategy achieved the dispersal, intimidation and wearing down of
> the enemy's forces and especially serious consequences resulting
> from our use of surprise.[30]

By concentrating on urban operations, as the Irgun had in Palestine,
EOKA also gained immediate access to the news media dispatched to
the island to cover the escalating violence. Had EOKA, like traditional
guerrilla forces, confined its operations to the island's rugged and
isolated rural areas and mountain ranges, it would arguably have lost this
access and forfeited the exposure so critical to Grivas's strategy. The
urban terrorist campaign was thus pivotal in securing the propaganda
platform required by the group to broadcast its cause to the world. In
this respect, Grivas was able to derive great satisfaction from the fact
that, within five months of the revolt's proclamation, EOKA had
succeeded in attaining what a decade of patient diplomacy and insistent
lobbying had failed to achieve: UN consideration of the Greek Cypriots'
nationalist claims. Hitherto, the General Assembly had upheld British
arguments that the situation in Cyprus was an entirely *internal* matter
and therefore outside the organization's remit. Now, for the first time,

Cyprus had been placed on the UN's agenda. 'This proved', Grivas later recalled, 'that inside this international body the idea was beginning to penetrate that something must be done about the Cyprus question.'[31]

Indeed, by the end of 1955, Grivas had succeeded in plunging the island into complete disorder. An average of two British soldiers or policemen were being killed each week. The security forces had been thrown on the defensive, kept off-balance by repeated EOKA hit-and-run attacks and unable to mount any effective offensive operations. Like Begin, Grivas also calculated that the unrelenting terrorist onslaught would sap the morale of British forces and compel them to over-react with counterproductive, self-defeating measures directed against the law-abiding Greek-Cypriot community. 'The "security forces" set about their work in a manner which might have been deliberately designed to drive the population into our arms,' Grivas recalled. 'These attempts to frighten the people away from EOKA always had exactly the opposite effect to that intended: the population were merely bound more closely to the Organisation.'[32] Once again, the fundamental asymmetry between the terrorists' apparent ability to strike anywhere, at any time, and the security forces' inability to protect all conceivable targets, all the time, was glaringly demonstrated. As in Palestine, the more visible and pervasive the security forces in Cyprus became, the greater the public frustration caused by disruption to daily life, and the more powerful and omnipresent the terrorists appeared. At the height of the conflict, British security forces on Cyprus totalled nearly 40,000 men, arrayed against a hard core of fewer than 400 active terrorists, backed by some 750 'auxiliaries'.[33] Again as in Palestine, this was not a war of 'numbers'. The massive deployment of British troops had little overall impact on the situation. As Grivas later reflected about his opponent commanding the British forces, Field Marshal Sir John Harding: 'He underrated his enemy on the one hand, and overweighted his forces on the other. But one does not use a tank to catch field mice – a cat will do the job better'.[34]

Throughout the campaign, Grivas coordinated his underground campaign with the above-ground diplomatic efforts of Archbishop Makarios III (Michael Christodoros Mouskos). As the appointed head of the Ethnarchy (Church Council) of Cyprus, Makarios was also the Greek-Cypriot community's de facto political leader. Both he and Grivas had met as early as 1950 to plan the general outline of the revolt, and prelate and soldier worked closely together throughout the struggle to achieve their shared goal of *enosis*. Thus the relationship that today exists between Sinn Fein and the IRA has an historical parallel in that between the Ethnarchy and EOKA forty years ago, with Makarios playing the role allegedly performed today by Gerry Adams. Like Adams, Makarios was interned; and in 1956 he was exiled to the Seychelles, being allowed to return to Cyprus two years later as a condition for Greek-Cypriot participation in British-sponsored multi-party talks on the island's future. It was not until February 1959 that agreement was reached.

Under intense pressure from Greece, Makarios reluctantly accepted the proposal for the creation of an independent republic of Cyprus, with Britain being allowed to retain two strategic bases on the island. Fears that Turkey would otherwise forcibly impose partition (as in fact occurred fifteen years later) led Makarios to acquiesce in the arrangement despite Grivas's vehement opposition. The revolt officially ended a month later, when EOKA surrendered a large enough quantity of arms to satisfy the government that the peace agreement could be implemented. Although *enosis* was never achieved, British rule was forcibly ended and Cyprus was granted its independence. The fruits of the terrorists' labours were also apparent in the new republic's general election: Makarios was elected the country's first president, polling 67 per cent of the popular vote.[35]

At the other end of the Mediterranean, the revolt against French rule over Algeria between 1954 and 1962 was the last of the immediate postwar anti-colonial struggles. For that reason, perhaps, it had the most direct and discernible impact on many later ethno-nationalist terrorist campaigns. Yassir Arafat, for example, in his authorized biography, cites the pivotal influence that the FLN had on the PLO's struggle and the critical material assistance that Algeria later provided to the Palestinians. 'I started my contacts with the Algerian revolutionaries in the early 1950s,' he recalled. 'I stayed in touch with them and they promised they would help us when they had achieved their independence. I never doubted for one moment that they would win, and that their victory would be very important for us.'[36] In his own candid memoir, Nelson Mandela similarly identifies the seminal influence that the FLN's struggle had on the decades-long effort of the African National Congress (ANC) to end minority white rule of South Africa. 'The situation in Algeria', Mandela wrote, 'was the closest model to our own in that the rebels faced a large white settler community that ruled the indigenous majority.' Accordingly, the ANC studied the Algerian conflict closely, deriving the main lesson that a pure military victory was impossible to achieve in such circumstances. Instead, Mandela assiduously applied the advice given to him by an Algerian revolutionary that 'international opinion . . . is sometimes worth more than a fleet of jet fighters'.[37] It was a lesson that the FLN itself had learned only belatedly.

By the middle of 1956, the rebellion against French rule had been raging for nearly two years; the FLN, however, had precious few tangible achievements to show for its efforts, and recent advances by the security forces in the countryside had seriously undermined the group's rural insurgent strategy. Accordingly, the FLN embarked on a new strategy that would, for the first time, focus on the country's capital, Algiers, and thereby apply pressure to France by appealing directly to international opinion. The architect of this new strategy, first unveiled during the August 1956 summit convened at Soummam, Morocco, in hopes of reversing the FLN's declining fortunes, was Ramdane Abane, a leading figure in the movement until his execution the following year during an internecine power struggle. As the group's chief theoretician, he was also its most potent intellect. From an impoverished background and entirely self-educated, he was as completely unsentimental as he was ruthless, maintaining an unalterable faith in the efficacy of violence. This was clearly evident in his famous directive number nine, wherein Abane succinctly explained not just the purpose of the FLN's new strategy but the elementary logic behind urban terrorism. 'Is it preferable for our cause to kill ten enemies in an oued [dry river bed] of Telergma when no one will talk of it,' he rhetorically asked, 'or a single man in Algiers which will be noted the next day by the American press?'[38]

The chain of events that led to the FLN's full-scale urban terrorist campaign, however, had actually begun two months earlier, in June, with the execution by guillotine of two convicted FLN fighters. As had occurred countless times elsewhere (Palestine and Cyprus included), such attempts by the ruling regime to deter further violence with a particularly harsh exemplary punishment backfired catastrophically. The recipients of this lesson, rather than serving as abject examples, as often as not become martyrs: emblematic rallying points for the revolutionary cause around which still greater sacrifice and still further blood-shed and destruction are demanded and justified. Thus it was in Algeria, where the FLN announced that for every FLN fighter executed, a hundred Frenchmen would meet a similar fate. Hitherto, the group could boast that its campaign in the capital had been deliberately non-lethal, its bombs directed against inanimate 'symbols' of French rule – government offices and buildings, military cantonments and police stations – but not deliberately against people. This now changed with Abane's instructions to the FLN's urban cadres to unleash a reign of unprecedented bombings and terror. Within seventy-two hours, forty-nine French civilians had been gunned down. Then, in August, as a result of the new strategic direction approved that same month at Soummam, the bombings began.

The campaign was spearheaded not by the group's hardened male fighters but by its attractive young female operatives – whose comely bearing and European looks, as Saadi Yacef, the group's operations officer in Algiers (who later reprised his real-life role in the Pontecorvo film), correctly guessed, would arouse far less suspicion than their male counterparts. Their targets, moreover, were neither military nor even governmental, but the crowded seaside milk bar frequented by *pied noir* (French colonist) families after a day at the beach; a cafeteria particularly favoured by European university students; and the downtown Air France passenger terminus. The coordinated operations killed three persons and injured some fifty others – including several children, some of them among the dozen or so victims requiring surgical amputation of mangled limbs. Throughout it all, Abane was unmoved. Drawing the same analogy between the terrorist bomb-in-the-dustbin and the 'poor man's air force' cited in chapter 1, Abane is said to have dismissively observed: 'I see hardly any difference between the girl who places a bomb in the Milk-Bar and the French aviator who bombards a *mechta* [village] or who drops napalm on a *zone interdite*.'[39]

The urban campaign continued throughout the remainder of the year, climaxing on 28 December 1956 with the assassination of the mayor of Algiers. Widespread anti-Muslim rioting broke out, only to be followed by a new round of FLN assassinations. This was the last straw. In despair over the deteriorating situation, the governor-general called out the army. On 7 January 1957, General Jacques Massu, commander of the elite 10th Parachute Division, assumed complete responsibility for maintaining order in the city. The FLN responded by declaring a general strike for 28 January, to coincide – as noted above – with the UN's annual opening session, its purpose (and that of the terrorist attacks that accompanied it) to focus international attention on Algeria. Once again, Yacef's bombers set about their work with startling efficiency. The FLN's target set now expanded to include popular bars and bistros, crowded city streets and sports stadia packed with spectators. Within two weeks fifteen persons had been killed and 105 others wounded.

Massu went on the offensive. Having fought in Indochina, he and his senior commanders prided themselves on having acquired a thorough understanding of revolutionary warfare – and how to counter it. Victory, they were convinced, would be entirely dependent on the acquisition of intelligence. 'The man who places the bomb', declared Colonel Yves Godard, one of Massu's sector commanders, 'is but an arm that tomorrow will be replaced by another arm': the key was to find the individual commanding the arm. Accordingly, Godard and his men set out to uproot and destroy the FLN's urban infrastructure. Their method was to build up a meticulously detailed picture of the FLN's apparatus in Algiers that would home in relentlessly on the terrorist campaign's mastermind. Godard's approach, dramatically depicted on screen by Pontecorvo, was described by the British historian Alistair Horne as a 'complex *organigramme* [that] began to take shape on a large blackboard, a kind of skeleton pyramid in which, as each fresh piece of information came from the interrogation centres, another name (and not always necessarily the right name) would be entered'.[40] That this system proved effective, there is no doubt. The problem was that it also depended on, and therefore encouraged, widespread abuses, including torture; for Massu and his men were not particularly concerned about *how* they obtained this information. Torture of both terrorists and *suspected* terrorists became routine. The French army in Algeria found it easy to justify such extraordinary measures, given the extraordinary conditions. The prevailing exculpatory philosophy among the Paras can be summed up by Massu's terse response to complaints, that 'the innocent [that is, the next victims of terrorist attacks] deserve more protection than the guilty'.[41]

The brutality of the army's campaign, however, completely alienated the native Algerian Muslim community. Hitherto mostly passive or apathetic, it was now driven into the arms of the FLN, swelling the organization's ranks and increasing its popular support. Domestic public opinion in France was similarly outraged, undercutting popular backing for continuing the struggle and creating deep fissures in French civil–military relations. Massu and his men stubbornly consoled themselves that they had achieved their mission and defeated the rebels' attempt to seize control of Algiers; but this military victory was bought at the cost of eventual political defeat. Five years later the French withdrew from Algeria and granted the country its independence.

Massu remained unrepentant, maintaining consistently that the ends justified the means used to destroy the FLN's urban insurrection. The battle was won and the terrorists' indiscriminate bombing campaign was ended. At the same time, there is no doubt that this 'success' cut both ways. The FLN's tactical defeat in the city resulted in yet another complete reassessment of its strategy. Large-scale urban terrorism was now abandoned alongside the FLN's belief that France could be defeated militarily. The group's high command also concluded that the struggle could not be won inside Algeria alone; accordingly, the rebels relocated their operational bases to Tunisia, from where they pursued a rural hit-and-run strategy, making cross-border raids from their newly established sanctuaries. But the 'Battle of Algiers' remains perhaps the most significant episode in bringing about the FLN's subsequent triumph, in that it succeeded in focusing world attention on the situation in Algeria, just as Abane had calculated. By provoking the government to over-react with torture, summary executions and other repressive tactics, it also revealed the bankruptcy of French rule, thereby hastening the complete destruction of *Algérie Française*.

Conclusion

The ethno-nationalist insurrections that followed the Second World War had a lasting influence on subsequent terrorist campaigns. Although governments throughout history and all over the world always claim that terrorism is ineffective as an instrument of political change, the examples of Israel, Cyprus and Algeria, and of Begin, Makarios and Ahmed Ben Bella (the FLN's leader, who became Algeria's first president), provide convincing evidence to the contrary. Admittedly the establishment of these independent countries was both confined to a distinct period of time and the product, in some cases, of powerful forces other than terrorism. At the same time, however, it is indisputable that, at the very least, the tactical 'successes' and political victories won through violence by groups like the Irgun, EOKA and the FLN clearly demonstrated that – notwithstanding the repeated denials of the governments they confronted – terrorism does 'work'. Even if this 'success' did not always manifest itself in terms of the actual acquisition of power in government, the respectability accorded to terrorist organizations hitherto branded as 'criminals' in fora like the United Nations and their success in attracting attention to themselves and their causes, in publicizing grievances that might otherwise have gone overlooked and perhaps even in compelling governments to address issues that, if not for the terrorists' violence, would have largely been ignored, cannot be disregarded.

In sum, the anti-colonial terrorism campaigns are critical to understanding the evolution and development of modern, contemporary terrorism. They were the first to recognize the publicity value inherent in terrorism and to choreograph their violence for an audience far beyond the immediate geographical loci of their respective struggles. The Irgun directed its message to New York and Washington, DC, as much as to London and Jerusalem. EOKA similarly appealed to opinion in New York and London as well as in Athens and Nicosia. And the FLN was especially concerned with influencing policy not only in Algiers but in New York and Paris too. The ability of these groups to mobilize sympathy and support outside the narrow confines of their actual 'theatres of operation' thus taught a powerful lesson to similarly aggrieved peoples elsewhere, who now saw in terrorism an effective means of transforming hitherto local conflicts into international issues. Thus the foundations were laid for the transformation of terrorism in the late 1960s from a primarily localized phenomenon into a security problem of global proportions.

3

The Internationalization of Terrorism

The advent of what is considered modern, international terrorism occurred on 22 July 1968. On that day three armed Palestinian terrorists, belonging to the Popular Front for the Liberation of Palestine (PFLP), one of the six groups then comprising the Palestine Liberation Organization (PLO), hijacked an Israeli El Al commercial flight en route from Rome to Tel Aviv. Although commercial aircraft had been hijacked before (this was the twelfth such incident in 1968 alone), the El Al hijacking differed significantly from all previous ones. First, its purpose was not simply the diversion of a scheduled flight from one destination to another, such as had been happening since 1959 with a seemingly endless succession of homesick Cubans or sympathetic revolutionaries from other countries commandeering domestic American passenger aircraft simply as a means to travel to Cuba. This hijacking was a bold political statement. The terrorists who seized the El Al flight had done so with the express purpose of trading the passengers they held hostage for Palestinian terrorists imprisoned in Israel. Second, unlike previous hijackings, where the origin or nationality of the aircraft that was being seized did not matter (as long as the plane itself was capable of transporting the hijacker(s) to a desired destination), El Al – as Israel's national airline and by extension, therefore, a readily evident national 'symbol' of the Israeli state – had been specifically and deliberately targeted by the terrorists. Third, by engineering a crisis where the consequences of a government ignoring or rejecting the terrorists' demands could prove catastrophic, leading to the destruction of the aircraft and the deaths of all persons on board, the terrorists succeeded in forcing their avowed enemy, Israel, to communicate directly with them and therefore with the organization to which they belonged, despite the Israeli government's previous declarations and policy pronouncements to the contrary. Finally, through the combination of dramatic political statement, 'symbolic' targeting and crisis-induced de facto recognition, the terrorists discovered that they had the power to create major media events – especially when innocent civilians were involved. As Zehdi Labib Terzi, the PLO's chief observer at the United Nations, reflected in a 1976 interview, 'The first several hijackings aroused the consciousness of the world and awakened the media and world opinion much more – and more effectively – than 20 years of pleading at the United Nations'.[1]

Many of the post-war anti-colonial terrorist campaigns, as noted above, also had a prominent international orientation. However, with the El Al hijacking the nature and character of terrorism demonstrably changed. For the first time, terrorists began to travel regularly from one country to another to carry out attacks. In addition, they also began to target innocent civilians from other countries who often had little if anything to do with the terrorists' cause or grievance, simply in order to endow their acts with the power to attract attention and publicity that attacks against their declared or avowed enemies often lacked. Their intent was to shock and, by shocking, to stimulate worldwide fear and alarm.

These dramatic tactical changes in terrorism were facilitated by the technological advances of the time that had transformed the speed and ease of international commercial air travel and vastly improved both the quality of television news footage and the promptness with which that footage could be broadcast around the globe. Accordingly, terrorists rapidly came to appreciate that operations perpetrated in countries other than their own and directly involving or affecting foreign nationals were a reliable means of attracting attention to themselves and their cause.

At the forefront of this transformation were the constituent groups of the PLO. Between 1968 and 1980, Palestinian terrorist groups were indisputably the world's most active, accounting for more *international* terrorist incidents than any other movement.[2] The success achieved by the PLO in publicizing the Palestinians' plight through the 'internation-alization' of its struggle with Israel has since served as a model for similarly aggrieved ethnic and nationalist minority groups everywhere, demonstrating how long-standing but hitherto ignored or forgotten causes can be resurrected and dramatically thrust on to the world's agenda through a series of well-orchestrated, attention-grabbing acts. In order to understand how revolutionary a development this was, it is necessary briefly to review the Palestinians' recent history and to appreciate the depths of obscurity and international neglect from which the PLO emerged.

The PLO and the Internationalization of Terrorism

The end of the First Arab–Israeli War in 1949 introduced two new factors into Middle Eastern politics: the Jewish State of Israel and the Palestinian refugees exiled from it. During the war, many of Palestine's Arab inhabitants had fled their homes for the safety of neighbouring countries. Some had left voluntarily; others had been forcibly expelled by the advancing Israeli forces. The exodus of Palestinian Arabs, however, did not end with the cessation of fighting. Fears of Israeli reprisals, coupled with the hope that the defeated Arab armies would shortly regroup and renew the fight against Israel, had convinced many Palestinians that they were better off as temporary exiles in the countries of their Arab brethren than remaining in the new Jewish state. The number of these displaced persons soon climbed beyond 700,000 (some estimates put the figure as high as 950,000).

Crowded into decrepit refugee camps in Jordan, Syria, Lebanon and Egypt, the Palestinians dreamed of the day when the Arab armies would arise to destroy Israel and return them to their homes. The Arab states, however, disheartened by the crushing defeat inflicted on them by the inferior Israeli forces, had no desire to launch another war. Furthermore, in the wretched conditions of the Palestinians' exile the region's Arab leaders seized upon an issue that could be exploited for their own ends. On the one hand, the Palestinian cause was a useful means by which to marshal international opprobrium against Israel and also to generate support among Arab states for greater regional unity against the common Zionist enemy; on the other, the refugee issue offered a convenient way to deflect attention away from domestic problems by focusing popular discontent outwards, against Israel, for the injustice done to the Palestinians. In any event, what the Palestinian refugees had once hoped would be a brief absence from their land evolved into indefinite displacement.

Meanwhile, inside the refugee camps, groups of desperate and disgruntled Palestinians were slowly banding together and establishing new political movements and associations. Out of these groups emerged new leaders, men who were untainted by the humiliation of the 1948–9 defeat and had not been party to the broken promises of their Arab hosts. These leaders argued that the Palestinians must henceforth rely on no one but themselves if they were ever to reclaim their homeland. Small groups of *fedayeen* (Arabic for 'commandos') began to sneak out of the refugee camps to carry out cross-border hit-and-run attacks inside Israel. At a time when Egypt, like all other 'front-line' Arab states, was militarily unprepared for another major war, its president, Nasser, saw in the raids a means through which he could both harass Israel and simultaneously advance his claim to leadership of the Arab world. Accordingly, Egypt began actively to train and arm the *fedayeen*. By 1953, Palestinian marauding had become both sufficiently frequent and sufficiently lethal to attract Israeli military reprisals. Thereafter a deadly cycle of raid and retaliation followed that culminated in the 1956 Suez crisis, providing Israel with the excuse it sought to invade the Sinai peninsula and eliminate the Egyptian bases supporting the *fedayeen* operations. Nearly a decade later, an almost identical tit-for-tat pattern of terrorist attack and Israeli reprisal set in motion a similar chain of events that resulted in the 1967 Six Day War.

Yet although Palestinian terrorist activities precipitated a significant international crisis (Suez) and eleven years later led to a major regional war – and notwithstanding the plight of hundreds of thousands of Palestinian refugees, many of whom were still living in the abject poverty of squalid refugee camps nearly two decades after their exile had begun – few outside the region took any notice of, much less cared about, the Palestinians. In fact, it was not until after 1968, when the *fedayeen* took their struggle against Israel outside the Middle East and began deliberately to enmesh citizens from more distant countries in their struggle, that the Palestinians discovered an effective means of broadcasting their cause to the world and attracting its attention and sympathy. 'When we hijack a plane it has more effect than if we killed a hundred Israelis in battle,' the PFLP's founder and leader Dr George Habash explained in a 1970 interview – echoing the same point made a decade earlier by the FLN's Ramdane Abane. 'For decades world opinion has been neither for nor against the Palestinians,' Habash noted.

'It simply ignored us. At least the world is talking about us now.'[3]

The premier example of terrorism's power to rocket a cause from obscurity to renown, however, was without doubt the murder of eleven Israeli athletes seized by Palestinian terrorists at the 1972 Munich Olympic Games. The purpose of the operation, according to Fuad al-Shamali, one of its architects, was to capture the world's attention by striking at a target of inestimable value (a country's star athletes), in a setting calculated to provide the terrorists with unparalleled exposure and publicity (the top global sporting event). 'Bombing attacks on El Al offices do not serve our cause,' al-Shamali had argued. 'We have to kill their most important and most famous people. Since we cannot come close to their statesmen, we have to kill artists and sportsmen.'[4]

The incident began on 5 September 1972, shortly before 5.00 a.m., when eight terrorists belonging to the PLO's Black September Organization (BSO) burst into the Israelis' dormitory, killing two athletes immediately and taking nine others hostage. As news of the attack spread and police rushed to the scene, the site was cordoned off and the terrorists issued their demands. They offered to exchange the hostages for 236 Palestinians imprisoned in Israeli gaols and five other terrorists being held in Germany (including Andreas Baader and Ulrike Meinhof, the founders of the radical left-wing West German terrorist group, the Red Army Faction); and they wanted a guarantee of safe passage to any Arab country (except Lebanon or Jordan). They also threatened to begin killing one hostage every two hours if their demands were not met. Fifteen hours of negotiations followed until a deal, brokered by the West Germans, was struck. The terrorists and their hostages, it was agreed, would be transported in two helicopters to the airbase at Fürstenfeldbruck, where they would then board a Lufthansa 727 aircraft and depart for Cairo. Once in Egypt, the exchange of prisoners would be effected and the terrorists allowed to proceed wherever they wished. The Egyptians, however, later changed their mind and decided to refuse the aircraft landing rights.

At 10.35 p.m. the two helicopters touched down at the German air base. Two terrorists emerged and went to inspect the airliner parked nearby. Two others took up positions outside the helicopters. The remaining four terrorists stayed inside, guarding the nine Israelis. Suddenly shots rang out. As part of a pre-arranged rescue plan, five West German police sharpshooters had opened fire. Three of the four terrorists outside the helicopters were cut down: the survivor, Mohammad Masalhah, the group's commander, took cover. The other terrorists immediately began to return fire and, according to some accounts, started to kill the hostages. A tense stand-off now ensued as appeals were broadcast over loudspeakers in Arabic, German and English to the remaining five terrorists to release their hostages and surrender. The terrorists again responded with gunfire. Finally, just after midnight, as German police prepared to mount a rescue assault, a terrorist leaped from one of the helicopters and tossed a hand grenade back into the cabin behind him. Pandemonium broke out when the grenade exploded. In the firefight that erupted, two more terrorists, including Masalhah, were killed. The three remaining terrorists, however, kept police at bay until nearly 1.30 a.m., when they finally surrendered and were taken into custody. All nine hostages lay dead, along with a West German policeman.

Both operations – the hostage seizure and the rescue attempt – were colossal failures. The Palestinians had not only failed to obtain their principal, stated demand – the release of terrorists imprisoned in Israel and West Germany – but, to many observers, had irredeemably tarnished the righteousness of their cause in the eyes of the world. Indeed, international opinion was virtually unanimous in its condemnation of the terrorists' operation. The grisly denouement on the airfield tarmac, broadcast via television and radio throughout the world, was initially regarded as disastrous to the Palestinian cause: a stunning failure and a grave miscalculation, generating revulsion rather than sympathy and condemnation instead of support.

As for the failure to save the hostages, for many other countries as well as for West Germany the botched rescue attempt provided stark evidence of both how serious a threat international terrorism had become and how woefully inadequate their own counterterrorist capabilities were. The embarrassed West Germans lost little time in establishing a special anti-terrorist detachment of their border police, known as GSG-9 (Grenzschutzgruppe Neun). Five years later, it acquitted itself brilliantly in Mogadishu, Somalia, rescuing all eighty-six hostages on board a Lufthansa flight hijacked en route from Mallorca by a mixed team of Palestinian and West German terrorists. In this incident, in marked contrast to the debacle at Fürstenfeldbruck, the GSG-9 commandos killed three of the hijackers and captured the fourth before they could harm any of the hostages (one GSG-9 officer was wounded in the rescue assault as well as four hostages). In France, the Groupe d'Intervention de la Gendarmerie Nationale (GIGN) was created within the Gendarmerie Nationale as that country's dedicated counterterrorist unit; in Britain, the elite Special Air Services Regiment (SAS) was given permission to establish a Counter-Revolutionary Warfare detachment with a specific counterterrorism mission. In 1980, these SAS units successfully resolved the six-day siege at the Iranian embassy in Princes Gate, London, rescuing nineteen of the twenty-one hostages (two died during the rescue operation) and killing five of the six terrorists. Curiously, at the time the United States decided *not* to follow the example of its European allies and established no special, elite counterterrorist unit of its own – thus courting the disaster that came eight years later in the failed attempt to rescue the fifty-two Americans held hostage at the US embassy in Tehran. Instead, President Richard Nixon ordered the formation of a special Inter-Departmental Working Group on Terrorism (chaired by the then secretary of state, Henry Kissinger) and elected to concentrate on diplomatic initiatives in the UN and elsewhere, focusing on the adoption of international conventions against terrorism.

The real lesson of Munich, however, was a somewhat counterintuitive one. The Olympic tragedy provided the first clear evidence that even terrorist attacks which fail to achieve their ostensible objectives can nonetheless still be counted successful provided that the operation is sufficiently dramatic to capture the media's attention. In terms of the publicity and exposure accorded to the Palestinian cause, Munich was an unequivocal success – a point conceded by even the most senior PLO officials. According to Abu Iyad, the organization's intelligence chief, long-time confidant of Arafat and co-founder with him of al-Fatah, the Black September terrorists admittedly 'didn't bring about the liberation of any of their comrades imprisoned in Israel as they had hoped, but they did attain the operation's other two objectives: World opinion was forced to take note of the Palestinian drama, and the Palestinian people imposed their presence on an international gathering that had sought to exclude them.'[5]

Indeed, despite the worldwide condemnation of the terrorists' actions at the time, it soon became apparent that, for the Palestinians, Munich was in fact a spectacular publicity coup. The undivided attention of some four thousand print and radio journalists and two thousand television reporters and crew already in place to cover the Olympiad was suddenly refocused on to Palestine and the Palestinian cause.[6] An estimated 900 million persons in at least a hundred different countries saw the crisis unfold on their television screens.[7] According to one observer, 'If one includes other forms of media it is safe to say that over a quarter of the world's population was at least aware of Black September's attack.'[8] It seems fair to suppose that few viewers who tuned in to watch the games would forget the image emblazoned on their television screen of a terrorist, his face concealed by a balaclava, standing on the balcony of the Israeli suite at the Olympic village, preening in front of the cameras. Henceforth, those persons throughout the world who before the games had neither known of the Palestinians nor been familiar with their cause were no longer as ignorant or dismissive. As an elderly Palestinian refugee remarked to a British reporter shortly after the attack, 'From Munich onwards nobody could ignore the Palestinians or their cause.'[9]

Further, the brutal dimensions of the operation, and its perpetrators' desperate plea for attention and recognition, convinced many across the world that the Palestinians were now a force to be reckoned with and possessed a cause that could no longer justifiably be denied. Black September was jubilant. In a communiqué published a week after the attack in a Beirut newspaper, the group proudly announced that

> In our assessment, and in light of the result, we have made one of the best achievements of Palestinian commando action. A bomb in the White House, a mine in the Vatican, the death of Mao tse-Tung, an earthquake in Paris could not have echoed through the consciousness of every man in the world like the operation at Munich. The Olympiad arouses the people's interest and attention more than anything else in the world. The choice of the Olympics, from the purely propagandistic view-point, was 100 percent successful. It was like painting the name of Palestine on a mountain that can be seen from the four corners of the earth.[10]

During the weeks that followed the incident, thousands of Palestinians rushed to join the terrorist organizations.[11]

It is perhaps not entirely coincidental, then, that eighteen months after Munich the PLO's leader, Yassir Arafat, was invited to address the UN General Assembly and shortly afterwards the PLO was granted special observer status in that international body. Indeed, by the end of the 1970s the PLO, a non-state actor, had formal diplomatic relations with more countries (eighty-six) than the actual established nation-state of Israel (seventy-two). It is doubtful whether the PLO could ever have achieved this success had it not resorted to international terrorism. Within four years, a handful of Palestinian terrorists had overcome a quarter-century of neglect and obscurity. They had achieved what diplomats and statesmen, lobbyists and humanitarian workers had persistently tried and failed to do: focus world attention on the Palestinian people and their plight. They had also provided a powerful example to similarly frustrated ethnic and nationalist groups elsewhere: within the decade, the number of terrorist groups either operating inter-nationally or committing attacks against foreign targets in their own country in order to attract international attention had more than quadrupled. According to the RAND–St Andrews Chronology of International Terrorism,[12] the number of organizations engaged in *international* terrorism grew from only eleven in 1968 (of which just three were ethno-nationalist/separatist organizations, the remainder radical Marxist-Leninist or left-wing groups) to an astonishing fifty-five in 1978. Of this total, more than half (thirty, or 54 per cent) were ethno-nationalist/separatist movements, all seeking to copy or capitalize on the PLO's success. They ranged from large, international communities of displaced persons with profound historical grievances, such as the Armenian diaspora, to minuscule, self-contained entities like the obscure expatriate South Moluccan community in the Netherlands. What they all had in common, however, was a burning sense of injustice and dispossession alongside a belief that through *international* terrorism they too could finally attract worldwide attention to themselves and their causes.

The Palestinians as Model:
The Rise of Ethno-nationalist Terrorism

The Armenians, as noted in an earlier chapter, had waged an inchoate armed struggle against Ottoman rule during the 1880s and 1890s in hopes of eliciting Western sympathy and intervention. Their revolt had culminated in 1896 with the daring but ill-fated seizure of the Ottoman Bank in Constantinople. This event was followed by three days of intense anti-Armenian rioting and bloodshed during which untold numbers of Armenians lost their lives. Thereafter, most overt manifestations of Armenian nationalism lapsed into temporary abeyance, and those that did surface were forcibly suppressed. Nationalist activity was rekindled, however, during the First World War, mostly as a result of Russian efforts to foment Armenian unrest and thereby undermine the common enemy, Turkey. Ottoman suspicions of their Armenian subjects' loyalty, already aggravated by these Russian interventions, were further inflamed by the Armenians' refusal to support the Turkish war effort. Accordingly, in 1915, Taalat Pasha, the Ottoman interior minister, ordered the Armenians' expulsion from their traditional homelands in eastern Turkey to Syria and Iraq. Although the exact number of Armenians who perished at this time of widespread war and upheaval remains a matter of considerable debate, the figure most commonly cited is 1.5 million people – roughly 60 per cent of Turkey's Armenian population. The events of 1915, therefore, are often cited as the first state 'genocide' of the twentieth century.

Despite the magnitude of this catastrophe, for sixty years thereafter the Armenians' tragic history remained either ignored or forgotten. This began to change in 1975 when two Armenian terrorist groups – known as ASALA (the Armenian Army for the Secret Liberation of Armenia) and the JCAG (Justice Commandos of the Armenian Genocide) – emerged from the civil war then engulfing Lebanon. When asked to account for the sudden re-emergence of Armenian terrorism, Hagop Hagopian, ASALA's founder and leader, unhesitatingly cited the Palestinian example. 'There are substantially two factors to be taken into consideration,' he stated in a 1975 interview: namely, the 'general discovery as to the failure of the policy of the traditional Armenian parties [to publicize the Armenians' cause and grievances] . . . and the fact that many Armenians since 1966 participated in the Palestinian Arab struggle from which they learned many things'.[13] Indeed, so important was the Palestinians' influence, and so close were their relations with the Armenian community in Lebanon, that ASALA can claim direct descent from both George Habash's PFLP and an even more radical splinter group of that organization, the PFLP Special Operations Group, led by Dr Wadi Haddad.[14]

The similarities and circumstances of these two dispossessed peoples' respective plights had an almost hypnotic effect on young Armenians living in Beirut. Indeed, nearly twenty years later the Palestinian influence still burned bright for a new generation of young Armenians fighting for control over the Caucasus enclave of Nagorno Karabakh. As one observer noted in 1994 after meeting with these men while on a visit to Yerevan, most of them 'viewed the "Palestinian cause" as a model that had attracted world wide attention. Palestinians were seen as people like themselves – persecuted without a homeland.'[15] In ASALA's case, the relationship between the two peoples was solidified through the PFLP's generous provision of arms, training and other forms of assistance.

It was ASALA's early success in re-invigorating the Armenian cause that prompted the formation of a rival group, the JCAG. Although the two differed in their ideology – ASALA was avowedly Marxist-Leninist, adhering to the PFLP's global revolutionary orientation, while the JCAG tended to represent more mainstream Armenian nationalist views – both had the same three goals: to exact revenge for the events of 1915; to force the present Turkish republic to recognize the genocide committed by its Ottoman predecessors and thereby accept responsibility for it; and to compel the Turkish government to make reparations payments to the survivors and their descendants. In pursuit of these ends, between 1975 and 1985 more than forty Turkish diplomats and members of their families were murdered by Armenian terrorists. Whereas the JCAG (and its splinter group, the Armenian Revolutionary Army) preferred individual assassinations of Turkish diplomats or non-lethal, 'symbolic' bombings of Turkish diplomatic and airline facilities, ASALA tended to employ more indiscriminate tactics and weapons, evincing little concern about who was killed or injured, Turk and non-Turk alike, as long as the operation succeeded in attracting attention. In July 1983, for example, ASALA bombed the Turkish airline's ticket counter at Orly Airport in Paris, killing seven persons and wounding fifty-six others. A month later an ASALA attack at Ankara's Esenboga Airport killed nine persons and injured seventy-eight, while an assault mounted in Istanbul's Grand Bazaar killed two and wounded twenty-seven. Indeed, ASALA's brutal tactics and desperate bids for attention drew comparisons with the ruthlessness of the Palestinian Black September Organization in general and the Olympic massacre in particular.[16] It was even reported that Hagopian himself had participated in the Munich operation.[17]

By the early 1980s, the Armenians' use of terrorism had apparently paid off. 'Thus it is true that the re-emergence of the Armenian question in the news – and especially of the Armenian genocide – is largely owing to Armenian terrorists,' wrote Gerard Chaliand, a French Armenian scholar and one of the world's foremost authorities on terrorism and guerrilla warfare, in 1983.[18] A year earlier, in a study of the Armenian terrorist movements, Andrew Corsun, one of the US State Department's leading analysts of terrorism, similarly argued that 'by resorting to terrorism, Armenian extremists were able to accomplish in 5 years what legitimate Armenian organizations have been trying to do for almost 70 years – internationalize the Armenian cause'.[19] However, while publicity and exposure proved to be easily gained through terrorism, the Armenian groups also found that attention does not necessarily translate into more tangible gains. For example, a detailed empirical study of American network news coverage of Armenian terrorism between 1968 and 1983 concluded that while the terrorist campaign had certainly increased public name-recognition of the Armenians, it had not engendered any meaningful awareness or sensitivity about the Armenians' cause, their historical condition, or their political aims.[20] More critical, perhaps, was the fact that, unlike the Palestinians, the vast majority of the worldwide Armenian diaspora did not rally to, much less actively support, the terrorists. Despite expressions of understanding of the terrorists' goals and motivations, the Armenian community offered them little overt assistance and became increasingly alienated by the violent acts committed in its name. What minimal actual support did exist began to dry up following the 1983 Orly Airport attack, to the point where, by the end of the decade, none of the Armenian terrorist groups was still actively engaged in international terrorism.

The tiny South Moluccan expatriate community in the Netherlands is yet another example of an ethno-nationalist group that sought to duplicate the Palestinians' success during the period following the Munich Olympics incident. Some 15,000 South Moluccans had emigrated to the Netherlands in 1951 from their native Indonesia, following the incorporation of their Republic of the South Moluccas into the Indonesian state of Negara Indonesia Timur. For more then twenty years they nursed increasingly futile hopes of returning to their homeland and re-establishing their independent nation. In 1977, militant elements within the mainstream Free South Moluccan Organization lost patience and prepared to embark on a campaign of terrorism designed to 'internationalize' their cause and realize their nationalist goals. In June that year, two groups of terrorists respectively hijacked a Dutch passenger train and seized a nearby schoolhouse, taking hostages in both cases. They had in fact got their idea of seizing the train from press coverage of a similar operation attempted by Palestinian terrorists.[21] Both hostage seizures were successfully resolved by Royal Dutch Marine commandos who stormed both the train (killing six of the nine terrorists and two of the fifty-one hostages) and the schoolhouse, where all four terrorists were apprehended without bloodshed. Like the Armenians, the South Moluccans too discovered the difficulties of converting publicity into actual political achievement. While the train and schoolhouse seizures brought the Moluccans more attention and publicity than they could otherwise ever have hoped to obtain, in the end this exposure did nothing to advance their cause or bring them any closer to obtaining their nationalist goals.

As a universally applicable model, therefore, the Palestinian archetype seems wanting. Nonetheless, nearly twenty years later, the Palestinian example continues to loom large for ethno-nationalist/separatist groups seeking international recognition and self-determination. In recent years, for example, Kurds fighting for autonomy in south-eastern Turkey have debated whether to adopt the Palestinian model for their own struggle. To date, the Kurdish Workers Party (PKK) has for the most part eschewed *international* terrorism as a means to advance its nationalist claims, concentrating instead on an internal campaign of rural guerrilla warfare coupled with occasional acts of urban terrorism inside Turkey only. But their failure to win the international attention and stature that other, similar movements such as the PLO enjoy has reportedly led to increasing discontent among younger Kurdish militants. 'Proponents of terrorism', one account noted, argue that 'the Palestinians have embassies in more than 100 countries while the Kurds, a far larger minority, have none.'[22] Accordingly, they press for the adoption of an aggressive campaign of international terrorism – against the advice of their more moderate elders, who argue that such a strategy would ultimately deprive their cause of both credibility and international sympathy. The debate has yet to be resolved.

The Palestinians as Mentors:
The Rise of Revolutionary Left-wing Terrorism

The 'internationalization' of terrorism that occurred in the late 1960s and early 1970s was not solely a product of Palestinian influence and success. Outside the Middle East, a combination of societal malaise and youthful idealism, rebelliousness and anti-militarism/anti-imperialism was rapidly transforming the collective political consciousness among the more affluent countries of Western Europe and North America. Perhaps the unprecedented economic prosperity of these years allowed the luxury of introspection and self-criticism that, in more radical political circles, generated a revulsion against the socio-economic inequities endemic to the modern, industrialized capitalist state. 'All they can think about', Ulrike Meinhof, the political activist and radical newspaper columnist turned Red Army Faction (RAF) terrorist, once dismissively remarked of her fellow Germans, 'is some hairspray, a vacation in Spain, and a tiled bathroom.'[23]

The sharp contrast between the highest and the lowest domestic levels of wealth and consumer consumption was further accentuated by the growing economic disparity between the developed world and the undeveloped world – as it came to be called, the 'Third World'. This was attributed by radicals as much to the 'neo-colonialist' ethos and economic exploitation inherent in capitalism as to the interventionist foreign policy championed by the United States under the banner of fighting the spread of communism. Thus, by the late 1960s, opposition to America's involvement in Indochina had emerged as the principal rallying cry for politically engaged, disaffected youth everywhere. 'Anti-imperialism meant first of all the protest against the Viet-nam war, but also [against] the American predominance over most countries of the Third World,' the former RAF terrorist Christoph Wackerngel explained in a recent speech recounting his own experience.[24]

Indeed, to a great extent, the Red Army Faction (German: Rote Armee Fraktion; more popularly known as the Baader–Meinhof Group) and its sister terrorist organization, the Second of June Movement, encapsulated the revolutionary spirit and anti-establishment attitudes typical of left-wing terrorists in other Western countries at the time. Both groups emerged from the communes and student associations that were part of

the 'counterculture' in late-1960s West Germany, and it was consequently impossible to separate their radical politics from their
'alternative' lifestyles. Revolution and armed struggle went hand-in-
hand with sexual promiscuity and drug use. 'You must understand',
Astrid Proll, a member of the RAF's 'first generation', later explained,
'that then the most fantastic thing in the world was not to be a rock star,
but a revolutionary.'[25] Michael 'Bommi' (the nickname given to him
because of his penchant for bombing) Baumann, a leading member of
the Second of June Movement, similarly describes in his memoir how

> with me it all began with rock music and long hair . . . it was like this:
> if you had long hair, things were suddenly like they are for the
> Blacks. Do you understand? They threw us out of joints, they cursed
> at us and ran after us – all you had was trouble . . . So you start
> building contact with a few people like yourself, other dropouts,
> or whatever you want to call them. You begin to orient yourself
> differently.[26]

Yet it would be a mistake to dismiss Proll and Baumann simply as apolitical narcissists or mere 'drop-outs' from society. Like many of their
generation, they too were animated by a profound sense of social injustice coupled with an intense enmity towards what they perceived as
worldwide American militarism and domination. 'To my mind, it wasn't
simply an international question,' the German terrorist Hans Joachim
Klein recalled in a 1978 interview,[27] 'but also an internal problem. The
B-52s stopped over at Wiesbaden on their way from Vietnam.'[28] The
pervasive influence of the Vietnam War on German terrorism can be
seen in several of the contemporary Second of June statements repro-
duced in Baumann's autobiography,[29] as well as in RAF communiqués
issued long after the war and American involvement in Indochina
ended. The RAF's first *actual* terrorist operation (that is, other than
bank robberies) was in retaliation for the US air force's mining of North
Vietnam's Haiphong harbour. The target was the US Fifth Army Corps
officers' mess at Frankfurt: one person was killed and thirteen other
injured in the bomb attack. As Brigitte Monhaupt, who later emerged as
one of the group's key leaders, explained to a German court in 1976,
'The strategic concept as developed by the RAF . . . was directed against
the US military presence in the Federal Republic . . . the concept was

developed by us all in the collective discussion process.'[30]

With the end of the Vietnam War, the German terrorists in both the RAF and other groups needed to find a new cause. Their choice again reflected the international orientation of West German radical politics: common cause was now to be made with the Palestinians. In his book, Baumann described the logic behind this decision. 'Since Vietnam is finished,' the argument ran, 'people should get involved with Palestine. It is actually much closer to us, which is apparent today with the oil business, and has more to do with us here in the European cities than does Vietnam. This was to become the new framework to carry on the struggle here.'[31]

The Palestinians were in fact the obvious candidates. As far back as 1968 the PLO – and Habash's PFLP especially – had welcomed terrorists from around the world to their guerrilla camps in Jordan for training, indoctrination and the general building of transnational revolutionary bridges. In this respect, the Palestinians pioneered the 'networking' dimension of international terrorism still in evidence among many groups today. In 1969 the Palestinians had welcomed the first delegation of West German terrorists – Baumann's comrades in the 'Blues' group, an early precursor of the Second of June Movement – to their guerrilla training camps in Jordan. 'They got some training there: how to shoot; how to make bombs; how to fight,' Baumann recalled. 'But the Palestinians told them to go back to Germany and make propaganda for them. That was all they were hot for – they offered no weapons.'[32] The following year another party of German terrorists – including Andreas Baader, Gudrun Ensslin, Ulrike Meinhof and six of their colleagues – secretly made their way to Beirut and thence to Palestinian terrorist camps in Jordan, as much to escape the police dragnet closing in on them at home as to receive training as 'urban guerrillas'. Although relations between the Germans and their Palestinian hosts were strained to the point where, after two months, the group was asked to leave, Baader and company had by this time learned enough to enable them formally to establish their own terrorist group – the RAF. According to Rapoport, this development marked a significant milestone in the history of terrorism, since it was probably the first time that one terrorist group had trained another.[33]

Thereafter, the relationship between the German and Palestinian groups flourished. Combined teams of German and Palestinian terror-

ists were involved in the 1975 seizure of the OPEC oil ministers' conference in Vienna, the 1976 hijacking of an Air France flight to Entebbe,
Uganda, and the hijacking (mentioned above) of a Lufthansa flight to
Somalia in 1977. The Germans also reportedly provided critical logistical assistance to the Palestinian Black September terrorists responsible
for the Munich massacre. Although the closest ties were forged with the
PFLP, Arafat's comparatively more moderate al-Fatah organization
played a particularly important role in supplying the RAF with
weapons. Its political agents in Germany, assigned primarily to fundraising activities, operated a profitable business on the side selling
hand-guns to the RAF. Indeed, according to the leading German–Israeli
counterterrorism analyst Dr David Schiller, without the assistance
provided by the Palestinian terrorists to their German counterparts the
latter could not have survived.[34]

The profound influence exercised by the Palestinians over the
Germans was perhaps never clearer than in 1985, when the RAF joined
forces with the French left-wing terrorist organization, Direct Action
(in French, Action Directe, thus AD), in hopes of creating a PLO-like
umbrella 'anti-imperialist front of Western European guerrillas' that
would include Italy's Red Brigades (RB) and the Belgian Communist
Combatant Cells (CCC) as well. But, just as the Armenians' and South
Moluccans' attempts to replicate the PLO's success had foundered, so
did the efforts of German and French organizations. Within two years,
the promised campaign of 'Euroterrorism' against NATO's politico-
military structure had fizzled out. The global conditions that had
produced and nurtured these organizations, indeed, had endowed them
with their fundamental *raison d'être*, were changing more rapidly than
they could adapt, thus threatening to turn them into hopeless anachro-
nisms. Crippled by the arrests of the leading members of the French and
Belgian groups, the 'anti-imperialist front' fell into disarray. Not
surprisingly, perhaps, the Red Brigades shortly afterwards drifted into
complete lassitude. The forty-year revolutionary struggle they had once
so proudly proclaimed for the Italian people less than a decade earlier
had run out of steam before even a generation had passed. In Germany,
meanwhile, the RAF disconsolately carried on, despite the political
revolutions then transforming the Soviet Union and Eastern Europe.
The fall of the Berlin Wall in 1989 and the national reunification that
followed deprived the group of their ideological resilience as well as a

convenient cross-border sanctuary. Politically marginalized and bereft of either patron or safe haven, the RAF finally collapsed in 1992 under the weight of its own exhaustion and the indifference of those in the newly united Germany whom the group still purported to represent.

Thus, of the four radical movements that only a decade ago attempted collectively to realize the revolution that they believed was inevitable, none remains. Yet, more than thirty years after its founding, the PLO – though still short of its ultimate goal of true sovereignty over a bona fide Palestinian state – has nonetheless survived expulsions and dislocations, internal rivalry and external enmity, to continue the struggle begun long ago in an equally transformed political environment.

Conclusion

The PLO, as a terrorist movement, is arguably unique in history. Not only was it the first truly 'international' terrorist organization, it also consistently embraced a far more internationalist orientation than most other terrorist groups. Some accounts suggest that by the early 1980s at least forty different terrorist groups – from Asia, Africa, North America, Europe and the Middle East – had been trained by the PLO at its camps in Jordan, Lebanon and the Yemen, among other places. The Palestinians' purpose in this tutelary role was not entirely philanthropic. The foreign participants in these courses were reportedly charged between $5,000 and $10,000 each for a six-week programme of instruction. In addition, many of them were later recruited to participate in joint operations alongside Palestinian terrorists. Thus, according to Israeli defence sources, the PLO in 1981 had active cooperative arrangements with some twenty-two different terrorist organizations that had previously benefited from Palestinian training, weapons supply and other logistical support.[35]

The PLO was also one of the first terrorist groups actively to pursue the accumulation of capital and wealth as an organizational priority. By the mid-1980s, it was estimated to have established an annual income flow of some $600 million, of which some $500 million was derived from investments.[36] The amassing of so vast a fortune is all the more astonishing given the fact that, when the PLO was established in 1964, it had no funds, no infrastructure and no real direction. It was not until Arafat's election as chairman in 1968 that the PLO started to become the major force in international politics that it is today. As the British journalist and acknowledged authority on terrorism James Adams has observed,

> as the PLO has grown in complexity and its income has risen accordingly, the organisation has had to adapt to a changing role and an altered image of itself. While the world still viewed the PLO as a bunch of terrorist fanatics robbing banks and blowing up aircraft to boost their cause, the secret side of the organisation was being rapidly transformed.[37]

Thus the attention that the PLO has received, the financial and political influence and power that it is has amassed and the stature that it has been accorded in the international community continues to send a powerful message to aggrieved peoples throughout the world. Ironically, this 'success' has also had a profound effect on the PLO's commitment to terrorism. It can be argued that, despite its fiery rhetoric, even an international terrorist organization like the PLO does not necessarily have an overriding interest in upsetting the international order of which it yearns to become an accepted part. This is not entirely surprising, given the PLO's unique international orientation. But what makes this process especially noteworthy is that the PLO's 'internationalist' efforts have long since expanded beyond the narrow goal of forging tactical alliances with other terrorist groups. Indeed, since the mid-1970s, al-Fatah in particular – but also the mainstream PLO in general – has actively sought to establish relations with as many countries as possible, regardless of their form of government or concern with the Palestinian cause. In pursuit of this policy, the PLO has often abjured from committing certain types of operations against non-Israeli targets, has attempted to impose restrictions on the geographical range of terrorist acts committed by its constituent groups (as, for example, in Arafat's 1988 prohibition on Palestinian terrorist activities outside of Israel and the occupied territories and his previous 1974 edict banning terrorist operations in Europe) and has frequently tried to cover up its involvement in or sponsorship of those terrorist incidents which have violated these declared self-imposed restraints. Over time, therefore, the most radical of its aims have been forsaken in favour of what the moderate leadership has defined as the organization's 'national interest'. Or, as

Abu Iyad has more dourly described this process, 'What we feared most of all . . . has happened. Our movement has become bureaucratized. What it gained in respectability it lost in militancy. We have acquired a taste for dealing with governments and men of power.'[38] Indeed, the PLO today, as the ruling party in the Palestine National Authority on the West Bank and in Gaza, must deal with the same daily complaints of incompetence, lethargy, inefficiency and corruption faced by governments the world over.[39]

4

Religion and Terrorism

Many historical and contemporary terrorist groups evidence a strong religious component, mostly by dint of their membership. Anti-colonial, nationalist movements such as the Jewish terrorist organizations active in pre-independence Israel and the Muslim-dominated FLN in Algeria come readily to mind, as do more recent examples such as the overwhelmingly Catholic IRA; their Protestant counterparts, arrayed in various loyalist paramilitary groups like the Ulster Freedom Fighters, the Ulster Volunteer Force and the Red Hand Commandos; and the predominantly Muslim PLO. However, in all these groups it is the political, not the religious aspect of their motivation that is dominant; the pre-eminence of their ethno-nationalist and/or irredentist aims is incontestable.

For others, however, the religious motive is overriding; and indeed, the religious imperative for terrorism is the most important defining characteristic of terrorist activity today. The consequences of the revolution that transformed Iran into an Islamic republic in 1979 have included its crucial role in the resurgence of this strand of terrorism; but, as we shall see, the modern advent of religious terrorism has not been confined exclusively to Iran, much less to the Middle East or to Islam: since the 1980s it has involved elements of all the world's major religions and, in some instances, smaller sects or cults as well. 'I have no regrets,' said Yigal Amir, the young Jewish extremist who assassinated Israeli prime minister Yitzhak Rabin, to the police. 'I acted alone and on orders from God.'[1] Today, Amir's words could just as easily have come from the mouths of the Islamic Hamas terrorists responsible for the wave of suicide bombings of civilian buses and public gathering-places that have convulsed Israel; the Muslim Algerian terrorists who have terrorized France with a campaign of indiscriminate bombings; the Japanese followers of Shoko Asahara in the Aum Shinrikyo sect who perpetrated the March 1995 nerve gas attack on the Tokyo subway in hopes of hastening a new millennium; or the American Christian Patriots who the following month – acting on an even more complex and less comprehensible mixture of seditious, millenarian, paranoiac and anti-government beliefs – bombed the Alfred P. Murrah Federal Office Building in Oklahoma City. As will become apparent, terrorism motivated either in whole or in part by a religious imperative, where violence is regarded by its practitioners as a divine duty or sacramental act, embraces markedly different means of legitimization and justification than that committed by secular terrorists; and these distinguishing features lead, in turn, to yet greater bloodshed and destruction.

The connection between religion and terrorism is not new. More than two thousand years ago the first acts of what we now describe as 'terrorism' were perpetrated by religious fanatics. Indeed, some of the words we use in the English language to describe terrorists and their actions are derived from the names of Jewish, Hindi and Muslim terrorist groups active long ago. The etymology of the word 'zealot',[2] for example, which to us means an 'immoderate partisan' or a 'fanatical enthusiast', can be traced back to a millenarian Jewish sect of the same name that fought in AD 66–73 against the Roman Empire's occupation of what is now Israel. The Zealots waged a ruthless campaign of assassination, mostly of individuals, relying on the *sica*, a primitive dagger. The Zealot would emerge from the anonymous obscurity of a crowded marketplace, draw the *sica* concealed beneath his robes and, in plain view of those present, dramatically slit the throat of a Roman legionnaire or of a Jewish citizen who had been judged by the group guilty of betrayal, apostasy or both. Thus, in an era long before CNN television news and the transmission of instantaneous live satellite images, the Zealots' dramatic, public acts of violence – precisely like those of terrorists today – were designed to have psychological repercussions far beyond the immediate victim(s) of the terrorist attack and thereby send a powerful message to a wider, watching target audience – namely, the Roman occupation administration and Jews who collaborated with the invaders. The Zealots are also reputed to have employed a primitive form of chemical warfare, poisoning wells and granaries used by the Romans and even sabotaging Jerusalem's water supply.[3]

Similarly, the word 'thug', now used to describe a 'a vicious or brutal ruffian',[4] is derived from a seventh-century religious cult that terrorized India until its suppression in the mid-nineteenth century. The Thugs engaged in acts of ritual murder designed to serve the Hindu goddess of terror and destruction, Kali. On specified holy days throughout the year, group members would forsake their daily occupations and lie in wait for innocent travellers who would be ritually strangled as sacrificial offerings to Kali. According to some accounts, the Thugs killed as many as a million persons during their twelve-hundred-year existence, or more than 800 individuals every year: a murder rate rarely achieved by their modern-day counterparts armed with far more efficient and destructively lethal weaponry.[5]

Finally, the word 'assassin' – 'one who undertakes to put another to death by treacherous violence'[6] – was the name of a radical offshoot of the Muslim Shi'a Ismaili sect who, between AD 1090 and 1272, fought to repel the Christian crusaders attempting to conquer present-day Syria and Iran. Literally translated, 'assassin' means 'hashish-eater': a reference to the ritual intoxication the Assassins undertook before embarking on their missions of murder. Violence for the Assassins was a sacramental act: a divine duty, commanded by religious text and communicated by clerical authorities. Accordingly, the Assassins' violence was meant not only to vanquish the sect's Christian enemies but to hasten the dawn of a new millennium as well. An important additional motivation for the Assassin was the promise that, should he himself perish in the course of carrying out his attack, he would ascend immediately to a glorious heaven. This same ethos of self-sacrifice and suicidal martyrdom can be seen in many Islamic – and indeed other religious – terrorist organizations today.

Until the nineteenth century, in fact, as Rapoport points out in his seminal study of what he terms 'holy terror', religion provided the only justification for terrorism.[7] Many of the political developments of this era discussed in chapter 1 – including the end of divine, monarchical rule in Europe at the beginning of the nineteenth century, followed by the emergence of new concepts redefining the role of both citizen and state, alongside emergent notions of nationalism and self-determination

– account for the shift in motivation and emphasis that then took place; and the growing popularity of various schools of radical political thought, embracing Marxist ideology (or its subsequent Leninist and Maoist interpretations), anarchism and nihilism, completed the transformation of terrorism from a mostly religious to a predominantly secular phenomenon. This process of 'secularization' was given fresh impetus by the anti-colonialist/national liberation movements that arose after the Second World War to challenge continued Western rule in Asia, the Middle East and Africa and subsequently exerted so profound an influence on ethno-nationalist/separatist and ideological terrorist organizations in the late 1960s and early 1970s.

While terrorism and religion share a long history, then, for the past century this particular manifestation has tended to be overshadowed by ethno-nationalist/separatist and ideologically motivated terrorism. For example, none of the eleven *identifiable* international terrorist groups active in 1968 – the year, as previously noted, credited with marking the advent of modern, international terrorism – could be classified as religious: that is, having aims and motivations reflecting a predominant religious character or influence.[8] This, perhaps, is only to be expected at the height of the Cold War, when the majority of terrorist groups (eight) were left-wing, revolutionary Marxist-Leninist ideological organizations, and the remaining three – including the various constituent groups of the PLO – reflected the emergence of the first post-colonial ethno-nationalist/separatist organizations. Not until 1980 – as a result of the repercussions of the revolution in Iran the previous year – do the first 'modern' religious terrorist groups appear. Even so, despite the large increase in the total number of identifiable international terrorist groups from eleven to sixty-four and the concomitant tenfold increase (from three to thirty-two) of ethno-nationalist/separatist organizations (for reasons described in chapter 3), only two of the sixty-four groups active in 1980 could be classified as predominantly religious in character and motivation: the Iranian-backed Shi'a organizations al-Dawa and the Committee for Safeguarding the Islamic Revolution.

However, while the re-emergence of modern religious terrorism was initially closely associated with the Islamic revolution in Iran, within a decade of that event none of the world's major religions could claim to be immune to the same volatile mixture of faith, fanaticism and violence. Twelve years later, in 1992, one finds that the number of religious terrorist groups has increased exponentially (from two to eleven groups) and moreover has expanded to embrace major world religions other than Islam as well as various obscure religious sects and cults.

Interestingly, as the number of religious terrorist groups was increasing, the number of ethno-nationalist/separatist terrorist groups declined appreciably. One explanation for this trend may be that many ethno-nationalist/separatist groups, suddenly finding themselves at the end of the Cold War enmeshed in bitter conflict and civil wars over their homelands (for example, in Bosnia, Chechnya, Nagorno Karabakh, and other parts of Eastern Europe and the former Soviet Union), consequently had little time or energy to engage in international terrorism. Another plausible explanation is that, at a time when the rigid bipolar structure of the Cold War that had throttled the United Nations for nearly half a century was breaking down, and new nations were obtaining sovereignty and rapidly gaining admission to the international community, there was perhaps less reason to resort to international terrorism in order to have one's own irredentist claims recognized. Also, in circumstances where previous impediments to UN membership no longer existed, many groups may have come to regard the use of international terrorism not only as an embarrassment (thus potentially vitiating their case for joining the community of nations), but possibly as counterproductive as well. Finally, it is also interesting to note that, notwithstanding the end of the Cold War and the demise of the Soviet Union and the Warsaw Pact, the number of groups espousing Marxist-Leninist-Maoist dogma (or some idiosyncratic interpretation of those ideological elements) remained unchanged, thus further challenging the Cold War myth of a global terrorist conspiracy directed by, and dependent upon, Moscow and its communist minions.

Significantly, during the 1990s the growth in the number of religious terrorist groups as a proportion of all active international terrorist organizations has not only continued but increased appreciably. In 1994, for example, a third (sixteen) of the forty-nine identifiable international terrorist groups active that year could be classified as religious in character and/or motivation; and in 1995, the most recent year for which complete statistics are available, their number grew yet again, to account for nearly half (twenty-six, or 46 per cent) of the fifty-six known, active international terrorist groups.

It is perhaps not surprising that religion should become a far more popular motivation for terrorism in the post-Cold War era as old ideologies lie discredited by the collapse of the Soviet Union and communist ideology, while the promise of munificent benefits from the liberal-democratic, capitalist state, apparently triumphant at what Francis Fukuyama in his famous aphorism has termed the 'end of history', fails to materialize in many countries throughout the world. The 'public sense of insecurity' engendered by these changes[9] – which has affected in equal measure the most economically disadvantaged (e.g. the Gaza Strip and the former Soviet Union) as well as the most prosperous (e.g. Japan and the United States) – has been deepened by other societal factors; including accelerated population growth, rapid urbanization and the breakdown of local services (e.g. medical care, housing, social welfare programmes and education), typically provided by the state.

The salience of religion as the major driving force behind international terrorism in the 1990s is further evidenced by the fact that the most serious terrorist acts of the decade – whether reckoned in terms of political implications and consequences or in the numbers of fatalities caused – have all had a significant religious dimension and/or motivation. They include:

- the March 1995 sarin nerve gas attack on the Tokyo subway system, perpetrated by an apocalyptic Japanese religious cult, which killed a dozen persons and wounded 3,796 others,[10] along with reports that the group also planned to carry out identical attacks in the United States;[11]
- the bombing in April 1995 of an Oklahoma City federal office building, where 168 persons perished, by Christian Patriots seeking to foment a nationwide revolution;
- the 1993 bombing of New York City's World Trade Center by Islamic radicals who deliberately attempted to topple one of the twin towers on to the other, reportedly while also simultaneously releasing a deadly cloud of poisonous gas;
- the assassination in November 1995, as mentioned above, of the Israeli premier Yitzhak Rabin by a Jewish religious extremist, intended as only the first step in a campaign of mass murder designed to disrupt the peace process;

- the June 1996 truck bombing of a US air force barracks in Dhahran, Saudi Arabia, where nineteen persons perished, by religious militants opposed to the reigning al-Saud regime;
- the string of bloody attacks by Hamas suicide bombers that turned the tide of Israel's national elections, killing sixty people, between February and March 1996;
- the brutal machine-gun and hand-grenade attack carried out by Egyptian Islamic militants on a group of Western tourists, killing eighteen, outside their Cairo hotel in April 1996;
- the massacre in November 1997 of fifty-eight foreign tourists and four Egyptians by terrorists belonging to the Gamat al-Islamiya (Islamic Group) at the Temple of Queen Hatshepsut in Luxor, Egypt;
- the series of thirteen near-simultaneous car and truck bombings that shook Bombay, India, in February 1993, killing 400 persons and injuring more than 1,000 others, in reprisal for the destruction of an Islamic shrine in that country;
- the December 1994 hijacking of an Air France passenger jet by Islamic terrorists belonging to the Algerian Armed Islamic Group (GIA), who plotted – unsuccessfully – to blow up themselves, the aircraft and the 283 passengers on board precisely when the plane was over Paris, causing the flaming wreckage to plunge into the crowded city below;[12]
- the wave of bombings unleashed by the GIA between the following July and October, in metro trains, outdoor markets, cafés, schools and popular tourist spots, during which eight persons were killed and more than 180 others wounded;
- the unrelenting bloodletting by Islamic extremists in Algeria itself, that has claimed the lives of an estimated 75,000 persons there since 1992.

As this list suggests, terrorism motivated in whole or in part by religious imperatives has often led to more intense acts of violence that have produced considerably higher levels of fatalities than the relatively more discriminating and less lethal incidents of violence perpetrated by secular terrorist organizations. Although religious terrorists committed only 25 per cent of the recorded international terrorist incidents in 1995 (the last calendar year for which complete data from the RAND–St Andrews chronology are currently available), their acts were responsible for 58 per cent of the total number of fatalities recorded that year;[13] and those attacks that caused the greatest numbers of deaths in 1995 – those that killed eight or more persons – were *all* perpetrated by religious terrorists.[14] The direct relationship between the religious motive for terrorism and higher numbers of deaths is even more starkly depicted by the record of violence perpetrated by Shi'a Islamic terrorists. Although these groups committed only 8 per cent of all international terrorist incidents between 1982 and 1989, they nonetheless were responsible for 30 per cent of the total number of fatalities arising from those incidents.[15]

Core Characteristics of Religious Terrorism

The reasons why terrorist incidents perpetrated for religious motives result in so many more deaths may be found in the radically different value systems, mechanisms of legitimization and justification, concepts of morality, and world-view embraced by the religious terrorist, compared with his secular counterpart.

For the religious terrorist, violence is first and foremost a sacramental act or divine duty executed in direct response to some theological demand or imperative. Terrorism thus assumes a transcendental dimension, and its perpetrators are consequently unconstrained by the political, moral or practical constraints that may affect other terrorists. Whereas secular terrorists, even if they have the capacity to do so, rarely attempt indiscriminate killing on a massive scale because such tactics are not consonant with their political aims and therefore are regarded as counterproductive, if not immoral, religious terrorists often seek the elimination of broadly defined categories of enemies and accordingly regard such large-scale violence not only as morally justified but as a necessary expedient for the attainment of their goals. Religion – conveyed by sacred text and imparted via clerical authorities claiming to speak for the divine – therefore serves as a legitimizing force. This explains why clerical sanction is so important to religious terrorists and why religious figures are often required to 'bless' (i.e. approve or sanction) terrorist operations before they are executed.

Religious and secular terrorists also differ in their constituencies. Whereas secular terrorists attempt to appeal to a constituency variously composed of actual and potential sympathizers, members of the communities they purport to 'defend' or the aggrieved people for whom they claim to speak, religious terrorists are at once activists and constituents engaged in what they regard as a total war. They seek to appeal to no other constituency than themselves. Thus the restraints on violence that are imposed on secular terrorists by the desire to appeal to a tacitly supportive or uncommitted constituency are not relevant to the religious terrorist. Moreover, this absence of a constituency in the secular terrorist sense leads to a sanctioning of almost limitless violence against a virtually open-ended category of targets: that is, anyone who is not a member of the terrorists' religion or religious sect. This explains the rhetoric common to 'holy terror' manifestos describing persons outside the terrorists' religious community in denigrating and dehumanizing terms as, for example, 'infidels', 'dogs', 'children of Satan' and 'mud people'. The deliberate use of such terminology to condone and justify terrorism is significant, in that it further erodes constraints on violence and bloodshed by portraying the terrorists' victims as either subhuman or unworthy of living.

Finally, religious and secular terrorists also have starkly different perceptions of themselves and their violent acts. Where secular terrorists regard violence either as a way of instigating the correction of a flaw in a system that is basically good or as a means to foment the creation of a new system, religious terrorists see themselves not as components of a system worth preserving but as 'outsiders', seeking fundamental changes in the existing order. This sense of alienation also enables the religious terrorist to contemplate far more destructive and deadly types of terrorist operations than secular terrorists, and indeed to embrace a far more open-ended category of 'enemies' for attack.

Islamic Groups

These core characteristics, while common to religious terrorists of all faiths, have nonetheless often been most closely associated with Islamic terrorist groups in general and Iranian-inspired ones in particular. At the root of the Iranian-backed Islamic terrorist campaign is the aim of extending the fundamentalist interpretation of Islamic law espoused in Iran to other Muslim countries. 'We must strive to export our Revolution throughout the world,' the Ayatollah Khomeini declared on the occasion of the Iranian new year in March 1980, just over a year after the establishment of the Islamic Republic in Iran, and must abandon all idea of not doing so, for not only does Islam refuse to recognize any difference between Muslim countries, it is the champion of all oppressed people . . . We must make plain our stance toward the powers and superpowers and demonstrate to them despite the arduous problems that burden us. Our attitude to the world is dictated by our beliefs.[16]

The Iranian revolution in Iran is held up as an example to Muslims throughout the world, exhorting them to reassert the fundamental teachings of the Qur'an and to resist the intrusion of Western – particularly United States – influence into the Middle East. This stance reflects the beliefs and history of Shi'a Islam as interpreted by Khomeini and subscribed to by his followers in Iran and other Middle Eastern countries. It begins with the notion of the Shi'a as a centuries-old minority within Islam, persecuted because of its special, revealed knowledge, but further entails an unswerving conviction of the inherent illegitimacy of all secular government. Under this rationale, legitimacy can be conferred only through the adoption of Islamic law in order to facilitate the return of the Prophet Mohammed to earth as the Messiah. Accordingly, since Iran is the only state to have begun the process of redemption by creating a 'true' Islamic state, it must be the advocate for the oppressed and aggrieved everywhere. Violence and coercion are not only permissible to achieve the worldwide spread of Islamic law, but a necessary means to this divinely sanctioned end.

The sense of alienation and of the necessity for far-reaching changes in the world order is apparent in the works of a number of Shi'a theologians. 'The world as it is today is how others shaped it,' wrote Ayatollah Baqer al-Sadr. 'We have two choices: either to accept it with submission, which means letting Islam die, or to destroy it, so that we can construct the world as Islam requires.' Mustafa Chamran has stated: 'We are not fighting within the rules of the world as it exists today. We reject all those rules.' Hussein Mussawi, the former leader of Lebanon's Hezbollah who was the victim of an Israeli helicopter-borne assassination in 1992, once remarked: 'We are not fighting so that the enemy recognizes us and offers us something. We are fighting to wipe out the enemy.'[17]

These statements also reflect the Shi'a perception of encirclement and concomitant predatory defensiveness. 'We, the sons of the community of Hezbollah [the Party of God],'[18] a 1985 communiqué from the

Lebanese Shi'a terrorist group of the same name declared, 'consider ourselves a part of the world Islamic community, attacked at once by the tyrants and the arrogant of the East and the West . . . Our way is one of radical combat against depravity,' it explained, 'and America is the original root of depravity.'[19] That Hezbollah perceives itself as fighting an entirely self-defensive struggle, sanctioned if not commanded by God, is also evident in the pronouncements of the group's spiritual leader, Sheikh Muhammad Hussein Fadlallah. 'We do not hold in our Islamic belief that violence is the solution to all types of problems,' he once told an interviewer; 'rather, we always see violence as a kind of surgical operation that a person should use only after trying all other means, and only when he finds his life imperilled . . . The violence began as the people, feeling themselves bound by impotence, stirred to shatter some of that enveloping powerlessness for the sake of liberty.' In this context, Fadlallah pointed out, Israel's invasion of Lebanon in 1982 was the embodiment of the West's hostility to revolutionary Islam:

This invasion was confronted by the Islamic factor, which had its roots in the Islamic Revolution in Iran. And throughout these affairs, America was the common denominator. America was generally perceived as the great nemesis behind the problems of the region, due to its support for Israel and many local reactionary regimes, and because it distanced itself from all causes of liberty and freedom in the area.[20]

As recently as 1996 Fadlallah justified Islamic terrorism on the grounds of self-defence. 'We are not preachers of violence,' he declared; 'Jihad [holy war] in Islam is a defensive movement against those who impose violence.'[21]

The role of clerical authority in sanctioning terrorist operations has always been critical to the Shi'a organizations. The *fatwa* issued in 1989 by the Ayatollah Khomeini imposing the death sentence on the author Salman Rushdie is precisely a case in point. Similarly, the Sunni extremists who bombed New York City's World Trade Center in 1993 specifically obtained a *fatwa* from Sheikh Omar Abdel-Rahman (who is now imprisoned in the United States) before planning their attack. Muslim clerics have lent their support and given their blessing even to self-martyrdom – though suicide is forbidden by Islamic law. For example, immediately after the 1983 suicide attacks on the US Marines and French paratroop headquarters, Hussein Mussawi said: 'I proclaim loud and clear that the double attack of Sunday is a valid act. And I salute, at Death's door, the heroism of the kamikazes, which they are; they are now under the protection of the All Powerful one and of the angels.'[22]

Nor are such sentiments restricted to radical Shi'a only. Militant Sunni fundamentalist organizations portray their struggle in similarly uncompromising terms. According to Antar Zouabri, one of the leaders of the GIA fighting to establish an Islamic republic in Algeria, there can never be either dialogue or truce in his organization's struggle against the illegitimate, secular Algerian government. The word of God, he maintains, is immutable on this point: God, Zouabri explained to an interviewer, does not negotiate or engage in discussion. Zouabri further couched the GIA's campaign in terms of an 'all-out war'. Its ineluctable mission, he said, is to 'found a true Islamic state': should innocents perish in the course of achieving this divinely commanded aim, then so be it. In the first instance, Zouabri explained, the killing of 'apostates', or those not a part of the Islamic movement, is a duty for him and his followers. In any event, the Prophet excuses the murder of innocents, as revealed in a verse from the Qur'an Zouabri quoted: 'I am innocent of those killed because they were associated with those who had to be fought.'[23]

The struggle being waged against Israel by the Islamic Resistance Movement, better known by its Arabic acronym, Hamas ('Zeal'),[24] is similarly cast in terms of an all-out war from which there can be no respite until the enemy is totally and utterly vanquished. The Hamas Covenant, for example, bluntly states, 'Israel will exist and will continue to exist until Islam will obliterate it, just as it obliterated others before it':[25] a view reflected in the words of a leader of the group's political wing, who told the American scholar Mark Juergensmeyer that 'Palestine is not completely free' – not in reference to the truncated sovereignty exercised over seven Palestinian urban centres by Yassir Arafat's Palestine National Authority,[26] but 'until it is an Islamic state'.[27] Moreover, the Covenant's article 7 displays clear millenarian overtones, declaring: 'The time [of Redemption] will not come until the Muslims fight the Jews and kill them, and until the Jews hide behind rocks and trees when the call is raised: "Oh Muslim, here is a Jew hiding!

Come and kill him.'"[28] The religious terrorist's preoccupation with the elimination of an almost open-ended category of enemies is further illustrated in the sermon preached at a Gaza City mosque in 1987 by Hamas's founder and spiritual leader, the Imam Sheikh Ahmad Ibrahim Yassin. Driving home the point that Hamas's war is not only against Israel, but against all Jews, Yassin reportedly declared: 'Six million descendants of monkeys [i.e. Jews] now rule in all the nations of the world, but their day, too, will come. Allah! Kill them all, do not leave even one.'[29]

The bloody suicide terrorist campaign that Hamas has prosecuted against Israel is ample testimony to the actual implications of these sentiments and indeed to the devotion of the organization's fighters. More than 150 persons have been killed in fourteen suicide attacks by members of Hamas and Palestine Islamic Jihad (another extremist Palestinian group) between April 1994 and July 1997. The logic behind the operations was explained by a leading Gaza Muslim activist interviewed on Israeli television in 1994. His exposition of this phenomenon accurately captured the logic or strategy of terrorism as the only weapon available to the weak, to the powerless, in confronting a stronger and exponentially more powerful opponent. 'We lack the arms possessed by the enemy,' he said;

> We have no planes or missiles, not even artillery with which to fight evil. The most effective instrument for inflicting harm with a minimum of losses is this type of operation. This is a legitimate technique based on martyrdom. Through such action, the 'martyr' acquires the right to enter heaven and liberate himself from all the pain and suffering of this world.[30]

The language and terminology are, of course, reminiscent of the medieval Assassins' doctrine, invoking the paradise that awaits the holy terrorists. This heaven is described today just as it was more than 700 years ago, as a place replete with 'rivers of milk and wine . . . lakes of honey, and the services of seventy-two virgins', where the martyr will see the face of Allah and later be joined by seventy chosen relatives.[31] Indeed, the pleasures of alcohol – which all Muslims are forbidden in their lives on earth – and sex are permitted in this glorious afterlife, where the commandments of the Shari'a (Islamic law) do not apply.[32]

Not surprisingly, perhaps, from the time of the first Islamic suicide bomb attacks in the early 1980s, witnesses and survivors have often recounted how the bombers were seen smiling just before blowing themselves and their victims up. The Marine corporal standing guard outside the barracks at Beirut International Airport on the morning of 23 October 1983, for example, recalled how the truck-bomb's driver, a young man with bushy black hair and a moustache, 'looked right at me . . . and smiled'.[33] This is known as the *bassamat al-Farah*, the 'smile of joy' – a tradition of the Shi'a denoting the joy of martyrdom. It is just as prevalent among Sunni terrorists as well. The statement issued by Hamas following the Israeli assassination of the group's master bomber, Yahya Ayyash, known as 'The Engineer', attests to the virtues of self-sacrifice.[34] 'Our valiant Palestinian people', it declared,

> Your militant movement, Hamas, while bringing you glad tidings that its leader hero Yahya Ayyash has ascended to heaven, congratulates its hero leader on winning the honor of martyrdom for the sake of God, and recalls the long series of sacrifices which were given as cheap offerings for the sake of God and the freedom of the homeland and the people . . .
>
> Martyrdom has been Yahya's long-pursued wish. It is the hope pursued by Hamas's heroes every hour.[35]

These sentiments were confirmed by Ayyash's own father, who observed, 'If he is dead, then God bless his soul. If he has acquired martyrdom, then congratulations.'[36]

Jewish Terrorism

Significantly, the same characteristics attributed to Islamic terrorist groups – the legitimization of violence by reference to religious precepts, the sense of alienation, the existence of a terrorist movement in which the activists are the constituents, and a preoccupation with the elimination of a broadly defined category of 'enemies' – are equally apparent among the Jewish terrorist movements that have surfaced in Israel since the early 1980s. To a great extent, many of the members of these groups draw their inspiration from the late Rabbi Meir Kahane.[37] A native of New York, Kahane preached a liturgy of virulent hatred of

Arabs that simultaneously extolled the virtues of Jewish aggressiveness and combativeness. He was a prolific author,[38] sermonizer, public speaker and newspaper columnist,[39] who founded his own (now outlawed) Israeli political party/vigilante organization, Kach ('Thus'), to disseminate his extreme, uncompromising views. Kahane's overriding obsession was to reverse the mythical image of the Jews as victim. From this flowed his conviction that the Jews were enmeshed in a continual struggle against an inherently anti-semitic world, surrounded by hate-mongers and closet anti-semites in the United States and predatory, bloodthirsty Arabs both inside and encircling Israel. 'And, above all,' he wrote in 1971 and reiterated throughout his life, 'let us understand that people, in the very best of times, do not like Jews.'[40] Kahane's prescription in the face of this eternally bleak Jewish condition was simple: a militant aggressiveness, portrayed as nothing more than the inalienable right of self-defence, that evoked images of Frantz Fanon's philosophy of the catharsis of violence.[41] 'Never again', Kahane declared, 'means that we have had it in the concept of being beaten and not hitting back. No one will respect us, and no one in the end will love us, if we don't respect ourselves.'[42]

When Kahane and his family emigrated to Israel in 1971, he began to apply his programme of strident self-assertion to the 'Palestinian problem'. This entailed repeated and vitriolic denunciations of governmental policies with respect both to the peace and to its alleged 'soft' approach to countering Palestinian terrorism. In 1980, for example, Kahane openly called upon the Israeli government to establish an official 'Jewish terrorist group' whose sole purpose would be to 'kill Arabs and drive them out of Israel and the Occupied Territories'.[43] For more than a decade afterwards, he unceasingly called for the forced expulsion of all Arabs from Eretz Yisrael (The Land of Israel – that is, the biblical lands of Greater Israel embracing both the current state's territory and the occupied West Bank as well) or for their physical annihilation if they refused to leave. In a speech before university students in a Los Angeles suburb in 1988, Kahane described the Arabs as 'dogs', as people who 'multiply like fleas' who must be expelled from Israel or eliminated.[44] In this manner, Kahane sought to dehumanize Arabs completely and thus make his odious policy prescriptions more tolerable and acceptable to Jews. 'I don't intend to sit quietly by while Arabs intend to liquidate my state – either by bullets or by having babies,' he declared. 'It's important that you know what the name "Kahane" means to the Arabs. It means terror.'[45]

Kahane's concerns, however, went far beyond practical matters of security to embrace mystical Judaic notions that condoned and justified ill-treatment of – even violence against – the Arabs. In this respect, the responsibility of all Jews to work actively to hasten redemption became immutably aligned with the 'sin' of returning to the Arabs the biblical lands (the West Bank) that God gave to Israel. 'Is there no longer a G–d in Israel?' Kahane asked in 1981:

> Have we so lost our bearings that we do not understand the ordained historical role of the State of Israel, a role that ensures that it can never be destroyed and that no further exile from it is possible? Why is it that we do not comprehend that *it is precisely our refusal to deal with the Arabs according to halakhic* [Jewish religious law] *obligation that will bring down on our heads terrible sufferings, whereas our courage in removing them will be one of the major factors in the hurrying of the final redemption?*[46]

When a Jewish *yeshiva* (Jewish religious school) student was murdered by Arabs two years later, a group of Kahane's followers in the ultra-nationalist West Bank settler movement Gush Emunim (Bloc of the Faithful) decided to take action. Their plan was to attack an Islamic college in Hebron in the Israeli-occupied West Bank at a time of day calculated to inflict the maximum casualties. Significantly, like their Islamic counterparts, the Jewish settlers similarly sought the specific approval and sanction of their own clerical authorities for the operation. Indeed, among the group it was axiomatic that they would not – indeed, that they could not – act without rabbinical blessing. Having secured this dispensation, the terrorists struck: opening fire with machine-guns on the Islamic students as they emerged from their classrooms for the noontime recess, they killed three and wounded another thirty-three.

Emboldened by the success of this operation – and armed once again with rabbinic sanction – the terrorists set in motion plans for an even more ambitious attack. They now plotted the simultaneous bombings of five Arab buses at a day and time when they were guaranteed to be packed with passengers but the roads were likely to be empty of Jews. The plan was to attach explosive devices to the gas tanks of the buses, setting them to detonate on a Friday evening, after the Jewish Sabbath had begun. However, just as the group was to about to act, they were all arrested. Only then did information come to light that for the preceding four years the group had also been plotting to blow up Jerusalem's Dome of the Rock – the third holiest shrine of Islam – which occupies the same grounds as the most sacred site in the Jewish religion, the Second Temple which was destroyed in AD 70.[47]

The so-called 'Temple Mount' operation represented a dramatic escalation in the terrorists' campaign, propelling it on a violent trajectory from simple vengeance wrought against mere mortals to genuine millenarian dimensions. The twenty-eight precision bombs that the terrorist cell had constructed were to them not mere instruments of death and destruction but the means by which miracles are attained.[48] Their goal was not just to destroy a Muslim holy place for reasons of blind hatred or petulant revenge, but to facilitate the resurrection of a Jewish Third Temple and thereby enable the Messiah's return. They were convinced that through their actions they could themselves hasten redemption. Even more alarming, though, was the terrorists' ancillary motive. By obliterating so venerated an Islamic shrine, they also sought to spark a cataclysmic war between Israel and the Muslim world. The terrorists' vision was that a beleaguered Jewish state, attacked on all sides by enraged, unrelenting, savage forces, would have no option but to unleash its nuclear arsenal. The result would be the complete annihilation of Israel's Arab enemies,[49] and the establishment on earth of a new 'Kingdom of Israel' – a theocracy governed by a divinely anointed Jewish king and held in judgement by a true 'Supreme Court'.[50] As with the terrorists' previous operations, this grand scheme was again entirely dependent on obtaining clerical approval.

The same volatile combination – messianic visions of redemption, legitimized by clerical dispensation and achieved through direct action entailing mass, indiscriminate murder – were also evident a decade later in the 1994 Cave of the Patriarchs massacre and the assassination of Rabin the following year. The first incident occurred on 25 February 1994 at a holy site revered (and shared) by both Judaism and Islam. Dr Baruch Goldstein, an American-born, ultra-nationalist, orthodox Jew and ardent disciple of Kahane, entered the Ibrahim (Abraham) Mosque, located at the Cave, and opened fire on Muslim worshippers who had gathered there for Friday (Sabbath) services. His attack was timed to coincide not only with the middle of Islam's holy month of Ramadan (when the mosque was certain to be filled to capacity) but also with the Jewish festival of Purim. Purim celebrates how a Jew named Mordecai, living in fifth-century BC Persia, single-handedly saved his people from their arch-enemy, Haman. Seeking to play the role of a modern-day saviour, Goldstein fired 119 bullets from his American-manufactured M-16 assault rifle into the crowd, killing twenty-nine and wounding 150, before he was set upon by the stunned congregants who beat him to death. Goldstein's grave is now a shrine, guarded over and revered by the ultra-religious nationalists who share his intense animus towards secular Israeli government and regard the peace accords as a blasphemous plan to hand over to the Palestinians the biblical lands that God gave to the Jewish people. Like the Temple Mount plotters, Goldstein too had sought to place himself in the vanguard of the actualization of the Jews' destiny. His mission, like theirs, was no less than to hasten redemption through the cataclysmic forces that his violent act was meant to unleash. This, Goldstein was certain, would ensure not only Israel's perennial possession of its biblical birthright, but the coming of the Messiah as foretold by Kahane.

The assassination in 1995 of Prime Minister Rabin exuded the same uncompromising blend of religious fervour coupled with intense enmity towards Israel's secular government, its elected leaders and the peace process that would return God-given lands to the Jews' most implacable opponents. Like Goldstein, Amir also believed that he was fulfilling God's will. Invoking the *halakhic* decree of the 'law of the pursuer' (*Din Rodef*), Amir explained to his police interrogators that he was completely justified in murdering the person he considered the architect of the Jewish people's doom. 'The minute a Jew betrays his people and country to the enemy,' Amir maintained, 'he must be killed.'[51] Amir appears to have been greatly influenced by extremist rabbis who had repeatedly condemned Rabin to death as a mortal enemy of the Jewish people. Amir, accordingly, felt a moral obligation – what he himself described as a 'mystical' urge – to kill a person declared by his religious authorities to pose so grave a danger to the Jewish people. 'Perhaps physically I acted alone,' Amir proclaimed during his trial, 'but it was not only my finger on the trigger but the entire nation which for two thousand years dreamed about this country and spilled its blood for it.'[52] Indeed, information that came to light after the assassination revealed that Amir had tried to murder Rabin on at least two previous occasions. The assassination, moreover, was intended by Amir and his alleged confederates to be only the first step in a campaign of mass murder, including car-bombings to avenge Palestinian suicide attacks as well as the murder of Palestinian terrorists released from Israeli gaols as part of the peace process.

Any hope that these uncompromisingly violent sentiments – backed and indeed encouraged by clerical decree – might have dissipated in the furore and national soul-searching that followed Rabin's assassination were dispelled by the call from an extremist rabbi in April 1997 for Jews to emulate Hamas and launch suicide attacks of their own against Arabs. 'Suicide during wartime is permissible for the sake of the victory of Israel,' wrote the rabbi from the West Bank settlement of Tapuah, advocating Jewish self-martyrdom in an article entitled 'Sacrificing Oneself for God'. 'A man who volunteers for such operations', he proclaimed, 'will be called a hero and a martyr.'[53]

American Christian White Supremacists

Half a world away from the Middle East in the heartland of America, the use of violence is similarly justified by theological imperative as a means to overthrow a reviled secular government and attain both racial purification and religious redemption. The bombing of the Alfred P. Murrah Federal Office building in Oklahoma City in April 1995 suddenly shed unaccustomed light on an indigenous, violent, Christian white supremacist movement that had been active long before this tragedy.

In June 1997 Timothy McVeigh, a 28-year-old US army veteran, was convicted in a Denver federal court of perpetrating the attack. Two months later he was sentenced to death by lethal injection. An anti-government, right-wing extremist, McVeigh engineered the attack – allegedly with the help of a friend, Terry L. Nichols, who is being tried separately – to commemorate the second anniversary of the FBI's bloody assault on the Branch Davidian's compound in Waco, Texas, in the course of which seventy-four persons, including twenty-one children, were killed.[54] He and his alleged accomplice(s) were apparently obsessed by the idea that the Waco assault – and a similar FBI siege of an alleged white supremacists' rural cabin at Ruby Ridge, Idaho, the previous year[55] – represented the opening salvo in US government plans to outlaw and seize all privately held firearms. There were other motivations as well – including vengeance, protest and armed resistance – which, it transpired, are shared by the members of the well-armed, militantly anti-government so-called 'citizens' militias' with whom McVeigh mixed. Zealous exponents, like those linked to the Oklahoma City bombing, of the American Constitution's second article, which provides for a well-regulated civilian militia and upholds the right to bear arms, many of these groups also evince the same combination of seditious, anti-semitic and racist views common to the broader American Christian Patriot (white supremacist) movement. In this respect, the militias have been described as part of a longer 'conveyor belt', in a phrase coined by Leonard Zeskind (the director of the Atlanta-based Center for Democratic Renewal, an organization which monitors militia activity). The metaphor is intended to depict a process whereby individuals are initially recruited into groups like the militias on the basis of their opposition to legislation outlawing firearms but gradually come to embrace increasingly extreme and violent positions that, in turn, are legitimized by appeals to scripture and theological imperatives.

Although organized hate groups and other bodies similarly preoccupied with far-fetched conspiracy theories have existed in the United States for decades, the advent of extremist white supremacist 'citizens' militias' and related Christian Patriot paramilitary groups orientated towards 'survivalism', outdoor skills, guerrilla training and outright sedition are a more recent development. Thus, while the various militia movements have only surfaced within the past seven years or so, they are in fact but the latest manifestations of a radical right-wing and white supremacist movement that has repeatedly 'repackaged' itself in a bid to attract new recruits and a larger number of adherents and supporters. With the militias, the wider anti-government movement discovered a powerful way of attracting people – like McVeigh – who are not only vehemently opposed to gun control but also subscribe to a variety of fantastic conspiracy theories that invariably involve the Clinton administration in some master-plan to seize all firearms held by American citizens and thereby proscribe fundamental, individual liberties. According to Michael Fortier, a close friend of McVeigh, who testified for the prosecution at McVeigh's trial, 'We both believed that the United Nations was actively trying to form a one-world government, disarm the American public, take away our weapons.'[56]

The Michigan Militia, the 12,000-strong paramilitary, survivalist organization to which McVeigh and Nichols have been linked, believes that the US government has already initiated a programme to control completely the life of every American. 'The Government is [already] in control,' explains Ray Southwell, the group's co-founder and information officer. 'And if you push back, if you cross the Government, they will come down on you hard. We are preparing to defend our freedom. The way things are going, I think bullets might be as valuable as gold and silver one day soon.'[57] Accordingly, through training in guerrilla warfare and survivalist techniques, the militia prepares to resist what it maintains are plans by the Clinton administration to deploy UN forces armed with cast-off Soviet military equipment or hordes of communist Chinese troops, backed by Latino and black inner-city American street gangs, to crush any opposition. Stripped bare of its conspiratorial explanations, the Michigan Militia's purpose is sedition, plain and simple: its other co-founder and commander, Norman E. Olson, makes no bones about that. 'My goal is not to plan a revolution,' he boasted in a message posted over the Internet (the favoured means of communication of militia members and other white supremacists), 'for revolution will come . . . my goal is to establish the Republican Provisional Government.'[58]

An estimated 800 other similarly orientated militias – with a total membership claimed to be over 5 million, though more realistically put at no more than 50,000 – have reportedly organized in almost every state of the union.[59] The difficulty in gauging even the rough dimensions of the American militia movement is a product not only of its geographical pervasiveness and its unimpeded growth in recent years, but also of critical differences between the two different types of militias that have emerged. On the one hand, there are the so-called 'talking' militias (also known as 'out-front' militias), to which the vast majority of the movement's adherents belong. The members of these groups are primarily concerned with opposing anti-gun legislation rather than with fomenting revolution, and consequently are neither especially nor explicitly violent. Their politics therefore tend to reflect the entirely secular conspiracy theories that have long been associated with various far-right American groups parodied in films such as Stanley Kubrick's *Dr Strangelove*. The 'marching' militias (also referred to as 'up-front' militias), on the other hand, are actively involved in violent, seditious activities, embracing the combination of revolutionary, racist and anti-semitic doctrines inherent in the wider American Christian Patriot movement today. It is this more radical element of the militia phenom-enon – whose members perhaps number no more than a dedicated hard core of 10,000 persons – who fervently believe in the impending UN invasion and takeover of America and have resolved to take violent action to prevent it from occurring.[60]

Among the more prominent of the 'marching' militia groups that have come to light since the Oklahoma bombing is the Militia of Montana or MOM. This organization embraces the same ineluctable revolutionary principles and harbours the same profound fears as its counterparts in Michigan and elsewhere. 'Gun control is people control,'[61] its founders, brothers John and David Trochmann, declare. The MOM's 12,000-plus members accordingly train in guerrilla warfare, survivalist techniques and other unconventional tactics in preparation to withstand the inevitable federal government onslaught to seize their weapons and deprive them of their inalienable right to bear arms, presaged by the Branch Davidian raid. The group also markets its own range of DIY manuals and tapes that not only explain how to manufacture bombs, but exhort listeners to prepare for the coming apocalypse that is sure to engulf the United States in retribution for its 'sins against God'.[62]

Montana is also home to other far-right groups, including the North American Volunteer Militia and the Almost Heaven 'survivalist' compound. While the North American Volunteer Militia rails against the 'mess' created by the US government and warns, 'We need cleansing . . . we need blood to cleanse us,'[63] the millenarian Almost Heaven residents await the inevitable Armageddon. Founded and led by Bo Gritz, formerly a presidential candidate for an extreme right-wing party and a US Special Forces Vietnam veteran (supposedly the model for Sylvester Stallone's 'Rambo' character), this group embraces the same zealous advocacy of firearms possession and anti-government senti-ments as the militias, but also believes in a coming apocalypse, for which it prepares by stockpiling weapons, food and valuables and training in survivalist techniques and guerrilla warfare.[64] Security is provided by Gritz's specially created elite SPIKE teams, which according to one knowledgeable observer bear as much resemblance to the mainstream militia organizations as the US army's Special Forces (Green Berets) do to the 'weekend warriors' of the local National Guards (the American equivalent of Britain's Territorial Army).[65] In April 1996 a tense stand-off between the FBI and yet another Montana militia, known as the Freemen, was defused and a repetition of the Branch Davidian debacle avoided when eighty-one days of negotiations led to the voluntary surrender of two of the group's members for whom federal arrest warrants had been issued.

To the south, the Texas-based Big Star One claims to have a military 'division-sized' following, with separate 'units' deployed across the northern part of the state and into Oklahoma and New Mexico; the Texas Constitutional Militia boasts membership in the thousands and chapters in some forty counties; and a third militia, known as the 'Republic of Texas', prosecutes a 'campaign of paper terrorism' – attempting to throttle state courts with bogus land claims and bad cheques – claiming that the US illegally annexed Texas in 1845 and therefore has no jurisdiction over the state.[66] The Indiana Militia is described by observers as a particularly militant anti-gun-control organization; its members proudly proclaim they are 'sick and tired of being raped and pillaged by the bunch of thieves that run the federal government',[67] and clamour to take matters into their own hands.

The militia movement's violent ambitions have been clearly illuminated by at least three separate, known conspiracies uncovered by federal authorities since the Oklahoma City bombing. In July 1996 twelve members of an Arizona group known as the 'Viper Militia' were arrested,[68] of whom six were later charged with illegal possession of explosives and machine-guns along with conspiracy to promote civil disorder. The group is alleged to have plotted over two years to blow up seven federal office buildings in Phoenix and to this end had carried out detailed reconnaissance, including videotaping of potential target sites. It was in the process of building up a stock of ammonium nitrate fertilizer – such as that used to construct the bomb that destroyed the Murrah building – for this purpose. At the time of the arrest, the Vipers had amassed 1,900 pounds of the fertilizer;[69] the Oklahoma City bomb contained an estimated 4,800 pounds mixed with high-powered racing fuel.[70] The second incident came to light four months later when agents of the Bureau of Alcohol, Tobacco and Firearms (BATF) arrested three members of the so-called Militia-at-Large for the Republic of Georgia. The three were subsequently convicted of conspiring to 'wage war with the government', with plans including the assassination of senior elected officials and possibly even attacks at the then forthcoming Olympic Games in Atlanta. Finally, in November 1995 seven members of the West Virginia Mountaineer Militia were arrested and charged with plotting to blow up the FBI's computer centre in that state.

The members of all these groups, it should be noted, are not full-time, 'professional' terrorists – like the more familiar Irish, Basque, Middle Eastern and left-wing extremists active in Europe throughout the past few decades – but consider themselves 'minutemen': ordinary citizens and patriots ready to take up arms at a moment's notice to defend their inalienable rights, self-styled heirs of the tradition of the American Revolution. It is therefore significant that the Oklahoma City bombing took place on the date that the American Revolution commenced in Boston 220 years earlier. Indeed, McVeigh himself used this analogy to describe himself and the reasons behind his actions. 'Any able-bodied adult male, any patriot,' McVeigh told a British journalist, 'is responsible for defending his liberty. Just like the Minutemen of the revolution.'[71]

Although the militias are a relatively recent phenomenon, their pedigree can be traced back to the Posse Comitatus (Latin for 'power of the county') movement founded during the 1970s and its 1980s offshoot – with which McVeigh is also believed to have had ties – the Arizona Patriots. These groups strenuously reject any form of government above the county level and specifically oppose federal and state income taxes, the existence of the Federal Reserve system and the supremacy of the federal judiciary over local courts. Over the past two decades, local chapters of the Posse Comitatus have been founded in almost every state in the US. The group became increasingly violent, particularly in the American mid-west and the far north-west, with members attacking local, state and federal law enforcement officers attempting to serve subpoenas or otherwise enforce the law. An attempt to serve a subpoena on North Dakota Posse Comitatus member Gordon Kahl in 1983 resulted in the first of many armed confrontations between the radical right and the authorities. In the ensuing shoot-out, Kahl killed two federal marshals before he himself was shot to death.[72] Undeterred by Kahl's death, in December 1986 six members of the Arizona Patriots were arrested and subsequently convicted on charges of plotting to bomb an Internal Revenue Service (IRS) office in Ogden, Utah, the Los Angeles Federal Building (specifically, the FBI offices located there) and a synagogue in Phoenix, Arizona. Now a new generation of Arizona Patriots is currently carrying on their predecessors' campaign. Nightly short-wave radio broadcasts by Patriot leader William Cooper exhort members to resist forcibly the imposition of the 'new world order' epitomized by institutions like the United Nations and treaties such as the General Agreement on Tariffs and Trade.

It would be a mistake, however, to view either the militias or the older Posse Comitatus and Arizona Patriots organizations as simply militant anti-federalist or extremist tax-resistance movements. The aims and motivations of these extremist groups in fact span a broad spectrum of anti-federalist and seditious beliefs coupled with religious hatred and racial intolerance, masked by a transparent veneer of religious precepts. They are bound together by the ethos of the broader Christian Patriot movement, which includes:

- hostility to any form of government above the county level;
- the vilification of Jews and non-whites as children of Satan;
- an obsession with achieving the religious and racial purification of the United States;
- belief in a conspiracy theory of powerful Jewish interests controlling the government, banks and the media;
- advocacy of the overthrow of the US government, or the ZOG (Zionist Occupation Government), as the Patriot/militia groups disparagingly refer to it.

Many militia groups' 'field manuals' (literally recycled and repackaged versions of US military training handbooks and genuine field manuals) and other literature quote liberally from Christian scripture in support of their violent activities and use biblical liturgy to justify their paranoid call to arms. One militia recruit, for example, recalled in an interview his initiation into the movement in a rural Missouri church: 'It was odd. It was extremely religious. There were people standing along the aisles carrying weapons, rifles, a few with pistols. We all stood up and walked to the front of the church in this strange procession. We were told that it was part of the ritual of becoming "God's soldiers" in this "holy war". One of the organizers of the event then mounted the pulpit declaring, "Soon we will be asked to kill, but we will kill with love in our hearts because God is with us."'[73]

The connecting thread in this seemingly diverse and disparate collection of citizens' militias, tax resisters, anti-federalists, bigots and racists is the white supremacist religious dogma espoused by the Christian Identity movement, itself based on the 'Anglo-Israelism' movement that emerged in Britain during the mid-nineteenth century. The core belief of Anglo-Israelism was that the ten lost tribes of ancient Israel were composed of Anglo-Saxons, not Jews. However, in marked contrast to the present-day Christian Identity movement in the United States, nineteenth-century Anglo-Israelism embraced an entirely pacifist doctrine. The basic tenets of the contemporary American version of the Identity movement include the beliefs that:

- Jesus Christ was not a Semite, but an Aryan;
- the lost tribes of Israel are composed not of Jews, but of 'blue-eyed Aryans';
- white Anglo-Saxons and not Jews are the true 'Chosen People';
- the United States is the 'Promised Land'.

In this context, Jews are viewed as impostors and children of Satan who must be exterminated.

Identity theology, combined with militant tax resistance and a form of regressive populism, figures prominently in the Christian Patriotism doctrine subscribed to by the 'marching' militia groups today. The ideological heir to the Posse Comitatus with its hard-line anti-federalist principles, Christian Patriotism goes one step further by embracing a salient theological component that combines Identity interpretation of scripture with the myth of the Illuminati – the global conspiracy theory, first promulgated in the late eighteenth century in respect of Freemasons and later adapted to include the Jews, worldwide banking interests and other dark, mystical forces. According to its modern-day American interpretation, the so-called 'two seed' theory embraced by Christian Patriotism, there are two races on earth: one godly and one satanic – the former comprised of white, Anglo-Saxon Christians and the latter of Jews and all non-whites. The movement further believes in the moral and legal force of a form of 'common law' derived from a synthesis of the Magna Carta, the original articles of the US Constitution and the American Bill of Rights, and also regards all paper money as 'fraudulent', gold and silver being the only legitimate means of trade. McVeigh, it should be noted, has openly admitted to interviewers his belief in Christian Patriotism and involvement in Patriot activities.[74]

At the nexus of Identity, Christian Patriotism and the militia movements is the organization called the Aryan Nations. An extremist, anti-semitic, neo-Nazi group of white supremacists, survivalists and militant tax resisters, the Aryan Nations has its headquarters on a secluded, fenced-in forty-acre site at the edge of the Coeur d'Alene National Forest in Hayden Lake, Idaho. It was founded in 1974 by the Reverend Richard Girnt Butler, a former aeronautical engineer from California who moved to Idaho the previous year. Under his direction, the Aryan Nations performs a similar function to the PLO, acting as an umbrella group for like-minded organizations among which it provides a coordinating and liaison function. To this end, Aryan Nations congresses have been held most every year since 1973 – except for 1985, when widespread arrests of members of a radical splinter group, calling itself The Order, dealt a stunning, albeit temporary blow to the white supremacist movement. The MOM's leader, John Trochmann, for example, was a featured speaker at the 1990 event.

The Aryan Nations ideology is precisely the same mixture of racist and seditious dicta common throughout the American Christian Patriot movement. '*WE BELIEVE*', a brochure entitled *This is Aryan Nations* explains,

> there is a battle being fought this day between the children of darkness (today known as Jews) and the children of light (God), the Aryan race, the true Israel of the Bible . . .
>
> *WE BELIEVE* in the preservation of our race individually and collectively as a people as demanded and directed by God. We believe a racial nation has a right and is under obligation to preserve itself and its members . . . As His divine race, we have been commissioned to fulfil His divine purpose and plans . . .
>
> *WE BELIEVE* that there is a day of reckoning. The usurper will be thrown out by the terrible might of Yahweh's people as they return to their roots and their special destiny.[75]

Indeed, the 'Aryan National State Platform' cites as Article VIII that 'A ruthless war must be waged against any whose activities are injurious to the common interest.'[76]

This 'cleansing' of the United States forms an immutable point of reference for the Christian Patriots' ideology. 'Aliens are pouring over as a flood into *each* of our ancestral lands,' Butler warns, 'threatening dispossession of the heritage, culture, and very life blood of our posterity . . . We know that as we return to our Father's natural Life Order, all power, prosperity, and liberty again comes to us as our possession, to establish justice forever on earth.'[77] In promotional literature, the group proclaims its desire to 'make clear to ourselves and our enemies what we intend to do: We will have a national racial state at whatever price in blood is necessary. Just as our forefathers purchased their freedom in blood, so must we.' The leaflet goes on to decry 'the leadership of malicious, bastardizing politicians . . . [in] modern, decadent America [where] millions of whites watch in abject dismay and hopelessness as their great culture, heritage and civilisation evaporates in the steaming stinking, seething milieu of so many alien races, cultures and gods'.[78] Robert Matthews, the deceased leader of The Order, once declared that in order to stem this tide, all Jews, blacks, Hispanics and other 'mud people', along with so-called white 'race traitors', must be exterminated in what he described as 'a racial and religious Armageddon'.[79]

It is particularly alarming that the Christian Patriots' expressed *raison d'être* – the cocktail of racism, anti-semitism and sedition – is justified and legitimized on theological grounds. It is at once a political and a grassroots religious movement. The leaders of individual groups within it are indeed often themselves clergymen – like the Michigan Militia's founder and 'general', *Pastor* Norman Olson, the Idaho-based Aryan Nations' leader, *Reverend* Richard Girnt Butler and the Ku Klux Klan's *Pastor* Thom Robb – who deliberately flaunt their clerical titles in order to endow their organizations with a theological veneer that condones and justifies violence. In an article entitled 'An All White Nation? – Why Not?', the *Reverend* Roy B. Masker, for example, explains how Aryan Nations members 'are in disobedience to our Father and God, Yahwey, for allowing the Nation He gave us to become the mongrelized cesspool in which we now find ourselves . . . Indeed, it is incumbent upon us to BUILD A NEW, ALL-WHITE NATION! We are under command to do so! All scripture demands it!' Masker concludes with the admonition, 'Woe to those who stand in the way of the Aryan juggernaut!'[80]

The Christian Patriots do not appear to recognize any of the political, moral or practical considerations that constrain most other terrorist groups from causing mass death and destruction. There are, in fact, striking parallels between these groups and religiously motivated Islamic Shi'a and messianic Jewish fanatics in the Middle East. All these groups transform abstract political ideologies and objectives into a religious imperative. Violence is not only sanctioned, it is divinely decreed. The killing of persons described as 'infidels' by the Shi'a, 'dogs' by the Jews or 'children of Satan' by the Christian Patriots becomes a sacramental act.

Although the Christian Patriots have so far caused far less death, destruction and bloodshed than the Islamic Shi'a terrorists, evidence has come to light that at least some of the movement's key figures had laid plans to engage in indiscriminate mass killing. For example, an indictment handed down by a US federal grand jury in 1987 alleged that fifteen representatives of groups from throughout the United States and Canada met at the Aryan Nations headquarters in Idaho in 1983 to plot the forcible overthrow of the federal government and the creation of a separate Aryan nation within the United States. The indictment stated that they planned to 'carry out assassinations of federal officials, politicians and Jews, *as well as bombings and polluting of municipal water supplies* [emphasis added]'.[81] Any doubts of their seriousness of purpose were dispelled when police and federal agents raided a white supremacist compound in rural Arkansas in April 1984 and discovered a stockpile of some thirty gallons of cyanide to be used to poison reservoirs in Chicago, Illinois, and Washington, DC.[82]

An identical scenario, in fact, is detailed in the novel *The Turner Diaries*,[83] written by William Pierce under the pseudonym Andrew MacDonald, which has been cited both as 'the Bible' of the Christian Patriots[84] and as a major influence on McVeigh in his planning of the Murrah building bombing.[85] The book describes a chain of events that begins with a white supremacist revolution in 1991 and culminates two years later in 'an all-out race war' and worldwide nuclear conflagration. A terrorist group called The Order embarks on a ruthless campaign of violence involving the assassination of public officials and prominent Jews, the shooting down of commercial airliners, the poisoning of water supplies and bombings of public utilities. The book reaches its climax when the terrorists seize the US nuclear arsenal and obliterate several American cities before turning the weapons against targets in Israel and the Soviet Union.

Turner's tale, although fictional, is in many ways of a kind with Adolf Hitler's *Mein Kampf*, which was not taken seriously at the time, only to be turned into terrible reality a mere ten years after its publication. In fact, as incredible and lunatic as the events described in *The Turner Diaries* may seem, the strategy of the inchoate terrorist campaign waged in the United States between 1983 and 1984 by Robert Matthews and the real-life Order was based entirely on the battle plan detailed in the book. In another example of life imitating art, the MOM's 200-page manual reportedly reads exactly like a blueprint for battle copied out of *The Turner Diaries*, detailing plans how to:

- paralyse America's entire economy, including its agricultural and industrial sectors and transport and communications systems;
- assassinate prominent 'artists and sports figures' and other leading personalities as a 'useful form of propaganda for the revolutionary and patriot principles';
- eliminate spies and traitorous government officials;
- generally foment 'an air of nervousness, discredit, insecurity, uncertainty and concern on the part of government'.[86]

The bizarre apocalyptic vision of *The Turner Diaries* has long formed an integral part of the beliefs of white supremacists, Christian Patriots and militia adherents. Whereas most people, for example, harbour deep fears of a nuclear war, many white supremacists appear to welcome the prospect as an opportunity to eliminate their avowed 'enemies' and permit the fulfilment of their objectives to create a new world order peopled exclusively by the white race. The self-described purpose of the Covenant, the Sword and the Arm of the Lord's former compound at Mountain Home, Arkansas (where the cyanide was discovered), was 'to build an Ark for God's people during the coming tribulations on the earth'.[87] Accordingly, the hundred or so men, women and children who lived in the compound prepared themselves for the coming Armageddon by stockpiling weapons, food and valuables, and undergoing training in survivalist techniques and guerrilla warfare. As *Pastor* Terry Noble, a spokesman for the group, once explained, 'We are Christian survivalists who believe in preparing for the ultimate holocaust . . . The coming war is a step toward God's government.'[88]

The continuing influence that apocalyptic revelations and millenarian imperatives exert over many of these groups today may be seen in the 'DIY apocalypse kit' marketed by the MOM. The kit reportedly contains such detailed instructions as the need to build at least two concealed and well-protected 'fall-out' shelters, stockpile enough food to last for at least a year and to arm oneself with, at the very minimum, a Colt AR-15 assault rifle and 600 rounds of .223 ammunition as well as at least one 9 mm type Beretta automatic pistol with no fewer than 200 bullets. A can-opener, toothbrush and thermal underwear are the other recommended essentials – with the MOM offering for sale such additional optional gear as a military surplus NBC (nuclear, biological and chemical) protective suit (available in green only) for $50.[89]

These beliefs involving the inevitability of Armageddon are actively encouraged by proselytizers of Dominion theology, the most recent re-interpretation of Christian Identity doctrine circulating among the Christian Patriots today. Dominion theology has been described by one knowledgeable observer as a 'post-millennial Bible-based doctrine' incorporating the main tenets of Identity dogma. Thus, in addition to anti-semitism and racism, Dominionists believe that it is incumbent upon each individual to hasten redemption by working actively to ensure the return of the Messiah (in the Dominionists' vision, Christ). Only by accelerating the inevitable apocalypse, Dominionists contend, will the tribulations that currently afflict the American Christian white man end. The apocalypse will be followed by a thousand-year period of rule by Christians, at the end of which Christ will return to earth.[90]

The abiding link between religion and violence was most clearly demonstrated at the conference sponsored by a leading Identity and Dominionist figure, the *Reverend* Pete Peters,[91] in Estes Park, Colorado, in October 1992.[92] At that meeting, Louis Beam – one of the pre-eminent figures in American white supremacism – defined the violent strategy of 'leaderless resistance' for the militia movement. Beam, a Vietnam veteran and former Grand Dragon of the Texas Ku Klux Klan, whose close ties with Butler led to his appointment as the Aryan Nations' ambassador-at-large, has long been at the cutting edge of white supremacist violent activism. It was he who, in the early 1980s, pioneered the use of computer bulletin boards as a means for like-minded hate-mongers both to communicate with one another and to circulate literature and information otherwise outlawed by the US and Canadian postal services. Beam was thus well positioned to take the American white supremacist movement into the twenty-first century, making full use of the advanced capabilities of the Internet and World-Wide Web. Even now, information and literature from obscure organizations that was once difficult to obtain is readily available over the net to millions; for example, the Aryan Nations can offer its materials to a huge audience via its website. Beam's concept of 'leaderless resistance' was designed to avoid the mistakes of the past, when traditional-type terrorist groups like The Order were created to prosecute the white-race revolution only to be undermined and ultimately neutralized by arrests and informants. Accordingly, Beam proposed that so-called 'phantom cell networks' or 'autonomous leadership units' (ALUs) be established that would operate completely independently of one another but, through their individual terrorist acts, would eventually join together to create a chain reaction leading to a nationwide white supremacist revolution.

The object of 'leaderless resistance', Beam has explained, is to 'defeat state tyranny'.[93] The concept is taken from the white supremacist adventure novel *Hunter*, William Pierce's sequel to *The Turner Diaries* (again written under the pseudonym Andrew MacDonald). The impact of the strategy on the militia movement has been profound. For example, the 'field manual' produced by 'The Free Militia' in Wisconsin – typical of the genre – states the following:

THE FUNDAMENTAL RULE GUIDING THE ORGANIZA-TION OF THE FREE MILITIA IS [NOT] GENERALIZED PRINCIPLES AND PLANNING BUT DECENTRALIZED TACTICS AND ACTION.
What is meant by this key statement is that the whole Militia must be committed to the same cause and coordinated in their joint defense of a community . . . The way a balance between these competing concerns is achieved in the Free Militia is to organize all elements into 'cells'.[94]

Similarly, the MOM's John Trochmann was quoted addressing a meeting of the Washington State Militia in January 1996: 'If the enemy forces have no idea what's . . . in store for them if they come to our backyard . . . Leave the element of surprise on your side. Not everyone has to stand up publicly. Go with the cell structure in some of your areas – have a ball. Let them guess what's going on for a change, instead of us.'[95]

The latest incarnation of the fusion of religion and hate is believed to be the shadowy militant Christian Patriot activist-warriors known as the Phineas Priesthood. The name is taken from the Old Testament (Numbers 25), which recounts how a man named Phineas became an avenger priest by murdering a Midianite woman (named Zimri) whom he discovered having sex with her Israelite (Jewish) lover. The biblical tale is taken by some modern-day Christian anti-abortion extremists cum Identity adherents as a decree against 'race-mixing' and a summons to 'strike down those who are viewed as enemies of the pure white race'.[96] The Phineas Priests' self-appointed mission is allegedly to impose what they believe is 'God's law' on earth: that is, the enforcement of prohibitions against inter-racial marriage, homosexuality and abortion and an end to the federal banking system. They are reported to be highly secretive: so little is known about the Priests that it is not even certain whether they are an actual group or organization or a loose association of like-minded individuals adhering to the wider movement's 'leaderless resistance' or 'phantom cells' strategy, or whether the name is simply a mysterious title adopted by individual Christian Patriot groups to confuse and mislead the authorities.[97] Joe Roy, the director of Klanwatch (a group that monitors hate crimes in America), believes that the Priests do genuinely exist, describing them as 'zealots who truly believe they are commanded by God to carry out a revolution in the United States to restore "God's law"'.[98]

Whatever the actual status of the Priesthood, a clear convergence of religious terrorism and violence against homosexuals and abortion clinics and their staffs has been evident on several occasions in recent years.[99] In 1994, for example, a Christian fundamentalist minister named Paul Hill shot to death a clinic doctor and his escort in Pensacola, Florida. In his book, *Should We Defend Born and Unborn Children With Force?*, Hill cites Phineas's biblical mission and writes of the need for a vigilante underground to punish all who 'disobey God's law' on abortion or homosexuality and engage in other forms of blasphemous behaviour.[100] The Priesthood was also invoked by Christian Patriots in defence of the slaying of three customers at a gay bookstore in Shelby, North Carolina, in 1991; and it surfaced again in connection with a series of bank robberies and bombings that took place between April and July 1996 in Spokane, Washington. Three men were subsequently convicted for bombing a Planned Parenthood clinic (where abortions are performed), a local newspaper's offices and a bank, as well as twice robbing the same bank to the tune of $108,000 (a sum which was never recovered). At the scene of some of their attacks the gang left a two-page printed document, signed with the mark of the 'Phineas Priests'. The document espouses both Dominionist and Identity liturgy, before concluding with the warning:

> Let the high praises of Yahweh [God] be in their mouth, and a two-edged sword in their hand; to execute vengeance upon the heathen, and punishments upon the people: To bind their kings with chains, and their nobles with fetters of iron: To execute upon them the judgement written . . .
>
> Flee you usurer from the face of our land, and all that would not that the Master should reign over them, for the end of Babylon is come. Praise Yahweh![101]

Finally, it should be noted that the uncompromising anti-government fervour, aggressive racism and strident anti-semitism espoused by the American Christian Patriot movement has not been restricted to the United States. The racist British group Combat 18 (which takes its name from the first and eighth letters of the alphabet – Adolf Hitler's initials), for example, apparently openly emulates the American militias and Christian Patriot movements, advocating attacks on the police and other symbols of governmental authority. Its founder, Harold Covington, is however an American, and the group's mailing address is a post office box number in Raleigh, North Carolina.[102] And in Australia, militia groups patterned on the American model have reportedly been established based on an organizational blueprint provided by the MOM.[103]

Cults

The especial potential of terrorism motivated by a religious imperative to cause mass, indiscriminate killing has been perhaps most clearly demonstrated by the ominous activities of various religious cults and sects in the United States, Japan and elsewhere since the 1980s. While the attention of law enforcement officials, government intelligence agencies and security services was focused firmly on the more visible threat presented by familiar terrorist adversaries in the traditional ideological and ethno-nationalist/separatist groups, members of these organizations were already poised to cross the threshold of terrorist use of either weapons of mass destruction (WMD) or mass annihilation.

In 1984, for example, a non-lethal but disturbingly portentous incident occurred in the small Oregon town of Dalles. Followers of the Bhagwan Shree Rajneesh (an ascetic Indian mystic who, in addition to amassing a collection of ninety-three Rolls-Royce automobiles, had established a large religious commune nearby) poisoned the local reservoir and contaminated the salad-bars of restaurants with salmonella bacteria in hopes of debilitating the local populace and thereby rigging a key municipal election in the cult's favour. Although their plot to 'take over the county' failed,[104] the group's successful cultivation and effective dispersal of the bacteria clearly suggested the ease with which even more lethal agents could potentially be produced and disseminated in even larger population centres.

The release of deadly nerve gas on the Tokyo underground in March 1995 not only confirmed those fears but marked a significant historical watershed in terrorist tactics and weaponry. Previously, most terrorists had shown an aversion to the esoteric and exotic weapons of mass destruction popularized in fictional thrillers or depicted in action-hero films and television shows. Radical in their politics, the majority of terrorists were equally conservative in their methods of operation. Indeed, from the time of the late nineteenth-century Russian revolutionaries and the Fenian dynamiters who terrorized Victorian-era London, terrorists have continued to rely almost exclusively on the same two weapons: the gun and the bomb. The sarin-induced deaths of a dozen Tokyo commuters and the injuries inflicted on nearly four thousand others may have changed that for ever.

The Aum Shinrikyo (Aum 'Supreme Truth' sect) arguably represents a new kind of terrorist threat, posed not by traditional secular adversaries but by a mass religious movement motivated by a mystical, almost transcendental, divinely inspired imperative. The group was founded in 1987 by Shoko Asahara. A partially blind, hitherto unexceptional purveyor of supposedly medicinal herbs (who in 1982 was fined $800 and sentenced to twenty days' incarceration after conviction for selling fake cures) and owner of a chain of yoga schools in Japan, Asahara had emerged the previous year from a trip to the Himalayas a self-anointed prophet. His messianic inclinations were subsequently encouraged by a vision he had while meditating on a beach after returning to Japan. According to Asahara, God sent a 'message' to him that he had been chosen to 'lead God's army'. Not long after this experience, Asahara fortuitously fell into conversation with an eccentric historian he met at a mountainside spiritual retreat. The historian told him that Armageddon would come at the end of the century, that 'only a merciful, godly race will survive', and that 'the leader of this race will emerge in Japan'. Asahara immediately knew that he was the person destined to be that leader. Transformed by this revelation, he changed his name from the plain-sounding Chizuo Matsumoto to the apparently more suitably spiritual 'Shoko Asahara'.[105]

Shortly afterwards, with just ten followers, Asahara opened up the first Aum office. The new sect grew rapidly, tapping into the peculiarly Japanese fascination with mystical, obscure religious sects that combine the spiritual with the supernatural. Indeed, according to one account, at that time approximately 183,000 different religious cults already existed in Japan.[106] Aum's highly idiosyncratic mixture of Buddhism and Hinduism fused with notions of apocalyptic redemption exerted a powerful attraction for young, intelligent Japanese alienated by society's preoccupation with work, success, technology and making money. Hence, by the end of 1987 Aum had 1,500 members with branches in several Japanese cities;[107] in less than a decade, it would have some 10,000 members, organized within twenty-four branches scattered throughout Japan, alongside an estimated twenty to thirty thousand followers in Russia alone,[108] with an additional ten to twenty thousand converts in at least six other countries,[109] and offices in New York, Germany, Australia and Sri Lanka.

From the start, Asahara preached about the inevitability of an impending apocalypse, stressing his unique messianic mission and variously describing himself as 'Today's Christ', 'the saviour of This Century',[110] and 'the one and only person who had acquired supreme truth'.[111] Particular emphasis was given to the Hindu god of destruction and subsequent regeneration, Shiva, whose fifteen-foot visage dominated the entrance to the Satian-7 laboratory where the group manufactured the sarin nerve gas used in the subway attack. To round out his preoccupation with prophesied cataclysmic events, Asahara also borrowed Judeo-Christian notions of Armageddon and frequently cited the apocalyptic predictions of the sixteenth-century French astrologer Nostradamus, whose recently translated works had become best-sellers in Japan. According to Asahara the world would end – he was never sure exactly when, variously fixing 1997, 1999, 2000 and 2003 as likely times. Whatever the date, Asahara was certain that Armageddon would be caused by a Third World War. Citing his other-worldly abilities of both 'astral vision and intuitive wisdom', he proclaimed before an Aum conference in 1987 that nuclear war was 'sure to break out' between 1999 and 2003. This catastrophe could be averted, Asahara assured his followers, provided that they worked actively to establish an Aum branch in every country in the world. 'Spread the training system of Aum on a global scale and scatter Buddhas over the world,' he advised. 'Then we can avoid World War III for sure. I guarantee it.'[112]

From these apocalyptic predictions sprang Asahara's obsession with American enmity towards the Japanese in general and himself in particular. 'As we move toward the year 2000,' an Aum pamphlet warned, 'there will be a series of events of inexpressible ferocity and terror. The lands of Japan will be transformed into a nuclear wasteland. Between 1996 and January 1998, America and its allies will attack Japan, and only 10 percent of the population of the major cities will survive.'[113] Indeed, Asahara regularly blamed the United States for all of Japan's economic and social problems, as well as for attempting to destroy his own health. An intrinsic element of all these claimed plots was Asahara's fascination with nerve gas. 'I come under a gas attack wherever I travel,' he reportedly once declared, drawing a connection between the 'jet fighters from the US forces [that] fly for exercises around Mt Fuji' and his alleged medical problems.[114]

Asahara thus deliberately fostered a climate of paranoiac expectation within the cult, driven by the same Manichean world-view embraced by other religious terrorist movements, with its conviction of the world as a battleground between good and evil. The sect's avowed enemies gradually expanded to include not only the predatory US government and its minions in the Japanese government (who, Asahara alleged, were responsible for causing the January 1995 Kobe earthquake), but a mysterious international cabal of Freemasons, Jews and financiers. Asahara's adherence to the same far-fetched conspiracy theories promulgated by the American Christian Patriots movement is perhaps not entirely surprising given that he was also an unabashed admirer of Hitler and a fervent believer in the conspiratorial fantasies spun by such well-known anti-semitic works as the turn-of-the-century forgery, the *Protocols of the Elders of Zion*.

In books such as *Disaster Approaches the Land of the Rising Sun: Shoko Asahara's Apocalyptic Predictions*, Asahara warned that Armageddon would be precipitated by a poisonous gas cloud dispatched from the United States that would engulf Japan.[115] Thereafter, a cataclysmic global conflict would erupt – involving both nerve gas and nuclear weapons – that, in words reminiscent of Hitler's proclaimed 'thousand-year Reich', would lead to a thousand years of peace, after which the appearance of a new messiah would create a 'paradise on earth'.[116] In 1993, however, Asahara suddenly began to proclaim that the forth-coming apocalypse could be averted if Aum took proper action. 'We need a lot of weapons to prevent Armageddon,' he reportedly told his closest aides. 'And we must prepare them quickly.'[117]

Thus Aum embarked on its programme to acquire an array of conven-tional and non-conventional weaponry that would effectively dwarf the arsenals of most established nation-states' standing forces. To achieve this goal, the group recruited scientists and technical experts from Japan, Russia (including two nuclear scientists) and other countries. These individuals brought to Aum's projects superb credentials, including advanced degrees from their respective countries' most prestigious universities and research institutions. Moreover, with its vast financial reserves (Aum's assets exceeded an estimated $1 billion;[118] and when police searched Asahara's office, they reportedly discovered 22 pounds of gold and about £5 million in cash[119]), the sect was able to purchase whatever additional knowledge and resources its members lacked. Prime contractors in this respect were the Russian KGB's elite Alpha Group, the equivalent of the British SAS or American Delta Force, whose expertise in counterterrorist tactics (the group was estab-lished as a direct result of the Munich Olympics incident) and clandestine warfare (including sabotage, assassination, kidnapping, and intelligence and counter-intelligence techniques), was imparted to Aum activists. Additional personnel from Russia's other military special operations force, known as Spetsnaz, reportedly provided further training in martial arts, escape and evasion techniques and the use of various small arms, including firing rocket launchers and assault rifles. Aum is also thought to have purchased large quantities of small arms from KGB stocks and to have been in the market for such advanced weaponry as T-72 tanks, MiG-29 jet fighters, an SL-13 Proton rocket launcher and even a nuclear bomb. What is known is that Aum succeeded in obtaining a surplus twin-turbine Mi-117 helicopter, complete with chemical spray dispersal devices. The group had ambitious plans – and had already acquired sophisticated robotic manufacturing devices – to produce at least 1,000 'knock-off' versions of Russia's world-famous AK-47 assault rifle, along with one million bullets. It had also perfected the manufacture of TNT and the central component of plastic explosives, RDX.

Aum's intentions, however, went far beyond a revolution facilitated by conventional armaments alone: it armed itself in addition with a panoply of chemical and biological warfare agents, and had (unrequited) nuclear aspirations. When police raided the sect's laboratories following the nerve gas attack on the Tokyo underground, they found enough sarin to kill an estimated 4.2 million persons.[120] In addition, Aum either had already produced or had plans to develop other nerve gases such as VX, tabun and soman; chemical warfare agents such as mustard gas and sodium cyanide; and biological warfare agents that included anthrax, the highly contagious disease known as Q-fever, and possibly the deadly Ebola virus as well.[121] Authorities also found 100 grams of the psychedelic drug LSD – the equivalent of one million doses – and 3 kilograms of mescaline, among other hallucinatory and stimulant drugs.[122]

Aum's most ambitious project was without doubt its attempt to develop a nuclear capability. To this end, the group had purchased a 500,000-acre sheep station (known as Banjawarn Station) in a remote part of Western Australia. There, they hoped to mine uranium that was to be shipped back to Aum's laboratories in Japan, where scientists using laser enrichment technology would convert it into weapons-grade nuclear material. The reason for a massive explosion that occurred near Aum's Australian holdings on 28 May 1993, which lit up the sky for miles and caused shock waves felt hundreds of miles away, is still unexplained, but may have been related to Aum's nuclear research and development activities.

'With the use of sarin we shall eradicate major cities,' Asahara had declared; and, on the morning of 20 March 1995, his disciples put his deadly plan into action. The date was much sooner than had been expected; but Aum informants inside the National Police Agency had warned that police were about to search the cult's compounds, and so Asahara suddenly ordered the planned attack to be brought forward in hopes of thwarting the impending raids and completely derailing the intensifying police investigation into Aum's activities.[123] At approximately 8.00 a.m., in the midst of the Monday morning rush hour, selected Aum cadres placed eleven packages containing sarin nerve gas on five subway trains on the Eidan Chiyoda, Hibiya and Marunouchi lines. The trains were scheduled to converge within four minutes of one another at Kasumigaseki central station: the terminus at the heart of the Japanese government, used daily by the thousands of office workers employed in the country's most important ministries – including the National Police Agency. Eyewitnesses reported that some of the containers appeared to be ordinary lunch-boxes or soft-drink flasks, while others were nylon rubbish bags wrapped in newspaper. In at least one instance, a man was observed to stab his package with the sharpened tip of an umbrella, thus releasing the nerve gas. Almost immediately, passengers were affected by the noxious fumes: some were quickly overcome, others were afflicted with nosebleeds, oral haemorrhaging, uncontrollable coughing fits or convulsions. In all, fifteen stations and three separate subway lines were affected. The casualties might even have been far greater had not favourable weather conditions fortuitously combined with hastened – and therefore perhaps botched – preparations to reduce the sarin's potency.

Amazingly, this was neither the first nor the last Aum attack to employ chemical or biological warfare agents. In April 1990, the group had attempted to realize one of Asahara's dire prophecies of an impending catastrophe by staging an attack with botulinus toxin. Using an aerosol device developed by Aum's scientists to disperse the poison over a wide area, the sect targeted downtown Tokyo and specifically the Diet (parliament) building. The toxin, however, proved ineffective. Another attempt to disperse botulinus in downtown Tokyo failed in June, as did a suspected Aum plot to spread anthrax the following month. Then, in June 1994, the group had tried to kill three judges presiding over a civil suit brought against Aum in the rural resort town of Matsumoto. The plan was to spray a block of flats where the judges were sleeping with sarin. Seven persons were killed and more than 250 others were admitted to hospital with nerve-gas-induced symptoms. Though taken seriously ill, the judges survived. Incredible as it seems, a report previously issued by a special unit of the Tokyo metropolitan police department's criminal investigation laboratory pointing to the presence of the nerve gas reportedly went ignored – despite repeated local complaints of strange odours emanating from the sect's nearby compound, alongside various unexplained disappearances of former Aum members and individuals who had attempted to investigate the sect's activities. Instead, the man who first reported the incident was branded as the culprit and accused of accidentally mixing some noxiously fatal concoction of weedkiller.[124] Finally, in a last spasm of activity designed to avert the governmental onslaught directed at Aum in the wake of the underground attacks, members of the sect attempted to stage a chemical attack using hydrogen cyanide – more infamously known as Zyklon B, the same type of gas used by the Nazis at Auschwitz during the Second World War to murder tens of thousands of persons – on 5 May, the national 'Children's Day' holiday.

On 15 December 1995 the Japanese prime minister, invoking a 1952 anti-subversion law, ordered Aum disbanded and seized all its assets. Asahara and his lieutenants are currently on trial in a Tokyo court. However, in recent months reports have surfaced that Aum is experiencing something of a revival in Japan. A hard core of at least 1,000 members – including even some new recruits – are said to be rebuilding the sect's profitable computer business and are engaged in various other commercial ventures, while continuing to worship their imprisoned leader.[125]

Conclusion

The emergence of obscure, idiosyncratic millenarian movements, zealously nationalist religious groups, and militantly anti-government, far-right paramilitary organizations arguably represents a different and potentially far more lethal threat than traditional terrorist adversaries; certainly a far more amorphous and diffuse one. The members of the Aum sect in Japan, the fanatical Jewish groups in Israel, the Christian Patriots in America and some of the radical Islamic organizations active in Algeria, Lebanon and Israel do not conform to our traditional stereo-types modelled on the secular terrorist organization. These groups had a defined set of political, social or economic objectives, and however disagreeable or distasteful their aims and motivations may have been, their ideology and intentions were at least comprehensible – albeit polit-ically radical and personally fanatical.

The identity of these new types of adversaries is also significant in terms of the countermeasures that the government, military, police and security services can employ against them. The most immediate challenge in countering or deterring these new adversaries is the problem simply of identifying them. These ethereal, amorphous entities will often lack the 'footprint' or *modus operandi* of an actual, existing terrorist organization, making it more difficult for intelligence, law enforcement and other security specialists to get a firm idea or build a complete picture of their intentions and capabilities, much less their capacity for violence, before they strike.

Second, these groups are mercurial and unpredictable. Knowledge is still lacking concerning the reasons why many 'fringe' movements or hitherto peaceful religious cults suddenly turn to violence or embark on lethal campaigns of indiscriminate terrorism. These are primarily intel-ligence, investigative and most importantly academic research issues that need to be addressed before effective countervailing, much less appropriately designed deterrent, measures can be considered. This leads on to a third point, which is that traditional counterterrorism approaches and policies may not be relevant, much less effective, in the face of this type of activity. Political concessions, financial rewards, amnesties and other personal inducements that have often been success-fully applied against secular terrorists would be not only irrelevant but impractical, given both the religious terrorists' fundamentally alienated world-views and often extreme, resolutely uncompromising demands.

A two-pronged course of action is needed. On the one hand, the profound sense of alienation and isolation of these cults and religious movements needs actively to be counteracted. A bridge needs to be found between mainstream society and the extremists so that they do not feel threatened and forced to withdraw into heavily armed, seething compounds or to engage in pre-emptive acts of violence directed against what they regard as a menacing, predatory society.

Finally, it must be contemplated that we may be on the cusp of a new, and potentially more dangerous, era of terrorism as the year 2000 – the literal millennium – approaches. One cannot predict the effect that this pivotal symbolic watershed might have on religion-inspired terrorist groups who feel impelled either to hasten the redemption associated with the millennium through acts of violence, as the Aum sect in Japan has already attempted to do, or, in the event that the year 2000 passes and redemption does not occur, to attempt to implement Armageddon by the apocalyptic use of weapons of mass destruction. The pattern of religion-inspired terrorism over the past two years alone suggests that the potential for still more and even greater acts of violence cannot be prudently discounted.

5

Terrorism, the Media and Public Opinion

The goals and motivations of terrorists, as we have seen in previous chapters, vary widely, from such grand schemes as the total remaking of society along doctrinaire ideological lines or the fulfilment of some divinely inspired millenarian imperative to comparatively more distinct aims such as the re-establishment of a national homeland or the unification of a divided nation. Still other terrorists are motivated by very issue-specific causes, such as the banning of abortion, animal rights or opposition to nuclear power, and seek to apply direct pressure on both the public and its representatives in government to either enact or repeal legislation directly affecting their particular interest. Despite these many differences, however, all terrorist groups have one trait in common: none commits actions randomly or senselessly. Each wants maximum publicity to be generated by its actions and, moreover, aims at intimidation and subjection to attain its objectives. In the words of the late Dr Frederick Hacker, a psychiatrist and noted authority on terrorism, terrorists seek to 'frighten and, by frightening to dominate and control. They want to impress. They play to and for an audience, and solicit audience participation.'[1]

Terrorism, therefore, may be seen as a violent act that is conceived specifically to attract attention and then, through the publicity it generates, to communicate a message. 'There is no other way for us,' a leader of the United Red Army (the 'parent group' of the Japanese Red Army) terrorist group once explained. 'Violent actions . . . are shocking. We *want* to shock people, everywhere . . . It is our way of communicating with the people.'[2] The modern news media, as the principal conduit of information about such acts, thus play a vital part in the terrorists' calculus. Indeed, without the media's coverage the act's impact is arguably wasted, remaining narrowly confined to the immediate victim(s) of the attack rather than reaching the wider 'target audience' at whom the terrorists' violence is actually aimed. Only by spreading the terror and outrage to a much larger audience can the terrorists gain the maximum potential leverage that they need to effect fundamental political change. 'Terrorism is theatre,' Jenkins famously declared in his seminal 1974 paper, explaining how 'terrorist attacks are often carefully choreographed to attract the attention of the electronic media and the international press'.[3]

Just as often, the media respond to these overtures with almost unbridled alacrity, proving unable to ignore what has been accurately described as 'an event . . . fashioned specifically for their needs'.[4] The American media's coverage of the hijacking of TWA flight 847 by Lebanese Shi'a terrorists in 1985 amply confirms that observation. Three terrorists belonging to Hezbollah had hijacked the aircraft en route from Rome to Cairo on 14 June. The hijackers originally demanded the release of 776 Shi'a held in Israeli gaols, although they later reduced that number. The commandeered aircraft was flown first to Beirut, then to Algiers, then back to Beirut. At each stop passengers who were not US citizens, along with the women and children travelling on board, were released until only thirty-nine American men remained. After the aircraft landed in Beirut for the second time, the hostages were spirited into hiding and scattered throughout the city to thwart any attempted rescue operation by US military forces. During the seventeen-day crisis, while the Americans were held hostage in Beirut, nearly 500 news segments – an average of 28.8 per day[5] – were broadcast by the three major US television networks (ABC, the American Broadcasting Corporation; NBC, the National Broadcasting Corporation; and CBS, the Columbia Broadcasting System). Indeed, on average, two-thirds of their daily early evening 'flagship' news shows (fourteen out of twenty-one minutes) focused on the hostage story;[6] and their regularly scheduled programmes were interrupted at least eighty times over those seventeen days with special reports or news bulletins.[7] This intense coverage was made possible by the small army of reporters, field producers, editors, camera crew and sound technicians whom the three networks rushed to the scene of the breaking story: within days, a total of eighty-five persons representing the three networks were on station in Beirut.[8] The message that they imparted to their viewers was clear: no other news of any significance was occurring anywhere else, except for that which concerned the hostages and their anxious families back home.

More disconcerting, perhaps, was the tenor of the coverage. As the hostage crisis dragged on day after day, at times with seemingly little or no progress towards a resolution, the vast media resources deployed for just this one story had to find or create 'news' to justify the expense and continued presence, even if no 'real news' was occurring. A gross imbalance therefore emerged: 'soft', human interest feature stories predominated (mostly interviews with the hostages and their families), accounting for slightly more than a third of all reports, with fewer than half as many stories addressing 'real' issues, such as the US government's reactions to various developments in the crisis or the Reagan administration's persistent efforts to reach a resolution.[9] The cloying and meretricious content of the reporting was clearly revealed in a contemporary *Washington Post* article. 'In the race for on-the-air scoops, which ABC-TV News seems to have won to date,' it began, 'the interview Friday morning between anchorman [news presenter] Dan Rather of "CBS Evening News" and TWA flight 847's hostage media star, Allyn Conwell, was distinctive.'[10] In possibly the most egregious perversion of news reporting during this episode, the 'news presenters' rather than the 'news makers' had become the story!

However, the most pernicious effect of the crisis was its validation of terrorism as a tactic. The Reagan administration, driven by intense domestic pressure generated by the hostages' plight, in turn compelled Israel to accede to the hijackers' demands and release 756 imprisoned Shi'a. The terrorists, in return, duly freed their thirty-nine American captives. The line of distraught hostage family members paraded before the three networks' cameras ensured that there was no let-up of pressure. 'Should the Reagan administration press Israel to release its Shi'a prisoners?' the son of one hostage was asked on a morning news show. 'That's what I'd like to see,' came the reply.[11] The networks professed little or no concern that they had moved beyond reporting the news to actively helping to determine policy. At times, presenters assumed for themselves the responsibility of negotiating with the terrorists. 'Any final words to President Reagan this morning?' the congenial host of ABC's *Good Morning America* asked the leader of one Lebanese group.[12] Justifying this type of active intervention in a story, CBS White House correspondent Lesley Stahl explained, 'We are an instrument for the hostages . . . We force the Administration to put their lives above policy.'[13]

Those responsible for determining and implementing that policy understandably took a very different view. Reflecting on a state of affairs where public emotions were seen to determine government policy, Senator Tom Lantos lamented that 'focusing on individual tragedies, interviewing the families of people in anguish, in horror, in nightmare, completely debilitates national policymakers from making rational decisions in the national interest'.[14] His complaint was echoed by former US secretary of state Henry Kissinger and Zbignew Brzezinski, President Carter's National Security Adviser during the Tehran hostage crisis. Both agreed that there was little doubt that the febrile television coverage afforded to hijackings and hostage situations involving American citizens complicates and undermines governmental efforts to obtain their release.[15]

That terrorism had indeed become a perverted form of show business is borne out by the experiences of other journalists who dealt with the hostage-takers' 'spin doctors' and therefore witnessed at first hand the terrorists' polished PR campaign. 'These guys are so sophisticated about the way they are getting through to the American viewer,' a senior Associated Press editor marvelled. 'These guys are street fighters [yet] they're making ground rules for the media.'[16] According to John Bullock, a British journalist who covered the story, throughout the crisis the terrorists knew exactly what they were doing. Their deft manipulation of the US networks, he recalls, 'was done quite consciously. There were graduates of media studies from American colleges at meetings at Nabih Berri's house in West Beirut while ['spin doctoring'] tactics were being worked out.'[17]

The fruit of the hijackers' labours may be seen in the abject capitulation of the American TV networks to the terrorists' point of view. On-air commentary repeatedly and unthinkingly equated the wanton kidnapping of entirely innocent airline passengers (who were singled out only because of the nationality of the passport they carried) with

Shi'a militiamen and suspected terrorists detained by Israeli troops during fighting in southern Lebanon. These invidious and inaccurate comparisons were all the more odious considering that one of the hostages, a US navy diver named Robert Dean Stethem, had been mercilessly beaten to death on board the aircraft shortly after the hijack began. As one critic noted, 'It's a cliché now that the Shi'ites got the networks to carry their political message back to America. When the TV coverage is replayed, it's clear just how well the Shi'ite line was delivered.' Indeed, so obvious was this perceived bias on the part of some reporters that it was said to be a standing joke among journalists in Beirut that the initials ABC stood for the 'Amal Broadcasting Company' (in recognition of the attention it showered on one of the Lebanese militias purportedly helping to effect the hostages' release), while NBC denoted the 'Nabih Berri Company' (the name of that militia's leader).[18]

While the American networks' response to the TWA flight 847 crisis is doubtless the most glaring example of terrorism's ability to capture media attention and manipulate and exploit it in ways amenable to the terrorists' cause, the problem is endemic to democratic countries with open and unrestricted press reporting everywhere. So pervasive was the influence exerted by West German terrorists over coverage of the 1972 deal that freed a kidnapped West Berlin politician, Peter Lorenz, in exchange for five imprisoned terrorists, that one executive was driven to admit that 'for seventy-two hours we lost control of our medium'.[19] In 1978 the same blanket coverage to the exclusion of almost all other news that would later be afforded to the TWA hijacking was evident in Italy throughout the 55-day state crisis engendered by the Red Brigades' kidnapping of former prime minister Aldo Moro. According to one analysis, during that time only two articles appeared on the front pages of that country's newspapers that did not have to do with the Moro case.[20] More recently, complaints have been voiced in Britain over the stranglehold exercised by Sinn Fein spin doctors on behalf of their IRA masters over reporting in Northern Ireland. Henry McDonald, BBC Northern Ireland security correspondent between 1994 and 1996, contends that the terrorists and their apologists orchestrated a public relations campaign that imposed a 'politically correct culture' on the reporting of both British and Irish print and electronic media. 'It is a culture', McDonald claims, 'where the commentators and opinion-formers blame John Major for resumed IRA violence, rather than the IRA itself.'[21]

Given that terrorism is inherently about attracting attention and publicity, and that in even its earliest manifestations centuries ago the Zealots and Assassins deliberately played to an audience far beyond the immediate victims of their attacks, why is it only comparatively recently that the media have been blamed for serving as the terrorists' willing apologists? The answer may be found in two technological advances in mass communication that occurred nearly 100 years apart and respectively altered the way that news is transmitted and made it accessible to exponentially larger audiences. These developments in turn have been ruthlessly and successfully exploited by terrorists.

Terrorism and the Transformation of Reporting

The invention of the steam-powered printing press in 1830 began the modern era of mass media and communication: within three years the first mass circulation newspaper was being produced in the United States. Subsequent technological refinements led to the introduction of the even more efficient rotary press the following decade. News became more timely (because of the speed with which newspapers could now be printed) and more accessible (as the economics of technological innovation created a more widely affordable product). By the 1870s the newspaper business had been completely transformed by the advent of electric power coupled with the development of curved stereotype printing plates, together resulting in the automatic rotary cylinder press – and the capability to print on both sides of a continuous roll of paper. The revolution in mass communication, begun less than fifty years earlier, was now complete, offering abundant new opportunities to communicate on a vaster scale than ever before. That terrorists were quick to recognize the potential of this new mass communications technology has already been noted in a previous chapter. It suffices simply to add here that the symbiotic relationship between terrorism and the media was forged during this era by both the Russian constitutionalists in the Narodnaya Volya and their anarchist contemporaries who, through 'propaganda by deed', deliberately sought to communicate their revolutionary message to a wide audience.

The second great revolution in mass communication that directly impacted terrorism occurred in 1968. That year marked not only, as previously noted, the birth of international terrorism – when Palestinian terrorists began to hijack airliners in Europe – but also the launching by the United States of the first television satellite. Now stories could be transmitted from local studios back to network news headquarters for editing and broadcast far more rapidly than was previously possible. It is perhaps not entirely coincidental that from this time forward, the United States became the number one target of terrorists throughout the world. Throughout the following thirty years, terrorists have attacked American citizens and interests more than any other country's.[22] While there are various reasons why terrorists find American targets so attractive,[23] a salient consideration has always been the unparalleled opportunities for publicity and exposure that terrorists the world over know they will get from the extensive US news media. This was made especially clear during the TWA flight 847 crisis when a British correspondent assigned to the story discovered that the hostage-takers paid no attention to 'non-American and non-television journalists'.[24] In retrospect, therefore, the US satellite launch was the first, critical step in facilitating the American news media's worldwide predominance through its ability to reach a numerically vast audience. Ironically, it was also this development that made the same audience exponentially more attractive to terrorists than any other nation's.

By the early 1970s the effect of this technological leap was further enhanced by the availability of three critical pieces of television equipment that made possible the reporting of events in 'real time'. These were the 'mini-cam' (the portable, lightweight video camera), the equally portable battery-powered video recorder, and the time-base corrector (which converts video footage into transmittable output that in turn can be broadcast over the airwaves). With this combination of technologies, live television transmissions could now be made directly from remote locations throughout the world and beamed instantaneously into the homes of viewers everywhere.[25] The dramatic potential of this breakthrough was, as previously described, spectacularly demonstrated at the 1972 Munich Olympics when Palestinian terrorists were able to monopolize the attention of a global television audience who had tuned in expecting to watch the Games.

The emergence of these broadcast technologies has had equally profound consequences for the content of the news and its impact on government. The ability to transmit a breaking story live spawned intense competition among rival networks to 'scoop' one another (as was illustrated by the *Washington Post* article quoted above). This could be accomplished basically in one of two ways: by being the first on the scene or by being the first to report some hitherto undisclosed information. The main problem with the former is that, even while it is the most sought-after prize of TV journalism it is also an inherently evanescent advantage. Hence, having broken the story and captured viewers' attention, the priority becomes to hold that attention with equally gripping follow-on reports. Accordingly, for the duration of an important story's life, the media's focus invariably shifts from the reporting of the limited and often dwindling quantity of 'hard' news to more human-interest-type 'feature' stories, mostly involving exclusive interviews (e.g. the aforementioned Rather–Conwell exchange) or the breathless revelation of some previously unknown or undocumented item of related news – no matter how trivial or irrelevant.

For the media-savvy terrorist, these conditions are ripe for exploitation. The networks' capability to broadcast instantaneously, coupled with the intense pressure to 'scoop' competitors, has meant that the responsibilities once exercised by a studio editor – with attendant opportunities for sober reflection or considered judgement – have long since passed in the rush to 'go live on air'.[26] The television medium thus presents itself as a vacuum waiting to be filled; a void of rolling cameras and open mikes susceptible to terrorist exploitation and manipulation. Indeed, in this key respect, the terrorists' and networks' interests are identical: having created the story, both are resolved to ensure its longevity. The overriding objective for the terrorists is to wring every last drop of exposure, publicity and coercive power from the incident, while for the networks it is to squeeze from the story every additional ratings point that their coverage can provide. 'Capturing the audience's attention may be easy,' political psychologists Jeffrey Z. Rubin and Nehemia Friedland note, 'but terrorist organizations need a flair for the dramatic to sustain that interest.'[27] Precisely the same can be said of television correspondents and field producers.

The quest to keep a story alive leads inevitably to a disproportionate fixation on the 'human interest angle': most often, the grief and anguish of family and friends of terrorist victims and/or hostages. In this manner, the vicarious dimension of a terrorist incident – the stimulation of thoughts in the minds of millions of television viewers and newspaper readers everywhere that 'there but for the grace of God go I' – is effectively and efficiently mined by terrorist and journalist alike. Beyond any doubt, the American networks during the TWA crisis served this diet on a platter to a waiting and watching public at home, made hungry both for every scrap of information on the hostages themselves and for each morsel doled out on the worried plight of their loved ones back home. This sort of coverage dovetailed perfectly with the terrorists' wish to apply the maximum pressure possible on the Reagan administration to force Israel to accede to the hijackers' demands. Day in and day out, as the hostages' uncertain fate was played out in the glare of the camera's lens, the administration was progressively compelled to abandon its publicly stated policy of refusing to negotiate with terrorists, undermine its relations with a close regional ally, embrace the recovery of the hostages as its only goal and believe that its sole option was the safe return of the thirty-nine American hostages in exchange for the release of the 700-plus Shi'a imprisoned in Israel. 'What the Shi'ite terrorists in Beirut achieved is spin control beyond the wildest dreams of any politician,' the American columnist Fred Barnes wrote in the wake of the crisis. 'How did this happen?' he asked, rhetorically. 'Easy,' came the reply:

> The terrorists exploited the normal lust of the media – particularly TV – for breaking events of international impact, and for high drama and a human dimension to the news . . . Media competition, always brutal, is especially fierce in this atmosphere, partly because the public is more attentive, partly because media stardom may be at stake for some.[28]

It will be recalled that the leading late-night American television news show *Nightline* grew out of the need to report at the end of each day, as viewers prepared for sleep, some new tit-bit of information from Tehran during the previous 444-day hostage crisis of 1979–80. This approach not only made the show's presenter, Ted Koppel, a media star,[29] but also spawned dozens of imitators in other countries.

One additional, even paramount, consideration influencing television news coverage that has emerged in recent years is financial cost. A once finite number of privately owned or state-run broadcasting corporations is now confronted with heightened competition not only from their traditional network rivals, but from a virtually unlimited plethora of upstart cable and satellite channels. Moreover, in addition to these traditional outlets, news is now broadcast over such diverse media as the Internet, e-mail and faxes, and via local telephone servers. Hence, on top of increasingly constrained news budgets (dating even from more than a decade ago), today foreign network news coverage especially must increasingly justify itself and its vast expense by winning larger audience shares. According to one veteran network foreign correspondent, the daily cost of the typical international television news team 'begins at around $3,000 a day. Air fare and excess baggage charges can easily reach $12,000' – in addition to the costs of satellite up-links and transmittal time.[30] There is accordingly a discernible proclivity among network executives to look more to the 'bottom line' than to journalistic priorities for guidance and hence to emphasize entertainment value over good reporting. 'They've got us putting more fuzz and wuzz on the air,' Dan Rather lamented in a 1993 speech, 'cop show stuff, so as to compete not with other news programs but with entertainment programs – including those posing as news programs – for dead bodies, mayhem and lurid tales'[31] – a view most recently reiterated by one of Rather's colleagues, Garrick Utley, the chief foreign correspondent for NBC and ABC TV news and a contributor to CNN, in a lead article in the prestigious American journal *Foreign Affairs*.[32] Immediacy, exclusivity and drama (the more violent or life-threatening the better) thus become the essential 'hooks' with which to reel in viewers and ensure a flow of advertising revenue. Terrorist incidents, inherently dramatic, replete with human interest and often of prolonged duration (whether the wrenching daily ordeal of hostages or reports on post-attack clean-up and repercussions in the aftermath of bombings), thus occupy centre-stage in network television's entertainment/news calculus. The result is a trivialization of television news that inevitably emphasizes aspects of the story that the wider viewing audience can 'relate to',[33] rather than genuine analysis or probing to gain an understanding of the background to a particular issue. The camera becomes tightly focused on the human drama at the expense of the 'bigger picture' that is what the story is really about. In essence, what is broadcast is the 'big picture' writ so small that the average television viewer can understand it, the story deliberately 'packaged' to suit the typical audience's short attention span.[34] 'Mindless gaga and emotional gush seem the mainstays of the moment,' the *Washington Post*'s television critic, Tom Shales, opined in the midst of the TWA crisis; bemoaning the debasement of broadcast news.[35]

This trend in American television news is by no means an inconsequential development, given that by 1978 television had become the primary source of news information for a majority (67 per cent) of Americans and the *only* source of news for 34 per cent.[36] The emphasis on entertainment and, in turn, the violence and 'blood and guts' aspects of news stories was demonstrated in a study of the three major American networks' reporting of Armenian terrorism between 1975 and 1983. It concluded that, while the coverage had indeed (as noted in chapter 3) provided unparalleled exposure to the terrorists and their cause, the 'networks tended to reduce Armenians to terrorists (not freedom fighters) shooting an American woman in the back as she tried to flee, taunting the police by holding a small child at gun point, and killing a young French boy with a gasoline bomb'. In this respect, virtually no attention was paid to the historical background, political context or attendant wider issues that would have shed light on the terrorists' reasoning and motivations.[37]

Unfortunately, the approach to terrorism coverage embraced by broadcast journalists is often emulated by their print counterparts. 'As the television media trivialise the news,' James Adams, CEO of United Press International (and former *Sunday Times* Washington Bureau chief, foreign manager and defence editor), argues, 'so newspapers have to seek ways of presenting their information in a lively and exciting way to their audience. That has meant not just a narrowing of the focus but a concentration on the trivial, the marginal and the irrelevant in the search for excitement.'[38] Colour photos, lurid images and sensational headlines splashed across the front pages of tabloids and their more serious counterparts is what now sells newspapers (and advertising copy) as much as commercial air-time. Accordingly, there is often the same abandonment in print as over the airwaves of any effort to understand the 'bigger picture'. Instead, an obsession with voyeuristic detail now predominates in many newspapers. It is an outcome dictated by the same financial pressures and declining revenues that have ravaged network television news, even while the broadcast media continue to erode the news-reading public. Adams, for example, draws a comparison between his stint at the *Sunday Times* as foreign manager during the 1980s and that of one his predecessors, Ian Fleming (the creator of the fictional spy, James Bond), in the 1950s. While Fleming could call on the services of 150 correspondents throughout the globe, thirty years later Adams had only eight at his disposal. 'What that means today', he writes, 'is that media coverage is highly selective and driven not necessarily by the importance of a story, but by the cost of covering it, or even by something as simple as who happens to be in the area at the time.'[39]

In these circumstances, news reporting is driven primarily by the imperative of speed in getting on air or into print and subsequently by the search for additional material to justify the initial expense and attention and thereby to continue to fill a broadcast slot or printed page. This is a situation that, however unwittingly, is tailor-made for terrorist manipulation and contrivance. '"Don't shoot, Abdul! We're not on prime time!"' is how terrorism expert J. Bowyer Bell describes the conscious efforts of terrorists to play to the modern media and the media's eagerness to respond. Sadly, this jocular observation is closer to reality than exaggeration. During the 1975 seizure of the OPEC headquarters in Vienna and kidnapping of the oil ministers, for example, Carlos 'The Jackal' obligingly waited for the arrival of the television camera crews before dramatically fleeing the building with his hostages.[40] Four years later, a sullen mob outside the American embassy in Tehran, where the fifty-two hostages were being held, suddenly came to life when a Canadian Broadcasting Company camera team showed up, turned on its klieg lights and began filming. As Schmid recounts, 'As soon as the cameras were on, the demonstrators began shouting "Death to Carter", raised their fists, looked angry and burned American flags. After two minutes, the cameraman signalled the end of the "take". Then the same scene was done once more for the French-speaking Canadians, with the crowd shouting "Mort à Carter".'[41]

Cause and Effect? Terrorism, the Media, and Public Opinion

Clearly, terrorism and the media are bound together in an inherently symbiotic relationship, each feeding off and exploiting the other for their own purposes. The real issue, however, is not so much the relationship itself, which is widely acknowledged to exist, as whether it actually affects public opinion and government decision-making, as the media's critics claim, in a manner that favours or assists terrorists. The answer is far more complex and ambiguous than the conventional wisdom on this subject suggests.

The view most commonly, if somewhat reflexively, advanced by statesmen,[42] scholars,[43] and other critics is of the media either as 'the terrorists' best friends'[44] or, in former British prime minister Margaret Thatcher's well-worn metaphor, as supplying 'the oxygen of publicity on which [terrorists] depend'.[45] The media are condemned for having 'made the terrorists' task all too easy',[46] or accused of having 'become the unwilling – and in some cases, willing – amplifier of the terrorists' publicity campaign'.[47] Indeed, Benjamin Netanyahu, the current Israeli prime minister, maintains that 'unreported, terrorist acts would be like the proverbial tree falling in the silent forest'.[48] The obvious implication being made in all these assertions is that if the terrorists could somehow be 'starved' of the publicity on which they 'thrive',[49] both their malignant influence and the frequency with which they act would be greatly reduced.[50]

This argument, while seductive in its simplicity, nonetheless ignores the fact that, for all the attention and sensationalist coverage that the media lavish on terrorism, rarely is it positive. 'I have seen no evidence', Lawrence K. Grossman, the president of NBC News, wrote in an article defending the media's coverage of the TWA hostage crisis, 'that audiences are ever taken in by the propaganda of terrorists who have blackmailed their way on to the television screen.'[51] However self-serving or self-exculpatory Grossman's argument may be, it is not without foundation. Even scholars like Laqueur, who in one breath criticize the media for its unstinting coverage of terrorism, concede in the next that this has not led to more favourable public attitudes towards either terrorists or their causes.[52]

This was precisely the conclusion of a study conducted between 1988 and 1989 by the renowned American think-tank, the RAND Corporation. By surveying a nationally representative sample, it sought to identify empirically public perceptions of both terrorism and terrorists and analyse how public opinion is affected by terrorist acts. The timing of the survey was particularly significant. It immediately followed a prolonged period of heightened international terrorist activity, characterized by repeated attacks on American targets abroad. These incidents (including the 1985 TWA hijacking) had also been heavily reported by the American press and broadcast media. Public awareness of the issue was therefore high. Indeed, terrorism had been a major news item throughout the five years preceding the study, and it had already been cited in a 1986 CBS News/*New York Times* opinion poll as the most important problem facing the United States by a margin of 15 percentage points above any other problem, domestic or international. However, despite the media's continual and often intense attention to their activities over a period of years, the RAND study found that public approval for terrorists '*was effectively zero* [emphasis added]'.[53]

At the same time, the study also revealed that, even though the vast majority of Americans have little sympathy towards groups that sponsor or commit terrorist acts,[54] they nonetheless evinced a profound and abiding fascination with both terrorists and terrorism. As Kellen explained, 'people [may not] approve of terrorists any more than they approve of murderers . . . But people are clearly intrigued by them.'[55] This was made abundantly clear on 5 May 1986 when NBC's *Nightly News* broadcast an in-depth interview with Abul Abbas, the leader of the Palestine Liberation Front (PLF). Just seven months earlier, the PLF had shocked the world when it had seized an Italian cruise ship, the *Achille Lauro*, and then attempted to trade the holidaymakers on board for fifty Palestinian terrorists imprisoned in Israel. In the course of the hijacking, the terrorists brutally murdered an American tourist confined to a wheelchair, Leon Klinghoffer, and cast his body into the Mediterranean. Eventually, the PLO's head, Yassir Arafat, intervened and brokered a deal whereby the terrorists would allow the ship to dock at Alexandria and release their hostages in return for receiving safe passage back to the PLF's base in Tunisia. US navy fighters, however, intercepted the EgyptAir plane carrying the four hijackers and forced it to land at a NATO air base in Sicily, where the terrorists were arrested by Italian police. The US State Department subsequently announced a $250,000 reward for Abbas's capture and launched an international man-hunt. In tracking down the fugitive terrorist leader and obtaining an 'exclusive interview' with him, NBC had therefore succeeded where the US government hitherto had failed. More to the point, the network disingenuously implied that its newsmen had accomplished this feat entirely on their own and without Abbas's encouragement or assistance.[56] The extent of the media's symbiotic relationship with terrorism, no less than the public fascination to which both media and terrorists actively cater, could hardly have been more blatantly evident.

However, what was particularly striking about the NBC interview was not simply the 'statesmanlike' status the network promiscuously accorded to a man whose hands, as the hijacking's mastermind, were arguably drenched in Klinghoffer's blood, but the preening self-importance that attended NBC's broadcast of this spectacle. 'We like to interview all leaders,' Grossman boasted. 'I think it is important for the American people to understand, be informed and make their own judgements.'[57] Yet by no stretch of the imagination could (or should) Abbas be ranked with those world 'leaders' whose views merit the most coveted prize on American television – a dedicated slot on a major prime-time news show. Abbas, in fact, was one of the least successful PLO commanders, whose group's previous operations had featured episodes redolent of the 'Keystone Kops', with terrorists flying hot-air balloons and hang-gliders, that had all failed as miserably as the attempt to free the fifty prisoners through hijacking a luxury liner. Nevertheless, while Abbas may have been a failure as a terrorist, he certainly had a flair for a form of macabre showmanship that suited NBC and its audience's interests perfectly. In the incandescent glare of the camera's lights, the public and media fascination with terrorism transformed Abbas into the 'media star of the moment' rather than the kidnapper and murderer that he really was.[58] Indeed, so far as many, perhaps most, viewers were concerned the interview was doubtless more 'entertainment' than news. Tasteless or inappropriate as the NBC broadcast may have been, then, it most probably had little or no impact on most viewers' attitudes towards terrorists or terrorism – except perhaps to re-affirm their overwhelming negative impressions.

The phenomenon of public fascination with terrorism is by no means confined to American news audiences only. A Royal Ulster Constabulary (RUC) divisional commander quoted at a conference on 'terrorism and the media' by his then boss, Chief Constable Sir John Hermon, rhetorically asked whether 'a rapist in Hampshire or a burglar in Berkshire [would] be accorded the freedom through the [British] media to justify rape and burglary and be allowed to threaten more of the same?'.[59] The answer, as we all know, is obviously that he would not. However, the point is less the publicity 'showered' on terrorism by the media than that terrorism patently *is* 'news' – often in an international as well as a national context – in a way that these other crimes, mostly, are not. Perhaps we should feel grateful that even after thirty years of violence and strife in Northern Ireland, terrorism remains so – relatively

– infrequent an occurrence that it is indeed still 'news'. But there is also an undeniably inherent element of drama in terrorism that seems to enable it genuinely to transcend the mundane and stimulate among audiences an almost insatiable interest, which the media of course actively encourage and feed. Thus, while the media may be guilty of constantly – perhaps at times even shamelessly – scrambling to fill a vacuum created by twenty-four-hour news channels, rolling news shows and intense competition, the media neither exist nor function in a vacuum and, like any business, respond naturally to 'consumer demand'. Whether this makes for good reporting or sound professional behaviour on the part of print and broadcast journalists is another question. On this issue, too, the opinions of critics and audiences differ considerably.

As the lightning rod for much of the criticism directed against the media over its coverage of terrorism, the TWA crisis epitomizes for many the corrosive effect of terrorism on journalistic standards.[60] Reagan administration officials railed against the 'media extravaganza' in Beirut that one senior political appointee claimed 'gave irresponsibility and tastelessness a new meaning'.[61] Even veteran newsmen, like NBC's Roger Mudd, cringed at what they too regarded as something of a 'media circus'.[62] Yet the American public disagreed completely. An ABC News/*Washington Post* poll conducted shortly after the TWA hostage crisis ended, for instance, found that over two-thirds of Americans approved of the way that television had reported the story,[63] while a Gallup poll from the same period revealed an even higher proportion in favour: 89 per cent.[64] Nor were these strongly positive ratings ephemeral aberrations of opinion. Three-quarters of Americans surveyed a year later in a poll conducted by Gallup and the Times Mirror Corporation (which publishes the *Los Angeles Times*, among other newspapers) similarly expressed satisfaction with both television and the print media's reporting of terrorist incidents. Moreover, 71 per cent of respondents regarded their country's news organizations as 'highly professional'.[65] These unequivocal responses, flying in the face of mostly genuinely deserved, if sometimes over-heated, criticism, seem to confirm viewers' interest in terrorism stories primarily for their entertainment value – and their lack of interest in the terrorists or their broader 'message'.

The media were further excoriated by both senior government officials and distinguished elder statesmen for the excessive attention focused on individual hostages and their families. 'TV is probably going to cost the lives of a number of people in a dangerous situation like this sometime in the future,'[66] one unidentified presidential aide declared, echoing the frequently heard criticism that the intense coverage compromised administration efforts to free the hostages. However, nearly half the persons surveyed in the Gallup/Times Mirror poll regarded the unrelenting attention devoted to the hostages as a positive development that ensured the hostages' safety and eventual release. As the wife of one hostage explained on a morning news show, 'If we like it or not, television is a way . . . to put pressure where pressure needs to be put.'[67] More than a few hostages wholeheartedly agreed. 'Thank the Lord we're on our way,' one declared as he boarded the flight that was to take him back to the United States, flashing the 'thumbs up' sign to a CNN camera crew filming his departure, and 'thanks for all the coverage'.[68] The American CNN reporter Jeremy Levin, who himself was kidnapped in Beirut by Hezbollah terrorists in March 1984, has made the exact same point. Levin maintains that the extensive media attention focused on his plight during the eleven months he was held captive actually deterred his captors from killing him.[69] He also makes the discomforting argument that the longest hostage crisis – that of the Americans and other Western nationals (including Terry Waite, the Archbishop of Canterbury's special envoy) kidnapped by terrorists in Lebanon between 1984 and 1992 – was also the one that had the least sustained media coverage.[70]

Seen in the light of the above discussion, the accepted wisdom about the symbiotic relationship between terrorism and the media appears far less self-evident than is commonly assumed. While most terrorists certainly crave the attention that the media eagerly provide, the publicity that they receive cuts both ways. On the one hand, terrorists are indeed assured of the notoriety that their actions are designed to achieve; but, on the other, the public attitudes and reactions that they hope to shape by their violent actions are both less predictable and less malleable than either the terrorists or the pundits believe. For example, one of the IRA's main aims in abandoning its ceasefire in February 1996 was to convince the British public that the government was to blame for the breakdown of negotiations and thereby to put pressure on the prime minister to grant concessions to the nationalist position that the government was hitherto unwilling or unable to make. The result was equivocal: in large measure, perhaps, because of the unanimous condemnation heaped on the IRA and Sinn Fein by the British (and, arguably, world) press for the Friday evening blast at London's Canary Wharf, which killed two persons and injured hundreds of others. While 63 per cent of persons polled a week later thought that the government should still be willing to talk with Sinn Fein in order to find a way to restore the ceasefire, 89 per cent nonetheless 'overwhelmingly blamed' the IRA for wrecking the peace process. Sinn Fein and the IRA's well-oiled public relations machine in Northern Ireland was eventually able to put their spin (as noted above) on the reporting of this issue in the province. Their failure to achieve the same result on the mainland, however, was palpable. As one analysis noted, 'In isolation, those figures suggest television appearances since last weekend of [Gerry] Adams and other prominent Sinn Fein leaders have had little success in deflecting criticism.'[71] This may also explain why the IRA was driven to escalate its bombing campaign throughout England during the weeks and months following the ceasefire's collapse. Indeed, until the change of government in May 1997, the IRA was resorting to the naked use of terrorism as a means to coerce the government back to the negotiating table, rather than to manipulate public attitudes in a manner usefully sympathetic to the nationalists' frustrations.

There are two areas in particular, however, where a clear causal relationship between terrorism and the attention it receives from the media impacts negatively on public and governmental behaviour. The first is the public's perception of personal risk from terrorism, and the consequent effect on willingness to travel; the second is the time pressures imposed by the media under which governments confronted with terrorist-created crises labour.

Action and Reaction: The Impact on Travel and Government Decision-making

When the above-mentioned RAND survey asked members of the public how likely they thought it that they might be involved in several low-probability events, the results on terrorism were revealing. Although the majority of respondents were able accurately to gauge the relative risk involved – realizing that they were more likely to be involved in an automobile accident than a terrorist incident – the perceived difference in the likelihood of the two eventualities was far smaller than the actual difference in probabilities. For example, 71 per cent thought it likely that they would be involved in a car crash – although the estimated actual probability is just 19.2 per 100,000 persons. By comparison, while only 14 per cent thought that they were likely to be flying on a plane that is hijacked or the victim of a terrorist bombing, the actual chances of being hijacked are fewer than one in 100,000 (no similar statistics for bombings were available). Viewed from another perspective, 47,087 persons were killed in automobile accidents in the United States during 1988 and 45,582 during 1989 (the two years during which the RAND study was conducted), while 203 Americans were killed in terrorist incidents throughout the world in 1988 (93 per cent of them perishing in a single incident, the December in-flight bombing of Pan Am flight 103 over Lockerbie) and 23 in 1989. Indeed, an American was just as likely to be killed by a dog as by a terrorist in 1989: yet nearly a third of those surveyed that year stated that they would refuse the opportunity to travel abroad because of the threat of terrorism. There is no statistical evidence whether an identical percentage had similarly concluded that it was now equally dangerous to keep dogs as pets.[72]

The distortion in perception that results in higher probabilities being accorded to terrorism than to other life-threatening acts is in large measure doubtless a direct reflection of the disproportionate coverage accorded to terrorism by the American media. Indeed, at one time during the 1980s the American television networks were devoting more attention to terrorism than to poverty, unemployment and crime combined – despite the fact that these were arguably more important political issues since they had a far greater and more immediate impact on most Americans' daily lives.[73] The role of media coverage in fuelling viewing and reading audiences' irrational fears of terrorism was dramatically demonstrated by the wave of cancellations of travel plans by Americans immediately following the TWA hijacking. Some 850,000 persons cancelled their travel and holiday reservations – both foreign and domestic – because of fears of becoming enmeshed in some terrorist incident (much as, in the wake of the November 1997 terrorist attack on foreign tourists at Luxor, many travellers were reported to be cancelling planned trips to Egypt). An additional 200,000 Americans rebooked their foreign holidays to US destinations on the assumption that their own country at least was still safe from terrorism.[74] Severe knock-on effects followed on local economies in foreign countries dependent on the tourist trade: 50 per cent of American bookings to Italy and 30 per cent to Greece were lost. While the reluctance of Americans to visit the country from which the ill-fated TWA flight had departed (Italy) is understandable, as, perhaps, are their reservations about travelling to and from a nearby country whose airports at the time were widely criticized for their poor security (Greece), it is more difficult to explain why the peaceful Netherlands experienced an only slightly less startling drop in the number of American visitors (20 per cent).[75]

To put the actual terrorist threat to Americans during 1985 into perspective: 6.5 million US citizens travelled abroad that year, of whom 6,000 died from a variety of natural causes, accidents and violence. Only seventeen of these 6,000 persons perished as a result of terrorist-related acts.[76] The chances of dying abroad were thus only one in 150,000 to begin with, and an almost infinitesimally smaller number so far as the risk from terrorism was concerned. Yet, despite these overwhelmingly low probabilities, by February 1986 a total of 1.8 million Americans had changed their plans to go on holiday outside the United States.[77] Cancellations of Greek holidays booked by Americans more than doubled from the previous year[78] – even while British and Scandinavian tourism to Greece increased respectively by 22 per cent and 25 per cent.[79] The number of American visitors to Britain itself fell by an astonishing 40 per cent compared to the previous year's figure.[80] Indeed, 76 per cent of Americans surveyed in April 1986 (following the in-flight bombing of a TWA passenger aircraft en route from Rome to Athens and the bombing of a West Berlin discotheque by Libyan agents) stated that the threat of terrorism had made it too dangerous to travel overseas that year – compared with 67 per cent who had felt that way the previous July.[81] By the end of 1986, some 80 per cent of Americans who had planned to travel abroad that year had cancelled[82] – despite the fact that the fears generated by the threat of terrorism were grossly divergent from the real risk.

The effects of the nexus between the news media and terrorism on decision-making go far beyond the question of US citizens' overseas travel plans. A third revolution in the communication of news has unfolded throughout the closing decades of the twentieth century to transform not only the way the world now gets its news, but the manner in which political leaders make decisions. This revolution has been less dependent than its two predecessors upon some new major technological breakthrough, deriving more from a concatenation of technological advances that have cumulatively changed the style rather than the mechanics of news presentation. The 'CNN Syndrome' – a catchphrase coined in recognition of the Atlanta-based Cable News Network – has revolutionized news broadcasting through the emergence of dedicated round-the-clock, 'all the news all the time' television stations on both satellite and cable. More recently, these have spawned a myriad of attendant, often connected, communications outlets – Internet news providers (e.g. CNN interactive), automated e-mail and fax news services, etc. – that feed a worldwide audience with an insatiable appetite for information transmitted in real time and furnishing immediate access to the actual locations and the people on the spot making the news.

The power of this latest expansion of the communications mass media is attested to by the multitude of television sets that can now be found in the office of virtually every functionary and politician in official Washington, DC – from mid-ranking civil servants to Pentagon flag officers, CIA spymasters to Commerce Department officials, and Congressmen to the president – their screens glowing silently throughout the day until some event of sufficient magnitude occurs to warrant both the attention of their owners and the volume knob's adjustment upward. 'Our best intelligence is invariably the media,' confessed Noel Koch, the deputy assistant secretary of defense responsible for counterterrorism during the Reagan administration, even as long ago as the mid-1980s. The ultimate accolade, however, was offered by Lieutenant-Colonel Oliver North, the former National Security Council aide made famous for his pivotal role in the 1986 arms-for-hostages deal, who said that 'CNN runs ten minutes ahead of NSA' – comparing the privately owned cable company to the National Security Agency, America's super-secret electronic and signals gathering intelligence agency.[83]

The effects of this immediacy, however, are such that television becomes not just an 'opinion shaper' but a 'policy driver', its presenters and on-air analysts racing to define the range of options at a government's disposal or interpret likely public reaction – and its repercussions. As Lloyd Cutler, counsellor to President Carter during the 1979–80 Iran hostage crisis, explained, 'If an ominous foreign event is featured on TV news, the President and his advisers feel bound to make a response in time for the next evening news program.'[84] Debate is not just precipitously joined, but abruptly rushed and then quickly truncated, depriving policy-makers, government officials and military commanders of the time needed to analyse critical issues thoroughly, reach well-thought-out decisions, craft coherent responses, and act with confidence based on exhaustive deliberation.[85] Governments are in consequence increasingly pressured to respond to events before they can be evaluated fully, taking their cue from the 'spin' that the media give them rather than working towards decisions based on all the available information. When asked in a 1993 interview specifically about the impact of the 'CNN Syndrome' on government decision-making, Prime Minister John Major replied that: 'I think it is bad for government. I think the idea that you automatically have to have a policy for everything before it happens and respond to things before you have had a chance to evaluate them isn't sensible.'[86]

The Clinton administration's experience during the last months of America's involvement in Somalia is a salutary reminder of both the overpowering influence of images flashed across the television screen and the hazards of decisions made on the basis of initial impressions and incomplete information. On 3 October 1993, a US military operation to arrest Somali warlord General Mohammed Farah Aideed's paymaster and chief lieutenants went disastrously awry. Fifteen US Rangers were killed and seventy-seven others wounded. In some of the most gripping footage broadcast on American television, an injured US army helicopter pilot was seen being paraded through the streets of Mogadishu by a chanting, gun-wielding Somali mob. Reacting quickly to the incident – while scrambling to pre-empt criticism by Congress, the media and the American public – President Clinton announced within days the immediate dispatch of military reinforcements to Somalia, but set 31 March 1994 as the firm date for the withdrawal of all American forces there – regardless of whether the multinational UN-led humanitarian aid mission to that country had in fact been successfully completed by that date. A USA Today/CNN/Gallup poll taken shortly after the incident validated the president's fears that a majority of Americans would hold him and his administration responsible for pursuing an ill-conceived humanitarian aid mission that had now cost the lives of more than a dozen troops. Fifty-two per cent of persons polled thought it was a mistake to have become involved in Somalia in the first place (a decision, in fact, made by the outgoing Bush administration) with 57 per cent opposing Clinton's decision to send reinforce-ments.[87] An ABC News poll revealed similar results.[88]

However, upon closer – and more sober – inspection, many of these 'results' appear less conclusive. For example, according to the *USA Today*/CNN/Gallup poll, 50 per cent of those questioned in their survey who stated that they wanted US troops immediately withdrawn had watched the television coverage of the injured helicopter pilot being led by Somali militiamen past jeering crowds and had been particularly incensed by the spectacle. But among those polled who hadn't seen the broadcasts, only 33 per cent favoured withdrawal.[89] In addition, 49 per cent of Americans surveyed in a subsequent ABC TV poll actually disap-proved of the president's decision to set a withdrawal date, compared with 45 per cent who approved it;[90] while a poll conducted later that same week by the University of Maryland's Program on International Policy Attitudes found that only 28 per cent of its nationwide sample favoured immediate withdrawal, with 43 per cent stating that they thought US forces should remain in Somalia 'until we have stabilized the country' – if necessary, even beyond the stated withdrawal deadline.[91] Accordingly, in retrospect it appears that the president may well have been stampeded into a decision that did not necessarily reflect public opinion because of the raw emotions generated by the widely televised scenes depicting the brutal treatment of the captive helicopter pilot. John Chancellor, senior commentator on NBC News and doyen of American network news, has tried to distinguish between television's perennial search for dramatic footage and the responsibilities incum-bent on reporters. 'You have journalism, which is thoughtful and considered,' Chancellor has observed, 'and you have what I call "electronics", which is the use of our facilities to transmit pictures and words, but does not have a lot to do with journalism.'[92] It is the conver-gence of the two that has fundamentally altered the context and content of the news today and has also at times exercised a distorted influence over both public opinion and official decision-making. In this new era of mass media, where the 'information revolution' has transformed communication worldwide as a result of breakthroughs in real-time, rapid communication, the rush to meet air-time and print deadlines, and the attendant inevitably hurried judgements and immediate decisions, may present still further opportunities for manipulation and influence by terrorists than have hitherto existed.

Conclusion

We live today in an age of soundbites and 'spin', in which arresting footage or pithy phrases are valued above considered analysis and detailed exegesis – and are frequently mistaken for good journalism. One of the enduring axioms of terrorism is that it is designed to generate publicity and attract attention to the terrorists and their cause. It is, accordingly, an activity custom-tailored to mass media communication at the end of the twentieth century. Terrorist acts are only too easily transformed into major, international media events – precisely because they are often staged specifically with this goal in mind. Their dramatic characteristics of sudden acts of violence exploding across the screen or printed page, rapidly unfolding into crises, pitting enigmatic adversaries against the forces of law and order make these episodes as ideal for television as they are irresistible for broadsheet and tabloid journalist alike.

In Britain, the media (and public) fascination with terrorists is second perhaps only to that with the country's royal family. How else can one explain the small article that was featured on page four of the London *Times* on 3 September 1997 as part of its coverage of the Princess of Wales's tragic death, and the repetition of its content the following day as part of a larger article on page six? Both described how Leila Khaled – the Palestinian terrorist who gained international notoriety as a result of her involvement in the in-flight hijacking of a TWA flight in 1969 and of an El Al passenger jet the following year – had been touched by the princess, to whom she dedicated a poem that she sent to the princess's two sons.[93] Apart from the fact that there could be no two persons more different than a former terrorist, whose actions on those two occasions deliberately endangered the lives of hundreds of innocent airline passengers, and a woman whose life was dedicated to ameliorating the suffering of the innocent and infirm, that Khaled and her thoughts should be considered newsworthy is testimony to the powerful magnetic attraction exercised by terrorists and terrorism for the media in even the most unlikely (and absurd) circumstances.

For terrorists, media coverage of their activities is, as we have seen, something of a double-edged sword, providing them with the attention and publicity that they invariably seek, but not always in a particularly useful or even helpful manner. In this respect, while the 1985 TWA hostage crisis provides a clear lesson of how terrorists exploit and prompt the media for their own advantage, the recent denouement of the so-called 'Unabomber's' seventeen-year terrorist campaign arguably demonstrates the opposite. The anonymous 'Unabomber', the name coined by the FBI in reference to his targeting of persons associated with either universities or the airline industry, who killed three people and wounded twenty-three others using simple yet ingeniously constructed home-made bombs sent through the post, had promised in June 1995 to restrict his lethal terrorist campaign provided that either the *New York Times* or *Washington Post* printed his entire manuscript and three annual follow-up messages. As a result of the publication in September of his 35,000-word diatribe against technology, modernity and the destruction of the environment in the *Washington Post*,[94] information subsequently came to light that led directly to the arrest of Theodore Kaczynski, a former University of California at Berkeley mathematician, who has now been charged with the bombings. Had the alleged 'Unabomber' not been as obsessed with publicity as he was, he might never have been unmasked and arrested. As Rapoport has observed,

> The relationship between publicity and terror is indeed paradoxical and complicated. Publicity focuses attention on a group, strengthening its morale and helping to attract recruits and sympathizers. But publicity is pernicious to the terrorist groups too. It helps an outraged public to mobilize its vast resources and produces information that the public needs to pierce the veil of secrecy all terrorist groups require.[95]

While not terrorism as most commonly understood, in that the 'Unabomber' was a lone individual acting from a frustration and animus so profound that no other person could share them, that bizarre case nonetheless demonstrates the complexity of terrorism's symbiotic relationship with the media. Moreover, it not only poses yet another formidable challenge to the almost unthinkingly accepted conventional wisdom about this relationship, but underscores the need for critical, however subtle, distinctions to be made in this area.

6

The Modern Terrorist Mindset:
Tactics, Targets and Technologies

The wrath of the terrorist is rarely uncontrolled. Contrary to both popular belief and media depiction, most terrorism is neither crazed nor capricious. Rather, terrorist attacks are generally both premeditated and carefully planned. As we saw in the previous chapter, the terrorist act is specifically designed to communicate a message. But, equally important, it is also conceived and executed in a manner that simultaneously reflects the terrorist group's particular aims and motivations, fits its resources and capabilities and takes into account the 'target audience' at which the act is directed. The tactics and targets of various terrorist movements, as well as the weapons they favour, are therefore ineluctably shaped by a group's ideology, its internal organizational dynamics and the personalities of its key members, as well as a variety of internal and external stimuli.

The Nexus of Ideological and Operational Imperatives

All terrorist groups seek targets that are rewarding from their point of view, and employ tactics that are consonant with their overriding political aims. Whereas left-wing terrorists like the German RAF and Italian RB have selectively kidnapped and assassinated persons whom they blamed for economic exploitation or political repression in order to attract publicity and promote a Marxist-Leninist revolution, terrorists motivated by a religious imperative have engaged in more indiscriminate

acts of violence, directed against a far wider category of targets encompassing not merely their declared enemies, but anyone who does not
share their religious faith. The actions of ethno-nationalist/separatist
groups arguably fall somewhere in between these two models. On the
one hand, the violent campaigns waged by groups like the PLO, the IRA
and the Basque separatist organization ETA have frequently been more
destructive and have caused far greater casualties than those of their
left-wing counterparts. But, on the other, their violence has largely been
restricted to a specifically defined 'target set': namely, the members of a
specific rival or dominant ethno-nationalist group.[1] Perhaps the least
consequential of all these terrorist group categories (in terms both of
frequency of incidents and of impact on public and governmental
attitudes) has been the disparate collection of recycled Nazis, racist
'political punk rockers' and other extreme right-wing elements that has
emerged over the years in various European countries. But even their
sporadic and uncoordinated, seemingly mindless violence – fuelled as
much by beer and bravado as by a discernible political agenda – is neither
completely random nor unthinkingly indiscriminate. Indeed, for all
these categories, the point is less their inherent differences than the fact
that their tactical and targeting choices correspond to, and are determined by, their respective ideologies and attendant mechanisms of
legitimization and justification; and, perhaps most critically, by their
relationship with the intended audience of their violent acts.

The overriding tactical – and, indeed ethical – imperative for left-
wing terrorists, for example, has been the deliberate tailoring of their
violent acts to appeal to their perceived 'constituencies'. In a 1978 interview, the German left-wing terrorist Michael 'Bommi' Baumann
denounced the hijacking of a Lufthansa passenger plane the previous
year by terrorists seeking the release of imprisoned RAF members as
'madness . . . you can't take your life and place it above that of children
and Majorca holiday-makers and say: *My* life is valuable! That is
elitarian madness, bordering on Fascism.'[2] For Baumann, the deliberate
involvement of innocent civilians in that terrorist operation was not only
counterproductive, but wrong. It was counterproductive in that it
tarnished the left-wing terrorists' image as a true 'revolutionary
vanguard' – using violence to draw attention to themselves and their
cause and 'educate' the public about what the terrorists perceived as the
inequities of the democratic-capitalist state. It was also wrong in itself

because innocent persons – no matter what the political justification – should not be the victims of terrorist acts directed against the state.

For this reason, left-wing terrorists' use of violence historically has been heavily constrained. Their self-styled crusade for social justice is typically directed against governmental or commercial institutions, or specific individuals who they believe represent capitalist exploitation and repression. They are therefore careful not to undertake actions that might alienate potential supporters or their perceived constituency. Accordingly, left-wing violence tends to be highly discriminate, selective and limited. Individuals epitomizing the focus of the terrorists' ideological hostility – wealthy industrialists like Hans Martin Schleyer (who was kidnapped and later murdered by the RAF in 1977) or leading parliamentarians like Aldo Moro (who similarly was kidnapped and subsequently murdered by the RB) – are deliberately selected and meticulously targeted for their intrinsic 'symbolic' value. 'You know that we did not kidnap Moro the man, but [rather] his function,' explained Mario Moretti, the leader of the RB Rome column who masterminded the operation, during his trial in November 1984. For Moretti, Moro was first and foremost a powerful symbol: a former prime minister and reigning Christian Democratic Party chief; a political wheeler-dealer *par excellence* and architect of the impending historic compromise with the Italian Communist Party that would fundamentally alter the country's political landscape and further marginalize the RB. He was, in the terrorists' eyes, the 'supreme manager of power in Italy' for the previous twenty years, a man whom Moretti described as the 'demiurge of bourgeois power'. By abducting so important a leader and so profound a symbol, the RB sought to galvanize the Italian left and thereby decisively transform the political situation in their favour.[3]

Even when less discriminate tactics such as bombing are employed, the violence is meant to be equally 'symbolic'. That is, while the damage inflicted is real, the terrorists' main purpose is not to destroy property or obliterate tangible assets, but to dramatize or call attention to a political cause. The decision-making process of the left-wing terrorist group is perhaps depicted most clearly in Baumann's description of the planning of a 1969 terrorist attack by the group known as the Tupamaros West Berlin (a precursor of both the Second of June Movement and the original RAF). Baumann and his colleagues wanted to stage an operation that would simultaneously attract attention to themselves and their cause, publicize the plight of the Palestinian people and demonstrate the West German left's solidarity and sympathy with the Palestinians' struggle. 'We sat down and pondered what would be a story that nobody could miss, that everyone would have to talk about and everyone would have to report,' Baumann recalled. 'And we came up with the right answer – a bomb in the Jewish Community Centre – and on the anniversary of the "Crystal Night"[4] during the Third Reich . . . Though it didn't explode, the story [still] went round the world.'[5] By striking on this particular date, against this specific target, with its deep – and unmistakable – symbolic significance, the group sought to draw a deliberate parallel between Israeli oppression of the Palestinians and Nazi persecution of the Jews.[6]

The use by left-wing terrorists of 'armed propaganda' (i.e. violent acts with clear symbolic content) is thus a critical element in their operational calculus. It is also the principal means by which these organizations 'educate' the masses through their self-anointed role as 'revolutionary vanguard'. The first official 'strategic resolution' of the RB, for example, stressed exactly this theme. 'It is not a question of organizing the class movement within the area of armed struggle,' the 1975 document stated, 'but of entrenching the organization of the armed struggle and the political realization of its historical necessity within the class movement.'[7] A less turgid explanation of this strategy was later offered by Patrizio Peci, leader of the group's Turin column, when he reflected how, 'As crazy as it might seem, the plan in a few words was this: First phase, armed propaganda . . . Second phase, that of armed support . . . Third phase, the civil war and victory. In essence, we were the embryo, the skeleton of the future . . . the ruling class of tomorrow in a communist society.'[8] The RAF drew similar parallels in its exegesis of the relationship between the terrorist vanguard and 'the people'. 'Our original conception of the organization implied a connection between the urban guerrilla and the work at the base', explained the document entitled 'Sur la Conception de la Guérilla Urbaine';

> We would like it if each and all of us could work at the neighborhoods and factories, in socialist groups that already exist, influence discussion, experience and learn. This has proved impossible . . .
>
> Some say that the possibilities for agitation, propaganda and organization are far from being eradicated and that only when they

Popular Front for the Liberation of Palestine hijacking of BOAC airliner –
Dawson's Field, Jordan, September 1970 *(Author's collection)*.

Lockerbie, December 1988 *(Popperfoto / Reuter)*.

Tokyo nerve gas attack, March 1995: troops decontaminating train
(Popperfoto / Reuter / Japan's Ground Self-Defence Force).

The IRA targets London: *above*, Hyde Park, July 1982 *(Author's collection)*;
below, Aldwych, February 1996 *(Popperfoto / Reuter / Andrew Shaw)*.

Four faces of terrorism:
top left, Carlos – 'The Jackal'; *top right*, Yassir Arafat;
bottom left, Leila Khaled; *bottom right*, George Habash *(all Author's collection)*.

Symbols of terrorism:
Red Army Faction

Red Brigades

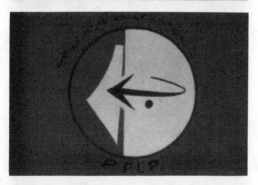

Popular Front for the
Liberation of Palestine

Justice Commandos for the
Armenian Genocide
(all Author's collection)

Americans held hostage in Iran, 1979–80 *(Author's collection)*.

Jerusalem, February 1996: the wreckage of the bombed bus in which
twenty-two Israelis were killed by Hamas *(Popperfoto/Reuter/David Silverman)*.

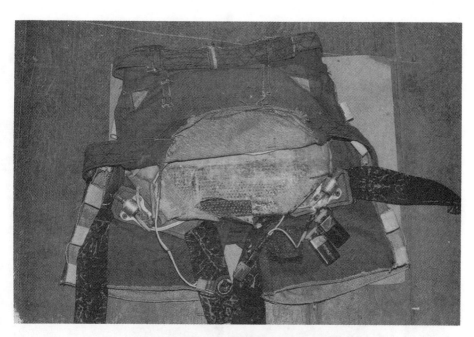

Terrorist suicide kit:
plastic explosive belt concealed in trousers, triggered by
(below) battery-powered detonator with plunger activator *(Author's collection)*.

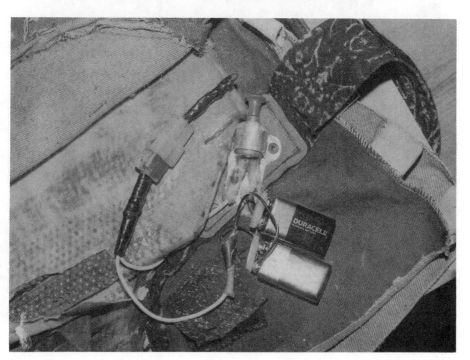

Oklahoma City, April 1995 *(Popperfoto / Reuter / Win McNamee)*.

are, should we pose the question of arms. We say: it will not really be possible to profit from any political actions as long as armed struggle does not appear clearly as the goal of the politicisation.[9]

This approach is not entirely dissimilar to that of many ethno-nationalist/separatist groups. These terrorist movements also see themselves as a revolutionary vanguard – if not in classic Marxist-Leninist terms, at least as a spearhead, similarly using violence to 'educate' fellow members of their national or ethnic group about the inequities imposed upon them by the ruling government and the need for communal resistance and rebellion. As one Basque nationalist bluntly told an interviewer, 'ETA is the vanguard of our revolution.'[10] Accordingly, like all ethno-nationalist/separatist terrorists, ETA uses demonstratively symbolic acts of violence to generate publicity and rally support by underscoring the powerlessness of the government to withstand the nationalist expression they champion, and thereby to embarrass and coerce it into acceding to the group's irredentist demands. Their 'target audience', however, is not just the local, indigenous population but often the international community as well. These groups, accordingly, recognize the need to tightly control and focus their operations in such a manner as to ensure both the continued support of their local 'constituencies' and the sympathy of the international community. What this essentially means is that their violence must always be perceived as both purposeful and deliberate, sustained and omnipresent. Gerry Adams himself expressed precisely this point in an article he wrote in 1976 to commemorate the sixtieth anniversary of the 1916 Easter Uprising. 'Rightly or wrongly, I am an IRA Volunteer,' Adams explained,

and, rightly or wrongly, I take a course of action as a means to bringing about a situation in which I believe the people of my country will prosper . . . The course I take involves the use of physical force, but only if I achieve the situation where my people can genuinely prosper can my course of action be seen, by me, to have been justified.[11]

Indeed, as the veteran Northern Ireland correspondent David McKittrick points out, 'Sinn Fein in its efforts to build a political machine in both parts of Ireland, has [always] been concerned to project IRA violence as the clinical and carefully directed use of force.'[12]

The more successful ethno-nationalist/separatist terrorist organization will be able to determine an effective level of violence that is at once 'tolerable' for the local populace, tacitly acceptable to international opinion and sufficiently modulated not to provoke massive governmental crackdown and reaction. The IRA has demonstrably mastered this synchronization of tactics to strategy. Since the mid-1980s, according to Patrick Bishop and Eamonn Mallie, the organization's military high command has clearly recognized that 'Republican strategy required a certain level of violence – but only enough to distort the private and public life of the North, and to make sure that the military arm was properly exercised.'[13] What this has often resulted in is the targeting of members of the security forces (ordinary policemen and soldiers) in preference to the terrorists' avowed enemies in some rival indigenous community. This is true in Northern Ireland, where fewer than 20 per cent of the IRA's victims between 1969 and 1993 were Protestant civilians,[14] and in Spain, where more than 60 per cent of fatalities inflicted by the Basque ETA have been members of the Spanish security forces.[15]

Certainly, 'traitors', informants, and other collaborators among their own brethren are regularly targeted; but here the terrorist group must be careful to strike another balance between salutary, if sporadic, 'lessons' that effectively intimidate and compel compliance from their own communities and more frequent and heavy-handed episodes that alienate popular support, encourage cooperation with the security forces and therefore prove counterproductive. By the same token, highly placed government officials and security force commanders will, when the opportunity presents itself and the political conditions are propitious, be attacked. But given the combination of uncertain – and possibly undesirable – political and security repercussions, the difficulties involved in gaining access to these VIPs and the considerable effort required of such operations, they are generally eschewed in favour of more productive, if less spectacular, operations that, moreover, conform to the terrorists' perceptions of what are regarded as 'legitimate' or 'acceptable' targets – however abhorrent the attacks may seem to the outside world.

The terrorist campaign is like a shark in the water: it must keep moving forward – no matter how slowly or incrementally – or die. Hence, when these more 'typical' targets fail to sustain the momentum of a terrorist campaign, or when other, perhaps even totally unrelated events overshadow the terrorists and shunt their cause out of the public eye, terrorists often have to resort to more violent and dramatic acts to refocus attention back upon themselves. But it would be a mistake to see these acts – which often involve the bombing of public gathering-places or the hijacking of airliners – as random or senseless. For example, we saw in chapter 3 how, following the Palestinian terrorists' failure to mount a concerted guerrilla campaign against Israel in the occupied West Bank and Gaza Strip after the 1967 Six Day War, the PFLP began hijacking international airliners. The purpose of these operations was not wantonly to kill or otherwise harm innocent persons (in contrast to many subsequent terrorists' targeting of civil aviation) but to use the passengers as pawns in pursuit of publicity and the extraction of concessions from unsympathetic governments. As one of the group's most famous hijackers, Leila Khaled, once explained, 'Look, I had orders to seize the plane, not to blow it up . . . I care about people. If I had wanted to blow up the plane no one could have prevented me.'[16]

Even when terrorists' actions are not as deliberate or discriminating, and when their purpose is in fact to kill innocent civilians, the target is still regarded as 'justified' because it represents the terrorists' defined 'enemy'. Although incidents may be quantitatively different in the volume of death or destruction caused, they are still qualitatively identical in that a widely known 'enemy' is being specifically targeted. This distinction is often accepted by the terrorists' constituents and at times by the international community as well. The recognition that the Palestinians obtained in the wake of the 1972 Munich Olympics massacre is a particularly prominent case in point. The poignant message left behind by the terrorist team struck precisely the sympathetic chord they had intended: 'We are neither killers nor bandits,' their letter stated. 'We are persecuted people who have no land and no homeland . . . We are not against any people, but why should our place here be taken by the flag of the occupiers . . . why should the whole world be having fun and entertainment while we suffer with all ears deaf to us?'[17] As the PFLP's Bassam Abu Sharif explained, 'For violence to become fruitful, for it to get us to our aims, it should not be undertaken without a proper political base and intention.'[18] While the logic in such a case may well be contrived, there is nonetheless a clear appreciation both that violence has its limits and that, if used properly, it can pay vast dividends. In other words, the level of violence must be kept within the bounds of what the terrorists' 'target audience' will accept.

But acts of terrorism, like battles in conventional wars, are difficult to limit and control once they are started, and often result in tragedy to civilians who are inadvertently caught up in the violence. One well-known example is the tragic bombing that occurred at Enniskillen, Northern Ireland, in November 1987, causing the deaths of eleven innocent bystanders attending a memorial ceremony and injuries to sixty-three others. The IRA was quick to describe the incident as an accident resulting from the 'catastrophic consequences' of an operation against British troops gone awry.[19] In this instance, there was an acceptance that some grievous wrong had been done, albeit clothed in layers of self-serving justifications. Eamon Collins, a former IRA terrorist, describes the organization's reaction to another botched attack that also accidentally claimed the lives of innocent civilians some years later:

> The IRA – regardless of their public utterances dismissing the condemnations of their behaviour from church and community leaders – tried to act in a way that would avoid severe censure from within the nationalist community; they knew they were operating within a sophisticated set of informal restrictions on their behaviour, no less powerful for being largely unspoken.[20]

The Basque ETA is no different: alternately threatening and remorseful in communiqués that seek to absolve itself of responsibility for its violent deeds and simultaneously to reap the rewards of introspection and self-criticism. 'We claim responsibility for the failed action against a member of the Spanish police,' reads one, 'following the placing of an explosive charge under his car. We very much deplore the accidental injuries involuntarily caused to his neighbor . . . and we wish his prompt and complete recovery.'[21]

Right-wing terrorism has often been characterized as the least discriminating, most senseless type of contemporary political violence. It has earned this reputation mostly as a result of the seemingly mindless 'street' violence and unsophisticated attacks that in recent years have increasingly targeted immigrants, refugees, guest workers and other foreigners in many European countries, especially in eastern Germany and other former communist-bloc states,[22] but also from an inchoate bombing campaign that briefly convulsed Western Europe in the early 1980s. If the means of the right-wing terrorists sometimes appear haphazardly planned and often spontaneously generated, their ends are hardly less indistinct. Essentially, their ostensible goal is the destruction of the liberal-democratic state to clear the way for a renascent National Socialist ('Nazi') or fascist one. But the extent to which this is simply an excuse for the egocentric pleasure derived from brawling and bombing, preening or parading in 1940s-era Nazi regalia is hard to judge, given that the majority of right-wing groups do not espouse any specific programme of reform, preferring to hide behind vague slogans of strident nationalism, the need for racial purity and the re-assertion of governmental strength. In sum, the democratic state is somewhat reflexively assailed for its manifold weaknesses – notably its liberal social welfare policies and tolerance of diverse opinion – alongside its permitting of dark-skinned immigrants in the national labour force and of Jews and other minorities in positions of power or influence. The right-wing terrorists believe that their nation's survival is dependent upon the exorcism of these elements from its environs; only by becoming politically, racially and culturally homogeneous can the state recover its strength and again work for its natural citizens rather than the variegated collection of interlopers and parasites who now sap the nation of its strength and greatness.

It should be noted that, while the European groups share many similarities (racism, anti-semitism, xenophobia and a hatred of liberal government) with their American counterparts, they differ fundamentally in their mechanisms of legitimization and justification. Whereas the US groups may be more accurately categorized as religious – rather than strictly as right-wing – terrorists because of the pivotal roles that liturgy, divine inferences and clerical sanction play in underpinning and motivating their violence, the foundations of the European right are avowedly secular, with neither theological imperatives nor clerics exerting any significant influence. Indeed, the ill-defined, amorphous contours of the contemporary European extreme right's political philosophy can be summed up by the refrain from a popular song by the British white power band 'White Noise': 'Two pints of lager and a packet of crisps. Wogs out! White Power!'[23] or the folk song composed by Gottfried Küssel, Führer of an Austrian neo-Nazi organization: 'Do you see his nose, no? Do you know his nose? His nose you do not know? It is crooked and ugly? Then hit him in the face. He is a Jew, a damned Jew, bloodsucker of the European race.'[24] By comparison, the lunatic and far-fetched millenarian views of American Christian white supremacists appear as deeply profound theological treatises.

It is for this reason, perhaps, that European right-wing terrorism has rarely transcended the boundaries of street brawls or the crude Molotov cocktail hurriedly tossed into a refugee shelter or a guest workers' dormitory (even though, of course, such crude acts of violence possess just the same tragic potential to kill and maim as much more sophisticated terrorist operations). Nonetheless, it would be a mistake to see right-wing violence as completely indiscriminate or entirely irrational. Indeed, the few occasions on which the neo-Nazis have attempted more ambitious types of operations have sent shock waves throughout the continent. In August 1980, for instance, a powerful explosion tore through the crowded rail station in Bologna, Italy, in the midst of the summer holiday crush. At the time, the total of eighty-four persons killed (and 180 wounded) was second only to the record ninety-one who had perished in a single terrorist act in the Irgun's bombing of the King David Hotel thirty-four years before. When it was followed less than a month later by a bombing at the popular Munich Oktoberfest celebration, killing fourteen and injuring another 215, fears were raised of a new terrorist onslaught more lethal and indiscriminate than that waged by either the European leftist terrorist organizations or the continent's various ethno-nationalist/separatist groups. But it did not materialize. Instead, the pattern of right-wing terrorism in Europe has remained largely the same since the 1970s: one of sporadic attacks, albeit specifically directed against particular types of targets – primarily refugee shelters and immigrant workers' hostels, anarchist houses and political party offices, and Arab and African immigrants walking along the street, as well as Jewish-owned property or businesses.

Crude and relatively unsophisticated and indeed intellectually depraved as this terrorist category may appear, then, like all forms of terrorism even right-wing violence is not based on some pathological obsession to kill or beat up as many people as possible, but rather on a deliberate policy of intimidating the general public into acceding to specific demands or pressures. The right-wing terrorists see themselves, if not as a revolutionary vanguard then as a catalyst of events that will lead to the imposition of an authoritarian form of government. Thus, like other terrorist movements, they too tailor their violence to appeal to their perceived constituency – be it fellow extreme nationalists, intransigent racists and xenophobes, reactionary conservatives or militant anti-communists – and, with the exception of a handful of noteworthy, but isolated, indiscriminate bombings, they seek to keep the violence they commit within the bounds of what the ruling government will tolerate without undertaking massive repressive actions against the terrorists themselves.

Moreover, the phenomenon by which terrorists consciously learn from one another, discussed in chapter 2, is evident in respect of at least some German right-wing terrorist elements. This suggests aspirations towards a more planned and coherent campaign of violence than has existed hitherto, raising the possibility of a more serious future threat. As long ago as 1981, Manfred Roeder, for a time Germany's leading neo-Nazi, advocated the emulation of left-wing terrorist targeting and tactics in hopes of endowing the movement with a clearer purpose and attainable goal. For the rightists, however, there was another factor: envy of the attention, status and occasional tactical victories won by left-wing terrorists in groups such as the RAF, alongside the realization that indiscriminate terrorist attacks would not result in the attainment of the neo-Nazis' goals. 'The RAF had brought terrorism to modern Europe,' Ingo Hasselbach, one of Roeder's successors, recently recalled, 'and even though they could not have been more opposed to our ideology, we respected them for their fanaticism and skill.' Hasselbach therefore advocated for his *Kameradschaft* (Nazi 'brotherhood'), before his own disillusionment forced him to break completely with the movement he had once so enthusiastically championed, a lethally discriminate campaign of terrorism mirroring that pursued by the RAF. Like the original founders of the Baader–Meinhof Group twenty years before, Hasselbach also believed that his National Alternative Berlin (NA) neo-Nazi organization could not achieve its political objectives by attempting to operate as a legal political party. Accordingly, he sought to mould the group into a terrorist organization modelled on the RAF and laid plans to assassinate prominent Jews and communists and leading politicians. 'We wanted to bring neo-Nazi terrorism up to the level of that carried out by the radical Left,' Hasselbach later explained,

> striking at targets that would be both better guarded and more significant – targets that would do serious damage to the democratic

German state while driving home our racial message. There was, for instance, talk of assassinating Gregor Gusi, the head of the reformed Communist Party, the PDS; he was East Germany's most prominent Jew and leader of the Communists to boot. He was not only a major politician but the political representative of the former GDR system. We also considered hitting Ignatz Bubis, the new head of the Jewish community, as well as a number of politicians in Bonn – including the interior minister and Chancellor Kohl himself.[25]

Like other terrorist organizations, the more sophisticated right-wing groups also seek targets that are likely to advance their cause. In this respect, their terrorist acts are as calculated as those of the left-wing organizations they try to emulate. Publicity and attention are of course paramount aims; but at the same time there is a conscious recognition that only if their violence is properly calculated and at least in some (however idiosyncratic) way regulated, will they be able to achieve the effect(s) they desire and the political objectives they seek. As an IRA terrorist once said, 'You don't bloody well kill people for the sake of killing them.'[26] This is not, however, the case with many of the religious terrorist movements discussed in chapter 4. For them, violence still has an instrumental purpose but, unlike secular terrorists, it is also often an end in itself – a sacred duty executed in direct response to some theological demand or imperative. A 1990 study of Lebanese Shi'a terrorists, for example, revealed that none of the sample was interested in influencing an actual or self-perceived constituency or in swaying popular opinion: their sole preoccupation was serving God through the fulfilment of their divinely ordained mission.[27] Hence, for religious terrorists there are demonstrably fewer constraints on the actual infliction of violence and the category of targets/enemies is much more open-ended. The leader of an Egyptian terrorist cell, for instance, professed absolutely no remorse when he was told that an attack he had planned against visiting Israeli Jews had instead killed nine German tourists. His matter-of-fact response was that 'infidels are all the same'.[28] Indeed, how else can one explain the mad plots of the American Christian white supremacists? Or the Aum sect's wanton and repeated attempts to use chemical warfare nerve agents indiscriminately in populous urban centres? Or the cataclysmic aim of the Jewish Temple Mount bombers in Israel? The willingness of religious terrorists to contemplate such wholesale acts of violence is a direct reflection of the fact that, unlike their secular counterparts, they do not seek to appeal to any constituency or authority other than their own god or religious figures, and therefore feel little need to regulate or calibrate their violence.

The Organizational Dynamics of Terrorist Groups

All terrorists, however, have one trait in common: they live in the future, live for that distant – yet imperceptibly close – point in time when they will assuredly triumph over their enemies and attain the ultimate realization of their political destiny. For the religious groups, this future is divinely decreed and the terrorists themselves specifically anointed to achieve it. The inevitability of their victory is taken for granted, as a 1996 communiqué issued by the Egyptian Gamat al-Islamiya (Islamic Group) reveals. Citing the Qur'an, the document brusquely dismisses even the possibility that its secular opponents might succeed. 'They plot and plan and God too plans,' it declares, 'but the best of planners is God.' Therefore the group must faithfully and resolutely 'pursue its battle . . . until such time as God would grant victory – just as the Prophet Mohammed did with the Quredish [his most implacable enemies] until God granted victory over Mecca'.[29]

For the secular terrorists, too, eventual victory is as inevitable as it is predetermined. Indeed, the innate righteousness of their cause itself assures success. 'Our struggle will be long and arduous because the enemy is powerful, well-organised, and well-sustained from abroad,' Leila Khaled wrote in her autobiography, published in 1973. 'We shall win because we represent the wave of the future . . . because mankind is on our side, and above all because we are determined to achieve victory.'[30] Comparatively small in number, limited in capabilities, isolated from society and dwarfed by both the vast resources of their enemy and the enormity of their task, secular terrorists necessarily function in an inverted reality where existence is defined by the sought-after, ardently pursued future rather than the oppressive, angst-driven and incomplete present. 'You convince yourself that to reach this utopia', the Red Brigades' Adriana Faranda later recalled of the group's collective mindset, 'it is necessary to pass through the destruction of society which prevents your ideas from being realised.'[31] By ignoring the present and literally 'soldiering on' despite hardship and adversity, terrorists are able to compensate for their abject weakness and thereby overcome the temporal apathy or hostility of a constituency whom they claim to represent. 'We made calculations,' Faranda's comrade-in-arms Patrizio Peci explained in his memoirs. 'The most pessimistic thought that within twenty years the war would be won, some said within five, ten. All, however, thought that we were living through the most difficult moment, that gradually things would become easier.'[32] The left-wing terrorists thus console themselves that the travails and isolation of life underground are but a mere transitory stage on the path to final victory.

The longevity of most modern terrorist groups, however, would suggest otherwise. Rapoport, for example, estimates that the life expectancy of at least 90 per cent of terrorist organizations is less than a year, and that nearly half of those that make it as far as that have ceased to exist within a decade.[33] Thus the optimistic clarion calls to battle issued by terrorist groups the world over in communiqués, treatises and other propaganda have a distinctly hollow ring given the grim reality of their organizational life cycles. 'NEVER BE DETERRED BY THE ENORMOUS DIMENSIONS OF YOUR OWN GOALS' proclaimed a communiqué issued by the left-wing French terrorist group Direct Action in 1985:[34] yet less than two years later the group had effectively been decapitated by the capture of virtually its entire leadership and shortly afterwards fell into complete lassitude. Similarly, in 1978 the RB leader, Renato Curio, bragged about a struggle that he envisioned would last forty years: but within a decade even this terrorist organization – for a time one of Europe's most formidable – had collapsed under the weight of arrests and defections.[35]

Some categories of terrorist groups admittedly have better chances of survival – and perhaps success – than others. Historically, although religious movements like the Assassins persisted for nearly two centuries and the Thugs remained active for more than six hundred years, in modern times ethno-nationalist/separatist terrorist groups have typically lasted the longest and been the most successful. Al-Fatah, the Palestinian terrorist organization led by Yassir Arafat, for example, was founded in 1957. The PLO itself is now thirty-four years old. The Basque group ETA was established in 1959, while the current incarnation of the IRA, formally known as the Provisional Irish Republican Army, is nearly thirty years old and is itself the successor of the older Official IRA that was founded nearly a century ago and can in turn be traced back to the various Fenian revolutionary brotherhoods that had surfaced periodically since Wolfe Tone's rebellion in 1789. However, except in the immediate post-war era of massive decolonization, success for ethno-nationalist terrorist organizations has rarely involved the actual realization of their stated, long-term goals of self-determination or nationhood. More often it has amounted to a string of key tactical victories that have sustained prolonged struggles and breathed new life into faltering – and in some instances, geriatric – terrorist movements.

The resilience of these groups is doubtless a product of the relative ease with which they are able to draw sustenance and support from an existing constituency – namely, the fellow members of their ethno-nationalist group. By contrast, both left- and right-wing terrorist organizations must actively proselytize among the politically aware and radical, though often uncommitted, for recruits and support, thus rendering themselves vulnerable to penetration and compromise. The ethno-nationalists derive a further advantage from their historical longevity by being able to appeal to a collective revolutionary tradition and even at times a predisposition to rebellion. This assures successive terrorist generations both a steady stream of recruits from their respective communities' youth and a ready pool of sympathizers and supporters among their more nostalgic elders. These groups' unique ability to replenish their ranks from within already close, tightly knit communities means that even when a continuing campaign shows signs of flagging, the mantle can be smoothly passed to a new generation. Abu Iyad, Arafat's intelligence chief, can therefore dismiss as mere ephemeral impediments the culs-de-sac and roundabouts that have long baulked the advance of the Palestinian liberation movement. 'Our people will bring forth a new revolution', he wrote some twenty years ago. 'They will engender a movement much more powerful than ours, better armed and thus more dangerous to the Zionists . . . And one day, we will have a country.'[36]

The ethno-nationalists' comparative success, however, may have as much to do with the clarity and tangibility of their envisioned future – the establishment (or re-establishment) of a national homeland from within some existing country – as to these other characteristics. The articulation of so concrete and comprehensible a goal is by far the most potent and persuasive rallying cry. It also makes the inevitable victory appear both palpable and readily attainable, even though the path to it be prolonged and protracted. Few would have doubted Martin McGuinness's 1977 pledge that the IRA would keep 'blattering on until Brits leave',[37] or Danny Morrison's declaration twelve years later that 'when it is politically costly for the British to remain in Ireland, they'll go . . . it won't be triggered until a large number of British soldiers are killed and that's what's going to happen'.[38]

Left-wing terrorist movements, by comparison, appear doubly disadvantaged. Not only do they lack the sizeable existing pool of potential recruits available to most ethno-nationalist groups, but among all the categories of terrorists they have formulated the least clear and most ill-defined vision of the future. Prolific and prodigious though their myriad denunciations of the evils of the militarist, capitalist state may be, precious little information is forthcoming about its envisioned successor. 'That is the most difficult question for revolutionaries,' replied Kozo Okamoto, the surviving member of the three-man JRA team that staged the 1972 Lod Airport massacre, when asked about the post-revolutionary society that his group sought to create. 'We really do not know what it will be like.'[39] The RAF's Gudrun Ensslin similarly brushed aside all questions about the group's long-term aims. 'As for the state of the future, the time after victory,' she once said, 'that is not our concern . . . we build the revolution, not the socialist model.'[40] This inability to articulate coherently, much less cogently, their future plans may explain why the left-wing terrorists' campaigns have historically been the least effectual.

Even when left-wing terrorists have attempted to conceptualize a concrete vision of the future, their efforts have rarely produced anything more lucid or edifying than verbose disquisitions espousing an idiosyncratic interpretation of Marxist doctrine. 'We have applied the Marxist analysis and method to the contemporary scene – not transferred it, but actually applied it,' Ensslin wrote in a collection of RAF statements published by the group in 1977 (and subsequently banned by the German government). Yet no further elucidation of the desired result is offered, except the belief that Marxism will be rendered obsolete when the revolution triumphs and the 'capitalist system has been abolished'.[41] Slightly more reflective is the exposition offered by the American radical Jane Alpert, who in her memoir explains how she and her comrades-in-arms believed that the world could be cleansed of all domination and submission, that perception itself could be purified of the division into subject and object, that power playing between nations, sexes, races, ages, between animals and humans, individuals and groups, could be brought to an end. Our revolution would create a universe in which all consciousness was cosmic, in which everyone would share the bliss we knew from acid [LSD], but untainted by fear, possessiveness, sickness, hunger, or the need for a drug to bring happiness.[42]

Nonetheless, this vision comes across as so vague and idyllic as to appear almost completely divorced from reality: an effect, perhaps, of its drug-induced influence. That drugs played a part in the formulation of other leftist terrorist strategies is an interesting, though perhaps exaggerated, sidelight. Baumann, for example, also recounts the centrality of drugs to the would-be revolution. 'We said integrate dope into praxis too,' he recalled, 'no more separate shit, but a total unification around this thing, so that a new person is born out of the struggle.'[43] It should be noted, though, that a study commissioned by the Italian secret services in the 1970s discovered (somewhat counterintuitively) that right-wing terrorists were in fact more prone to abuse[44] and indeed to use drugs than their left-wing counterparts. Two Italian psychiatrists conducting a related study attributed this tendency to the rightists' innate psychological instability, at least compared to Italian left-wing terrorists. 'In the right-wing terrorism', wrote Drs Franco Ferracuti and Francesco Bruno, 'the individual terrorists are frequently psychopathological and the ideology is empty; in left-wing terrorism, ideology is outside of reality and terrorists are more normal and fanatical.'[45]

But it would be a grave error to dismiss the left-wing terrorists as either totally feckless and frivolous or completely devoid of introspection or seriousness of purpose. For them, the future was simply too large and abstract a concept to comprehend: instead, action – terrorist attacks specifically designed to effect the revolution – was embraced as a far more rewarding pursuit. Accordingly, it was Fanon, and not Marx, who arguably exerted the greater influence. For example, Susan Stern, a member of the 1970s-era American left-wing terrorist group, The Weathermen, recalled the dynamic tension between thought and action that permeated the group and affected all internal debate. 'Once we tore down capitalism, who would empty the garbage, and teach the children and who would decide that?' she and her comrades would often consider.

> Would the world be Communist? Would the Third World control it? Would all whites die? Would all sex perverts die? Who would run the prisons – would there be prisons? Endless questions like these were *raised* by the Weathermen, but we didn't have the answers. *And we were tired of trying to wait until we understood everything* [emphasis added].[46]

The RAF's seminal treatise, 'Sur la Conception de la Guérilla Urbaine', reflects the same frustration. Quoting fellow revolutionary Eldridge Cleaver, a leader of the Black Panther Party, an African-American radical political organization active during the 1960s, it states: 'For centuries and generations we have contemplated and examined the shit from all sides. "Me, I'm convinced that most things which happen in this country don't need to be analysed much longer", said Cleaver. The RAF put the words of Cleaver into practice.'[47]

Indeed, all terrorists are driven by this burning impatience, coupled with an unswerving belief in the efficacy of violence. The future that they look forward to is neither temporal nor born of the natural progression of mankind: rather, it is contrived and shaped, forged and moulded and ultimately determined and achieved by violence. 'What use was there in writing memoranda?' Begin rhetorically enquired to explain the Irgun's decision to resume its revolt in 1944.

> What value in speeches? . . . No, there was no other way. If we did not fight we should be destroyed. To fight was the only way to salvation.
>
> When Descartes said: 'I think, therefore, I am,' he uttered a very profound thought. But there are times in the history of peoples when thought alone does not prove their existence . . . There are times when everything in you cries out: your very self-respect as a human being lies in your resistance to evil.
>
> We fight, therefore we are![48]

Thirty years later, Leila Khaled similarly invoked the primacy of action over talk and bullets over words: 'We must act, not just talk and memorise the arguments against Zionism,' she counselled.[49] This view was echoed by Yoyes, an ETA terrorist who lost faith in the endless promises that 'independence can be won by peaceful means. It's all a lie . . . The only possibility we have of gaining our liberty is through violence.'[50] As the former neo-Nazi Ingo Hasselbach recalled of his own experience, 'The time for legal work and patience was through. The only thing to do was to turn our *Kameradschaft* into a real terrorist organization.'[51]

For some terrorists, however, the desire for action can lead to an obsession with violence itself. Abu Nidal, for example, was once known and admired for his 'fiery and unbending nationalism', whereas today he is universally disdained as little more than an 'outlaw and killer'.[52] Eamon Collins describes a similar transformation in his IRA-gunman cousin Mickey, who, Collins realized, had gradually 'lost any sense of the wider perspective, and was just obsessively absorbed by the details of the next killing'.[53] Andreas Baader is perhaps a different type altogether. From the very start of the RAF's campaign, he never wavered from his conviction that the terrorist's only 'language is action'.[54] Baumann, who knew Baader well, remembers the RAF's founder as a 'weapons maniac, [who] later developed an almost sexual relationship with pistols (the Heckler and Koch type in particular)'.[55] Indeed, according to Baader himself, 'Fucking and shooting [were] the same thing.'[56] Unquestionably a man of action and not words, he preferred, in the terrorist vernacular, 'direct actions' – bank robberies, vandalism and arson, bombings and armed attacks – to debate and discourse. 'Let's go, then!' was Baader's immediate response, for example, when his lover and co-leader Ensslin suggested that the group bomb an American military base in retaliation for the US air force's mining of North Vietnam's Haiphong harbour in 1972. Despite being the leading figure of an organization dedicated to achieve profound political change, he had absolutely no time for politics, which he derisively dismissed as a load of 'shit'.[57] Baader's whole approach can be summed up in the advice he gave to a wavering RAF recruit. 'Either you come along [and join the revolution and fight],' he said, 'or you stay forever an empty chatterbox.'[58]

Although Baader may perhaps be an extreme example of this phenomenon, action is the undeniable cynosure for all terrorists – perhaps even more so, the thrill and heady excitement that accompany it. Far more of Peci's 222-page account of his life as a Red Brigadist, for instance, is devoted to recounting in obsessive detail the types of weapons (and their technical specifications) used on particular RB operations and which group members actually did the shooting than to elucidating the organization's ideological aims and political goals.[59] Baumann is particularly candid about the cathartic relief that an operation brought to a small group of individuals living underground, in close proximity to one another, constantly on the run and fearful of arrest and betrayal. The real stress, he said, came from life in the group – not from the planning and execution of attacks.[60] Others, like Stern, Collins, the RAF's Silke Maier-Witt and the RB's Susana Ronconi, are even more explicit about the 'rush' and the sense of power and accomplishment they derived from the violence they inflicted. 'Nothing in my life had ever been this exciting,' Stern enthused as she drifted deeper into terrorism.[61] Collins similarly recalls how he led an 'action-packed existence' during his six years in the IRA, 'living each day with the excitement of feeling I was playing a part in taking on the Orange State'.[62] For Maier-Witt, the intoxicating allure of action was sufficient to overcome the misgivings she had about the murder of Schleyer's four bodyguards in order to kidnap the man himself. 'At the time I felt the brutality of that action . . . [But it] was a kind of excitement too because something had happened. The real thing', she consoled herself, had 'started now'.[63] Ronconi is the most expansive and incisive in analysing the terrorist's psychology. 'The main thing was that you felt you were able to influence the world about you, instead of experiencing it passively,' thereby combining intrinsic excitement with profound satisfaction. 'It was this ability to make an impact on the reality of everyday life that was important,' she explained, 'and obviously still is important.'[64]

For the terrorist, success in making this impact is most often measured in terms of the amount of publicity and attention received. Newsprint and air-time are thus the coin of the realm in the terrorists' mindset: the only tangible or empirical means they have by which to gauge their success and assess their progress. In this respect, little distinction or discrimination is made between good or bad publicity: the satisfaction of simply being noticed is often regarded as sufficient reward. 'The only way to achieve results,' boasted the JRA in its communiqué claiming credit for the 1972 Lod Airport massacre, in which twenty-six people were slain (including sixteen Puerto Rican Christians on a pilgrimage to the Holy Land), 'is to shock the world right down to its socks.'[65] The arch-terrorist Carlos 'The Jackal' reportedly meticulously clipped and had translated newspaper accounts about him and his deeds.[66] 'The more I'm talked about,' Carlos once explained to his terrorist colleague – later turned apostate – Hans Joachim Klein, 'the more dangerous I appear. That's all the better for me.'[67] Similarly, when Ramzi Ahmed Yousef, the alleged mastermind behind the 1993 bombing of New York's World Trade Center, was apprehended in Pakistan two years later, police found in his possession two remote-control explosive devices along with a collection of newspaper articles detailing his exploits.[68]

However, for Carlos and Yousef as for many other terrorists, this equation of publicity and attention with success and self-gratification has the effect of locking them into an unrelenting upward spiral of violence in order to keep the eye of the media and the public on them.[69] Yousef, for example, planned to follow the World Trade Center bombing with the assassinations of Pope John Paul II and the then prime minister of Pakistan, Benazir Bhutto, and the near-simultaneous in-flight bombings of eleven US passenger airliners. Klein in fact describes escalation as a 'force of habit' among terrorists; an intrinsic product of their perennial need for validation which in turn is routinely assessed and appraised on the basis of media coverage. The effect is that terrorists today feel driven to undertake ever more dramatic and destructively lethal deeds in order to achieve the same effect that a less ambitious or bloody action may have had in the past. To their minds at least, the media and public have become progressively inured or desensitized to the seemingly endless litany of successive terrorist incidents; thus a continuous upward ratcheting of the violence is required in order to retain media and public interest and attention. As Klein once observed, the 'more violent things get, the more people will respect you. The greater the chance of achieving your demands.'[70] Timothy McVeigh, the convicted Oklahoma City bomber, seemed to be offering the same explanation when responding to his attorney's question whether he could not have achieved the same effect of drawing attention to his grievances against the US government without killing anyone. 'That would not have gotten the point across,' McVeigh reportedly replied. 'We needed a body count to make our point.'[71] In this respect, although the Murrah building bombing was doubtless planned well in advance of the portentously symbolic date of 19 April deliberately chosen by McVeigh, he may nonetheless have felt driven to surpass in terms of death and destruction the previous month's dramatic and more exotic nerve gas attack on the

Tokyo underground in order to guarantee that his attack too received the requisite media coverage and public attention.

The terrorists' ability to attract – and, moreover, to continue to attract – attention is most often predicated on the success of their attacks. The most feared terrorists are arguably those who are the most successful in translating thought into action: ruthless and efficient, demonstrating that they are able to make good on their threats and back up their demands with violence. This organizational imperative to succeed, however, in turn imposes on some terrorist groups an operational conservatism that makes an ironic contrast with their political radicalism, decreeing that they adhere to an established *modus operandi* that, to their minds at least, minimizes the chances of failure and maximizes the chances of success. 'The main point is to select targets where success is 100% assured,' the doyen of modern international terrorism, George Habash, once explained.[72] For the terrorist, therefore, a combination of solid training, sound planning, good intelligence and technological competence are the essential prerequisites for a successful operation. 'I learned how to be an effective IRA member,' Collins reminisced about his two-year training and induction period: 'how to gather intelligence, how to set up operations, how to avoid mistakes.'[73] Similarly, an unidentified American left-wing radical who specialized in bombings described in a 1970 interview the procedures and extreme care that governed all his group's operations. The 'first decision', he said, is

> political – determining appropriate and possible targets. Once a set of targets is decided on, they must be reconnoitered and information gathered on how to approach the targets, how to place the bomb, how the security of the individuals and the explosives is to be protected. Then the time is chosen and a specific target. Next there was a preliminary run-through – in our case a number of practice sessions ... The discipline during the actual operation is not to alter any of the agreed-upon plans or to discuss the action until everyone's safe within the group again. Our desire is not just for one success but to continue as long as possible.[74]

Good intelligence, therefore, is as critical for the success of an operation as it is for the terrorists' own survival. An almost Darwinian

principle of natural selection thus seems to affect terrorist organizations, whereby (as noted above) every new terrorist generation learns
from its predecessors, becoming smarter, tougher and more difficult to
capture or eliminate. In this respect, terrorists also analyse the 'lessons'
to be drawn from mistakes made by former comrades who have been
either killed or apprehended. Press accounts, judicial indictments,
courtroom testimony and trial transcripts are meticulously culled for
information on security force tactics and methods and then absorbed by
surviving group members. The third generation of the RAF that
emerged in the late 1980s is a classic example of this phenomenon.
According to a senior German official, group members routinely study
'every court case against them to discover their weak spots'. Having
learned about the techniques used against them by the authorities from
testimony presented by law enforcement personnel in open court (in
some instances having been deliberately questioned on these matters by
sympathetic attorneys), the terrorists are consequently able to undertake the requisite countermeasures to avoid detection. For example,
learning that the German police could usually obtain fingerprints from
the bottom of toilet seats or the inside of refrigerators, surviving RAF
members began to apply a special ointment to their fingers that, after
drying, prevents fingerprints and thus thwarted their identification and
incrimination.[75] As a spokesperson for the Bundeskriminalamt (BKA or
Federal Investigation Department) lamented in the months immediately preceding the RAF's unilateral declaration of a ceasefire in April
1992, the '"Third Generation" learnt a lot from the mistakes of its
predecessors – and about how the police works . . . they now know how to
operate very carefully'.[76] Indeed, according to a former member of the
group, Peter-Jürgen Brock, now serving a life sentence for murder, the
RAF before the ceasefire had 'reached maximum efficiency'.[77]

Similar accolades have also been bestowed on the current generation
of IRA fighters. At the end of his tour of duty in 1992 as General Officer
Commanding British Forces in Northern Ireland, General Sir John
Wilsey described the IRA as 'an absolutely formidable enemy. The
essential attributes of their leaders are better than ever before. Some of
their operations are brilliant in terrorist terms.'[78] By this time, too, even
the IRA's once comparatively unsophisticated loyalist terrorist counterparts had absorbed the lessons of their own past mistakes and had
consciously emulated the IRA to become disquietingly more 'profes-

One senior RUC officer noted this change in the loyalist ... bilities, observing that they too were now increasingly ... operations from small cells, on a need to know basis. They ... down on loose talk. They have learned how to destroy ... nce. And if you bring them in for questioning, they say

The Technological Treadmill

Finally, success for the terrorist is dependent on their ability to keep one step ahead not only of the authorities but also of counterterrorist technology. The terrorist group's fundamental organizational imperative to act also drives this persistent search for new ways to overcome or circumvent or defeat governmental security and countermeasures. The IRA's own relentless quest to pierce the armour protecting both the security forces in Northern Ireland and the most senior government officials in England illustrates the professional evolution and increasing operational sophistication of a terrorist group. The first generation of early 1970s IRA devices were often little more than crude anti-personnel bombs, consisting of a handful of roofing nails wrapped around a lump of plastic explosive and detonated simply by lighting a fuse. Time-bombs from the same era were hardly more sophisticated. Typically, they were constructed from a few sticks of dynamite and commercial detonators stolen from construction sites or rock quarries attached to ordinary battery-powered alarm clocks. Neither device was terribly reliable and often put the bomber at considerable risk. The process of placing and actually lighting the first type of device carried with it the potential to attract undesired attention while affording the bomber little time to effect the attack and make good his or her escape. Although the second type of device was designed to mitigate precisely this danger, its timing and detonation mechanism was often so crude that accidental or premature explosions were not infrequent, thus causing some terrorists inadvertently to kill themselves – what is known in Belfast as 'own goals'. About 120 IRA members have been killed in this way since 1969.[80]

In hopes of obviating, or at least reducing, these risks, the IRA's bomb-makers invented a means of detonating bombs from a safe distance using the radio controls for model aircraft purchased at hobby shops.

Scientists and engineers working in the scientific research and dev
ment division of the British Ministry of Defence (MoD) in tu
developed a system of electronic countermeasures and jamming
techniques for the army that effectively thwarted this means of attack.
However, rather than abandon this tactic completely, the IRA began to
search for a solution. In contrast to the state-of-the art laboratories,
huge budgets and academic credentials of their government counterparts, the IRA's own 'R&D' department toiled in cellars beneath
cross-border safe houses and the back rooms of urban tenements for five
years before devising a network of sophisticated electronic switches for
their bombs that would ignore or bypass the army's electronic counter-
measures. Once again, the MoD scientists returned to their laboratories;
emerging with a new system of electronic scanners able to detect radio
emissions the moment the radio is switched on – and, critically, just tens
of seconds before the bomber can actually transmit the detonation
signal. The almost infinitesimal window of time provided by this 'early
warning' of impending attack was just sufficient to allow army technicians to activate a series of additional electronic measures to neutralize
the transmission signal and render detonation impossible.

For a time, this mechanism in its turn proved effective. But then the
IRA discovered a means to outwit even this countermeasure. Using
radar detectors like those used by motorists in the United States to evade
speed traps, in 1991 the group's bomb-makers fabricated a detonating
system that can be triggered by the same type of hand-held radar gun
used by police throughout the world to catch speeding drivers. Since the
radar gun can be aimed at its target before being switched on, and the
signal that it transmits is nearly instantaneous, no practical means
currently exists either to detect or to intercept the transmission signal.
Moreover, shortly after making this breakthrough the IRA's 'R&D'
units developed yet another means to detonate bombs, using a photoflash 'slave' unit that can be triggered from a distance of up to 800 metres
by a flash of light. This device, which sells for between £60 and £70, is
used by commercial photographers to produce simultaneous flashes
during photo shoots. The IRA bombers attach the unit to the detonating
system on a bomb and then simply activate it with an ordinary, commercially available, flash gun.

Not surprisingly, therefore, the IRA bombers have earned a reputation
for their innovative expertise, adaptability and cunning. 'There are some

e around,' the British army's Chief Ammunitions
(CATO) in Northern Ireland commented. 'I would
hly for improvisation. IRA bombs are very well
colade was offered by the staff officer of the British
es and Ordnance Disposal Company: 'We are
livision,' he said. 'I don't think there is any organi-
as cunning as the IRA. They have had twenty years at
they have learned from their experience. We have a great deal of
respect for their skills . . . not as individuals, but their skills.'[82] While not
yet nearly as good as the IRA, the province's loyalist terrorist groups
have themselves been on a 'learning curve' with regard to bomb-making,
and are said to have become increasingly adept in the construction,
concealment and surreptitious placement of bombs.

In certain circumstances, even attacks that are not successful in
conventionally understood military terms of casualties inflicted or assets
destroyed can still be counted a success for the terrorists provided that
they are technologically daring enough to garner media and public
attention.[83] Although the IRA failed to kill the prime minister, Margaret
Thatcher, at the Conservative Party's 1984 conference in Brighton, the
technological ingenuity of the attempt, involving the bomb's placement
at the conference site weeks before the event and its detonation timing
device powered by a computer microchip, nonetheless succeeded in
capturing the world's headlines and providing the IRA with a platform
from which to warn Mrs Thatcher and all other British leaders: 'Today
we were unlucky, but remember we only have to be lucky once – you will
have to be lucky always.'[84] Similarly, although the remote-control
mortar attack staged by the IRA on No. 10 Downing Street as Mrs
Thatcher's successor John Major and his cabinet met at the height of the
1991 Gulf War failed to hit its intended target, it nonetheless successfully elbowed the war out of the limelight and shone renewed media
attention on the terrorists, their cause and their impressive ability to
strike at the nerve-centre of the British government even at a time of
heightened security. 'The Provies are always that step ahead of you,' a
senior RUC officer has commented. 'They are very innovative.'[85]
Although the technological mastery employed by the IRA is arguably
unique among terrorist organizations, experience has nonetheless
demonstrated repeatedly that, when confronted by new security
measures, terrorists will seek to identify and exploit new vulnerabilities,

adjusting their means of attack accordingly and often carrying on despite the obstacles placed in their path.

Conclusion

'All politics is a struggle for power,' wrote C. Wright Mills, and 'the ultimate kind of power is violence.'[86] Terrorism is where politics and violence intersect in the hope of delivering power. All terrorism involves the quest for power: power to dominate and coerce, to intimidate and control, and ultimately to effect fundamental political change. Violence (or the threat of violence) is thus the *sine qua non* of terrorists, who are unswervingly convinced that only through violence can their cause triumph and their long-term political aims be attained. Terrorists therefore plan their operations in a manner that will shock, impress and intimidate, ensuring that their acts are sufficiently daring and violent to capture the attention of the media and, in turn, of the public and government as well. Often erroneously seen as indiscriminate or senseless, terrorism is actually a very deliberate and planned application of violence. It may be represented as a concatenation of five individual processes, designed to achieve, sequentially, the following key objectives:

1 *Attention*. Through dramatic, attention-riveting acts of violence, terrorists seek to focus attention on themselves and their causes through the publicity they receive, most often from news media coverage.
2 *Acknowledgement*. Having attracted this attention, and thrust some otherwise previously ignored or hitherto forgotten cause on to the state's – or, often more desirably, the international community's – agenda, terrorists seek to translate their new-found notoriety into acknowledgement (and perhaps even sympathy and support) of their cause.
3 *Recognition*. Terrorists attempt to capitalize on the interest and acknowledgement their violent acts have generated by obtaining recognition of their rights (i.e. acceptance of the justification of their cause) and of their particular organization as *the* spokesman of the constituency whom the terrorists purport to, or in some cases actually do, represent.

4 *Authority*. Armed with this recognition, terrorists seek the authority
   to effect the changes in government and/or society that lie at the heart
   of their movement's struggle: this may involve a change in government or in the entire state structure, or the redistribution of wealth,
   re-adjustment of geographical boundaries, assertion of minority
   rights, etc.

5 *Governance*. Having acquired authority, terrorists seek to consolidate
   their direct and complete control over the state, their homeland
   and/or their people.

While some terrorist movements have been successful in achieving the
first three objectives, rarely in modern times has any group attained the
latter two. Nonetheless, all terrorists exist and function in hopes of
reaching this ultimate end. For them, the future rather than the present
defines their reality. Indeed, they can console themselves that it was only
a decade ago that the British prime minister, Margaret Thatcher, said of
the African National Congress, 'Anyone who thinks it is going to run the
government in South Africa is living in cloud-cuckoo land.'[87] Exactly
ten years after that remark was uttered, Queen Elizabeth II greeted
President Nelson Mandela on his first official state visit to London.

7

Terrorism Today and Tomorrow

Terrorism today is dominated by several different trends that in recent years have become increasingly intertwined – with often unsettling consequences. The re-emergence in the early 1980s of terrorism motivated by a religious imperative and state-sponsored terrorism set in motion profound changes in the nature, motivations and capabilities of terrorists that are still unfolding. The appearance later in the decade of a professional subculture of terrorist 'guns for hire', coupled with the proliferation during the 1990s of so-called 'amateur' terrorists (with little or no formal connection to an existing terrorist group), continued this process, transforming terrorism into the arguably more diffuse and amorphous phenomenon that it has now become. This concluding chapter discusses some of the implications of these trends within the context of the rise and persistence of state-sponsored terrorism and for the light that they shed on potential terrorist use of weapons of mass destruction.

The Emergence of Modern State-sponsored Terrorism

Certainly, governments have long engaged in various types of illicit, clandestine activities – including the systematic use of terror – against their enemies, both domestic and foreign. The Nazis' victimization of Jews, gypsies, communists and homosexuals, political rivals and other 'enemies of the state' in Germany, and the Serbian military's intimate involvement in fomenting anti-Habsburg unrest in Bosnia on the eve of the First World War are two clear examples of past state sponsorship or indeed outright use of terrorism. But what sets these (and indeed many other historical) cases apart from the type of state-sponsored terrorism that has emerged since the early 1980s is the way in which some governments have now come to embrace terrorism as a deliberate instrument of foreign policy: a cost-effective means of waging war covertly, through the use of surrogate warriors or 'guns for hire' – terrorists.

The pivotal event in the emergence of state-sponsored terrorism as a weapon of state and instrument of foreign policy was doubtless the seizure in November 1979 of fifty-two American hostages at the United States embassy in Tehran by a group of militant Iranian 'students'. For 444 days these so-called students – who claimed to have acted independently, without government support or encouragement – held the world's most powerful state at bay. Throughout that protracted episode they focused unparalleled worldwide media attention on both themselves and their anti-American cause, ultimately costing an American president his re-election to office. As events would later show, this incident was only the beginning of an increasingly serious and extensive state-sponsored terrorist campaign directed by the Khomeini regime in Iran against the United States as well as other Western countries. Its lessons, moreover, were absorbed not only by Iran's clerical rulers, who sought to expunge Western (and especially American) influence from the Middle East, but by the leaders of the region's other 'pariah states' – Libya, Syria and Iraq – and by foreign governments elsewhere. Acts of violence, perpetrated by terrorists secretly working for governments, were shown to be a relatively inexpensive and, if executed properly, potentially risk-free means of anonymously attacking stronger enemies and thereby avoiding the threat of international punishment or reprisal.

For the terrorist, the benefits of state sponsorship were even greater. Such a relationship appreciably enhanced the capabilities and operational capacity of otherwise limited terrorist groups, placing at their disposal the resources of an established nation-state's entire diplomatic, military and intelligence apparatus and thus greatly facilitating planning and intelligence. The logistical support provided by states assured the terrorists of otherwise unobtainable luxuries such as the use of diplomatic pouches for the transport of weapons and explosives, false identification in the form of genuine passports, and the use of embassies and other diplomatic facilities as safe houses or staging bases. State sponsorship also afforded terrorists greater training opportunities: thus some groups were transformed into entities more akin to elite commando units than to the stereotypical conspiratorial cell of anarchists wielding Molotov cocktails or radicals manufacturing crude pipe-bombs. Finally, terrorists were often paid handsomely for their services, turning hitherto financially destitute entities into well-endowed organizations with investment profiles and bulging balance sheets.

For all these reasons, it was not necessary for the state-sponsored terrorist to identify with his patron's cause. Nor did he necessarily have to be the rabid ideologue, religious zealot or extreme nationalist common to ideologically and religiously motivated groups or ethno-nationalist/separatist organizations. All the state-sponsored terrorist needed to be was willing to perform a service for a price, as an independent mercenary – a mere 'hired gun'. The Abu Nidal Organization (ANO) is a prominent case in point. This group, founded and led by the Palestinian terrorist Sabri al-Banna, has been variously employed by Syria, Iraq and Libya (three countries who have been on the US State Department's list of state sponsors of terrorism since the list was established in 1979).[1] As it has profited from its mercenary role, so the group has progressively relinquished its original revolutionary/political motivations in favour of activities devoted almost entirely to making money. The ANO, accordingly, has reputedly amassed a considerable fortune: initially through its 'for-hire' terrorist activities, but then through exploiting its gains from these deals in shrewd commercial and real estate investments, including the profitable operation of a multinational arms trading company based in Poland. In 1988 the ANO's assets were said to be worth an estimated $400 million. Given the vast profits involved, not surprisingly the group's financial portfolio is administered by a separate 'finance directorate' within the organization – with Abu Nidal himself at its head.[2]

Even supposedly ideologically 'pure' Marxist-Leninist organizations, like the Japanese Red Army (JRA), built up a fortune during the 1980s through commissioned terrorism. The JRA, which has been based in Lebanon's Bekaa valley since its founding in 1971 by a former Meiji University student named Fusako Shigenobu, has in fact always sought outside patrons. Initially, the PFLP filled this role, with the JRA

performing operations – such as the 1972 suicide machine-gun and
hand-grenade attack on Israel's Lod Airport, where twenty-six persons
were killed and eighty others wounded – on the PFLP's behalf. Later,
the group was taken under the wing of the world's legendary master
terrorist, Carlos 'The Jackal', for whom it carried out operations
including the takeover of the French embassy in The Hague in 1974 and
the bombing that same year of a popular discotheque on the rue St
Germain in Paris, where two persons were killed and thirty-five injured.
In 1986, Shigenobu decided to diversify the JRA's income stream still
further by cutting a lucrative deal with Libyan leader Muammar
Qaddafi. Only a few months earlier, US air force jets had bombed Tripoli
and Benghazi in retaliation for Libya's alleged involvement in a terrorist
attack on a West Berlin night-club popular with American GIs that had
killed two persons and wounded some 200 others. Qaddafi was
desperate for revenge; fearing further American retaliatory air
strikes were he to take direct action, he turned to the JRA for help.
The group was only too happy to oblige, adopting the alias 'Anti-
Imperialist International Brigades' (AIIB) as a cover for those
operations specifically executed on Libya's behalf.

The JRA mounted the first AIIB attack in June 1986, targeting the
American and Japanese embassies in Jakarta, Indonesia, with remote-
controlled mortars positioned in a nearby hotel room. The following
year the group 'commemorated' the first anniversary of the US air
strike with an identical attack on three US diplomatic facilities in
Madrid. They struck again in June, detonating a car-bomb outside the
US embassy in Rome, and shortly afterwards launched rocket attacks
against both the same target and the British embassy nearby. To mark
the second anniversary of the 1986 US air strike the JRA/AIIB initiated its most ambitious plan: simultaneous attacks against American
military targets in the United States and Europe. The American arm of
the plan, however, went seriously awry a month before the attacks were
to commence when a veteran JRA terrorist, Yu Kikumura, was arrested
by a New Jersey state police officer in March while en route to New
York. In the back seat of Kikumura's car, the police officer found
several hollowed-out fire extinguishers, packed with explosive material
and roofing nails. Kikumura had planned to place these crude but
effective anti-personnel bombs outside a US navy recruiting station in
lower Manhattan's Wall Street financial district and time them to

explode precisely at the crowded noon-time lunch hour. The carnage that would have ensued almost certainly would have dwarfed the six deaths caused by the World Trade Center bombing five years later. Kikumura was subsequently convicted and sentenced to thirty years' imprisonment.

The other JRA/AIIB attacks scheduled for that day in Europe, however, went off almost as planned. In Naples, a car-bomb exploded outside a US military club, killing five persons and wounding seventeen others, while in Spain the group bombed a US air base. Then, in July, the AIIB attacks suddenly ended, with a failed remote-controlled rocket attack on the US embassy in Madrid. Thereafter, the JRA itself mysteriously ceased active terrorist operations, its twenty or so members presumably having 'retired' to the group's base in the Bekaa valley or to its sanctuary in North Korea to live off the sizeable nest egg that Shigenobu had accumulated for herself and her followers.

State-sponsored terrorism has had a profound impact on patterns of terrorism more broadly. Since state-sponsored terrorism is geared less to obtaining publicity than to pursuing specific foreign policy objectives – by covertly bringing pressure to bear on the sponsor's opponents through acts of violence – it operates under fewer constraints than does ordinary terrorism. In addition, because state-sponsored terrorists do not depend on the local population for support, they need not concern themselves with the risk of alienating popular support or provoking a public backlash. Thus the state-sponsored terrorist and his patron can engage in acts of violence that are typically more destructive and bloodier than those carried out by groups acting on their own behalf. Indeed, given the enhanced resources that state-supported groups can command, it is not surprising to find that identifiable state-sponsored terrorist attacks during the 1980s were overall eight times more lethal than those carried out by groups without state support or assistance. Among them were:

- the April 1983 suicide car-bomb explosion outside the US embassy in Beirut that killed 69 persons and was claimed by Islamic Jihad (Islamic Holy War), a cover-name used by Iranian-backed Lebanese Shi'a terrorists;
- the simultaneous suicide truck bombings of the US Marine headquarters at Beirut International Airport and the French paratroop

headquarters in that city, which killed respectively 241 Marines and 58 paratroopers in October 1983, and for which Islamic Jihad also took credit, boasting in a communiqué how 'two martyr *mujahidin* [holy warriors] set out to inflict upon the US Administration an utter defeat not experienced since Vietnam, and a similar one upon the French Administration';[3]

- the identical attack carried out by Islamic Jihad on the Israeli military government building in Sidon the following month that resulted in the deaths of 67 persons;
- the coordinated car-bomb attacks in Karachi, Pakistan, carried out by agents of Afghanistan's secret intelligence service, WAD, in July 1987, killing 72 persons and wounding more than 250 others;
- the bomb placed by two North Korean agents on a Korean Air Lines plane en route from Baghdad to Seoul that killed all 115 persons on board in November 1987;
- the sabotage of a munitions dump in Islamabad, Pakistan, in April 1988 by Afghani WAD operatives that killed more than 100 persons and wounded 1,100;
- the mid-air explosion aboard Pan Am flight 103 in December 1988 over Lockerbie, Scotland, that claimed the lives of all 259 passengers as well as of 11 persons on the ground and has been linked to two Libyan intelligence agents, acting not only with official Libyan state sanction but possibly at the behest of Iran as well;
- the in-flight bombing of a French UTA passenger jet over Chad in August 1989 that killed 171 persons and was claimed by Islamic Jihad.

State-sponsored terrorism has also been employed on a far more discriminating scale to stifle external dissent. Exiled opposition figures, political dissidents, human rights activists, journalists, political cartoonists and others have been intimidated and, in some instances, murdered at the behest of various foreign governments. In one especially notorious case, Bulgarian agents used a poison-tipped umbrella to murder dissident exile Georgi Markov on a London bridge in 1978.[4] Libyan, Iranian and Iraqi agents have also allegedly carried out operations against opponents of their respective regimes residing in the United States, France, Germany, Italy, Switzerland, Austria, South Africa and the United Kingdom. In 1991, for example, an Iranian 'hit team', using diplomatic cover, assassinated the former prime minister and outspoken critic of the Khomeini regime, Shahpur Baktiar, in Paris; and since 1989 Salman Rushdie, the Pakistani-born British author of *The Satanic Verses*, has lived under the *fatwa* (religious edict) death sentence imposed on him and his publishers for blasphemy by the Ayatollah Khomeini, in pursuit of which a group of Iranian clerics have offered a $2.5 million bounty to whomever fulfils the ayatollah's decree. Thus far, the book's Japanese translator has been stabbed to death, its Norwegian publisher shot and its Italian translator knifed, while Rushdie himself continues to lead a life on the run, protected round the clock by Scotland Yard's Special Branch at a cost to the British taxpayer of more than £7 million as of 1997.[5] The most serious – and daring – state-sponsored terrorist incident of the 1980s was the attempt on the life of Pope John Paul II as he greeted the crowd gathered in St Peter's Square on 13 May 1981. Although a young Turkish terrorist, Mehmet Ali Agca, was apprehended on the spot and subsequently convicted of the attack, it is widely believed that the Bulgarian secret service was behind the assassination plot – allegedly acting on instructions from KGB head and later premier of the Soviet Union, Yuri Andropov.[6]

A Persistent Phenomenon

Today, state sponsorship of terrorism continues unabated. In 1996, for example, the US State Department designated seven countries as terrorism sponsors: Cuba, Iran, Iraq, Libya, North Korea, Sudan and Syria. With the exception of Sudan, which was added in 1993, each of these countries has remained on the list of terrorism's patron states for more than a decade. The reason, as noted above, is that neither economic sanctions nor military reprisals have proven completely successful in effecting positive changes to these countries' policies on terrorism. Even seasoned US government counterterrorist analysts are somewhat dismissive of their effects. A recent high-level discussion paper circulated within the American intelligence community noted that

In theory, the threat or imposition of embargoes and sanctions would appear to be a powerful leveraging tool in the conduct of foreign relations between countries. In practice, no state sponsor of international terrorism against which the US has enacted an embargo or sanctions has renounced it[s] role of sponsorship or denounced terrorism as a tool of its foreign policy. Nor has any state once placed on the state sponsors list ever been removed.[7]

Military reprisals against state sponsors of terrorism have arguably proved no more effective; worse still, in some respects they have been counterproductive. For example, the aforementioned 1986 US air strike against Libya is frequently cited as proof of the effectiveness of military retaliation; yet, rather than having deterred the Qaddafi regime from engaging in state-sponsored terrorism, it appears that it may have had precisely the opposite effect. In the first place, so far from stopping Libyan-backed terrorism, the US air strike goaded the Libyan dictator to undertake even more serious and heinous acts of terrorism against the United States and its citizens. Indeed, after a brief lull, Libya not only resumed but actually increased its international terrorist activities. According to the RAND–St Andrews University Chronology of International Terrorism, at least fifteen identifiable state-sponsored terrorist incidents in 1987 and eight in 1988 – including the previously cited 'for hire' terrorist incidents perpetrated by the JRA/AIIB – have been conclusively linked to Libya.[8] The incident involving Kikumura, related above, is especially noteworthy as evidence that Qaddafi was not only continuing his terrorist campaign against the United States but significantly escalating it in dispatching the veteran JRA terrorist to New York on the (failed) bombing mission.

The United States was not the only country to suffer continued acts of Libyan-sponsored international terrorism. In retaliation for Britain's role in allowing the US warplanes that bombed Tripoli and Benghazi to take off from bases in that country, Qaddafi deliberately increased his supply of weapons to the IRA. During the months following the air-strike, the Irish terrorist group reportedly took delivery of some five to ten tons of Semtex-H plastic explosive (investigators believe that about eight ounces of Semtex-H was used in the bomb that exploded on board Pan Am flight 103) in addition to 120 tons of other arms and explosives, including twelve SAM-7 ground-to-air missiles, stocks of RPG-7 rocket-propelled grenades, and anti-aircraft and anti-tank guns.[9] British authorities largely credit the Libyan weapons shipments with having appreciably facilitated the IRA's terror campaign over the following months and years.

As for the air strikes sending a powerful deterrent message to other terrorists elsewhere, as the Reagan administration claimed at the time, the evidence is similarly wanting. Indeed, more terrorist attacks against American targets occurred during the three-month period following the US action (fifty-three) than during the three months preceding it (forty-one).[10] Indeed, the US State Department admitted in the 1996 edition of its *Patterns of Global Terrorism* that Libya had continued throughout the period to provide support for the most 'rejectionist' (that is, the most vehemently opposed to the Israeli–Palestinian peace process and dialogue) and extreme of the Palestinian terrorist groups, including the ANO, the Palestine Islamic Jihad (PIJ) and Ahmed Jibril's PFLP-GC (General Command). Indeed, Abu Nidal reportedly makes his home – and has his organization's headquarters – in Libya.[11]

Finally, even the oft-repeated claims of the attack's surgical precision and the immense technological sophistication of American precision-guided air-delivered ordnance fall down under examination. Despite the particularly careful selection of military targets for the US fighter-bombers, thirty-six civilians were killed in the air strike and ninety-three others wounded. These civilian deaths and injuries were not only tragic in themselves, but deprived the United States of the moral high ground it often claims to occupy above terrorists and terrorism and thereby engendered further domestic and international criticism. However, perhaps the most incontrovertible – and obvious, if ignored – refutation of 'the myth of military retaliation' is the 1988 in-flight bombing of Pan Am flight 103. After what has been described as the 'the most extensive criminal investigation in history', the joint FBI and Scottish police investigation resulted in the indictment of two Libyan employees of that country's national airline, who are alleged to have been agents of Qaddafi's intelligence service.[12]

Today, though, it is not Libya but Iran that is deemed by the US State Department to be the 'premier state sponsor of terrorism', actively planning and facilitating the execution of attacks by both its agents and surrogates in groups such as the Lebanese Hezbollah.[13] According to Israeli and American intelligence sources, during 1996 at least three 747 jumbo cargo jets were landing in Damascus every month ferrying weapons sent by Tehran to its minions in Hezbollah. Among the armaments were long-range Katyusha rockets, Russian-made Sagger anti-tank weapons and other sophisticated ordnance. Mixed in with the weapons were humanitarian supplies for the group and nascent political party to dispense to its Lebanese Shi'a constituents, thereby strengthening its political position.[14] Iran is alleged to provide a total of about $100 million a year to various Islamic terrorist organizations across the world, with the lion's share going to Hezbollah.[15]

Like Libya, Iran reportedly also provides training and sanctuary for the most hard-line Palestinian factions, including Hamas and the PIJ, as well as the Kurdish PKK. Tehran is also alleged to be behind the subversive activities occurring in several Gulf states, including a planned coup in Bahrain that was foiled in June 1996. The authorities arrested nearly thirty members of the Bahraini branch of Hezbollah who confessed to having been plotting since 1993 to overthrow the emirate's al-Khalifa ruling family, which belongs to the minority Sunni branch of Islam. Conclusive proof of Iran's continued sponsorship of international terrorism was revealed in a Berlin court in April 1997, when convictions were obtained for an Iranian and four Lebanese accused of the killing in 1992 of three Iranian Kurdish dissidents and their translator, murders carried out on instructions from Tehran. As a result of evidence presented during the trial, which lasted nearly four years, the German authorities issued an arrest warrant for Ali Fallahian, the Iranian minister of intelligence, for his role in the murders, and accused the Iranian government's Committee for Special Operations – which reportedly comprised the highest echelon of Iran's ruling elite, including President Hashemi Rafsanjani and the country's supreme religious leader, the Ayatollah Ali Khamenei – of actually having issued orders for the dissidents' murder. Exile sources say that Tehran is directly responsible for the murder of at least twenty Iranian opposition figures in Europe since 1979.[16] And yet, as with Libya, American efforts to dissuade Iran from sponsoring terrorism have proven largely ineffective. In 1995, for example, the CIA's deputy director for intelligence testified before Congress that the US economic embargo imposed the previous April had been 'a failure' and would be unlikely ever to have any impact without more widespread international support. At the time, only Israel, El Salvador and the Ivory Coast had answered President Clinton's call for sanctions.[17]

Even those countries on the State Department's list that may not be current active sponsors of international terrorism – Syria, Cuba, North Korea and the Sudan – nevertheless play a critical role in abetting and

facilitating terrorist operations. Without their provision of training facilities, sanctuary, safe havens and other 'passive' forms of support, many
groups would find it far more difficult to continue to operate. For
example, although there is no evidence that either Syria or Syrian
government officials have been directly involved in the planning or
execution of international terrorist attacks since 1986, that country
continues to provide sanctuary and assistance to terrorists. The PFLP-
GC, a Palestinian faction firmly opposed to the Arab–Israeli peace
process, which was implicated just prior to the 1988 bombing of Pan Am
flight 103 in a plot to bomb American and Israeli commercial aircraft
flying from Europe,[18] has had its headquarters in Damascus for more
than three decades. Other groups, such as Hamas (the Palestine Islamic
Resistance Movement), the PIJ, the JRA and the PKK, also maintain
bases either in Syria or just across the border in the Syrian-controlled
Bekaa valley.[19] Indeed, only a few years ago the State Department alleged
that at least sixteen different international terrorist organizations
maintained training facilities under Syria's aegis in the Bekaa valley.[20]

For all seven of the countries identified by the State Department,
then, terrorism remains a useful and integral tool of their respective
foreign policies: a clandestine weapon to be wielded whenever the situation is appropriate and the benefits palpable, but remaining sheathed
when the risks of using it appear to outweigh the potential gains and the
possible repercussions are likely to prove counterproductive. For the
state sponsor, much as for the terrorist group itself, terrorism – contrary
to popular perception – is not a mindless act of fanatical or indiscriminate violence, but a purposefully targeted, deliberately calibrated
method of pursuing specific objectives at acceptable cost. In this
respect, the attractions of terrorists as 'surrogate warriors' or merce-
naries for various renegade regimes may in fact have increased since the
1991 Gulf War. The lesson of Iraq's *overt* invasion of Kuwait, in
response to which a UN-backed multinational coalition was almost
immediately arrayed against Saddam Hussein, suggests that future
aggressors may prefer to accomplish clandestinely with a handful of
armed men and a limited amount of weaponry what traditionally whole
armies, navies and air forces have been deployed to achieve. Not only
could such small bands facilitate the conquest of neighbouring or rival
states, but if this action is carried out covertly – and successfully – the
state sponsor might escape identification, and hence international

military response and economic sanction. Accordingly, terrorists may in the future come to be regarded by the globe's rogue states as the 'ultimate fifth column' – a clandestine, cost-effective force used to wage war covertly against more powerful rivals or to subvert neighbouring countries or hostile regimes. Recent accusations of Iran's fomenting subversion in Bahrain, along with its suspected role in the bombing of an American military housing complex in Dhahran, Saudi Arabia, in June 1996 and of a joint Saudi–American military training facility in Riyadh in November 1995 may already be indicative of this trend.

The Future: Terrorist Use of Weapons of Mass Destruction

Meanwhile, the face of terrorism is changing in other ways. New adversaries, new motivations and new rationales have emerged in recent years to challenge at least some of the conventional wisdom on both terrorists and terrorism. More critically, perhaps, many of our old preconceptions – as well as government policies – date from the emergence of terrorism as a global security problem more than a quarter of a century ago. They originated, and took hold, during the Cold War, when radical left-wing terrorist groups then active throughout the world were widely regarded as posing the most serious threat to Western security. Even such modifications or 'fine-tuning' as have been undertaken since that time are arguably no less dated by now, having been implemented a decade ago in response to the series of suicide bombings against American diplomatic and military targets in the Middle East that at the time had underscored the rising threat of state-sponsored terrorism.

In no area, perhaps, is the potential irrelevance of much of this thinking clearer, or the critical lacuna more apparent, than with regard to the potential use by terrorists of weapons of mass destruction (WMD): that is, nuclear, chemical or biological weapons. Most of the handful of publications that have authoritatively addressed this issue are themselves now seriously dated, having been conceived and written in some instances nearly two decades ago when very different situations, circumstances and international dynamics existed. Indeed, much of the research on potential uses of WMD during the Cold War understandably concentrated on nuclear confrontation involving almost exclusively the two superpowers and their allies. Potential terrorist use of such devices was either addressed within the Cold War/superpowers framework or else dismissed, given the prevailing patterns of substate violence and the aims and objectives of violent non-state groups active at the time.

Today, the threat of a general war – nuclear and/or conventional – between the superpowers of the Cold War era and their respective alliances has faded. But it has been replaced by new security challenges of a potentially far more amorphous, less quantifiable and perhaps even more ominous character, that may also be far more difficult to meet. As we saw in chapter 4, the increasing salience of religious motives for terrorist activity has already contributed to the increasing lethality of international terrorism. Moreover, many of the constraints (both self-imposed and technical) which previously inhibited terrorist use of WMD are eroding. The particular characteristics, justifications and mindsets of religious and quasi-religious – as compared with secular – terrorists suggest that religious terrorists will be among the most likely of the potential categories of non-state perpetrators to use WMD.

The Changing Characteristics of International Terrorism

In the past, terrorist groups were recognizable mostly as collections of individuals belonging to an organization with a well-defined command and control apparatus, who had been previously trained (in however rudimentary a fashion) in the techniques and tactics of terrorism, were engaged in conspiracy as a full-time avocation, living underground while constantly planning and plotting terrorist attacks, and who at times were under the direct control, or operated at the express behest, of a foreign government (as, for example, in the case of Libya's sponsorship of JRA operations claimed in the name of the 'Anti-Imperialist International Brigades'). Radical leftist organizations such as the JRA, RAF, RB, etc., as well as ethno-nationalist/separatist terrorist movements like the PLO, IRA and ETA, conformed to this stereotype of the 'traditional' terrorist group. These organizations engaged in highly selective and mostly discriminate acts of violence. They targeted for bombing various 'symbolic' targets representing the source of their hostility (e.g. embassies, banks, national airline carriers), or kidnapped and assassinated specific persons whom they considered guilty of economic exploitation or political repression in order to attract attention to themselves and their causes.

However, radical or revolutionary as these groups were politically, the vast majority were equally conservative in their operations. These types of terrorists were said to be demonstrably more 'imitative than innovative', having a very limited tactical repertoire directed against a similarly narrow target set.[21] They were judged as hesitant to take advantage of new situations, let alone to create new opportunities. What little innovation was observed lay more in the terrorists' choice of targets (e.g. the 1985 hijacking of the Italian cruise ship *Achille Lauro* by Palestinian terrorists, as opposed to the more typical terrorist hijacking of passenger aircraft), or in the methods used to conceal and detonate explosive devices, than in their tactics or their interest in using non-conventional weapons – particularly chemical, biological, radiological or nuclear.[22]

Although various terrorist groups – including the RAF, RB and some Palestinian organizations – had occasionally toyed with the idea of using such indiscriminately lethal weapons, none had ever crossed the critical psychological threshold of actually implementing their heinous daydreams or executing their half-baked plots. Admittedly, in 1979 Palestinian terrorists poisoned some Jaffa oranges exported to Europe in hopes of sabotaging Israel's economy; and a police raid on an RAF safe house in Paris the following year discovered a miniature laboratory designed to be used for the culture of *clostridium botulinum*.[23] But these two isolated incidents represented virtually the total extent of either *actual* use or serious *attempts* at the use by terrorists of such non-conventional weapons and tactics. Instead, most terrorists seemed relatively content with the limited killing potential of their hand-guns and machine-guns, and the slightly higher casualty rates that their bombs achieved. Like most people, terrorists themselves appeared to fear powerful contaminants and toxins about which they knew little and which they were uncertain how to fabricate and safely handle, much less effectively deploy and disperse. Indeed, of more than 8,000 incidents recorded in the RAND–St Andrews University Chronology of International Terrorist Incidents since 1968, fewer than sixty offer any indication of terrorists plotting such attacks, attempting to use chemical or biological agents, or intending to steal or fabricate their own nuclear devices.[24]

There has also been a general acceptance of Brian Jenkins's previously cited observation that 'Terrorists want a lot of people watching and a lot of people listening and not a lot of people dead.' Even after the events of the mid-1980s, when a series of high-profile and particularly lethal suicide car- and truck-bombings were directed against American diplomatic and military targets in the Middle East (in one instance resulting in the deaths of 241 Marines), Jenkins still saw no need to revise his thinking, reiterating that 'simply killing a lot of people has seldom been one terrorist objective . . . Terrorists operate on the principle of the minimum force necessary. They find it unnecessary to kill many, as long as killing a few suffices for their purposes.'[25] This maxim was further applied to the question of potential terrorist use of WMD, in respect of which it was used to explain the paucity of actual known plots, much less verifiable incidents. Within the context of potential terrorist use of radiological or nuclear weapons, for example, Jenkins had noted in 1975 that

> Scenarios involving the deliberate dispersal of toxic radioactive material . . . do not appear to fit the pattern of any terrorist actions carried out thus far . . . Terrorist actions have tended to be aimed at producing immediate dramatic effects, a handful of violent deaths – not lingering illness, and certainly not a population of ill, vengeance-seeking victims . . . If terrorists were to employ radioactive contaminants, they could not halt the continuing effects of their act, not even long after they may have achieved their ultimate political objectives. It has not been the style of terrorists to kill hundreds or thousands. To make hundreds or thousands of persons terminally ill would be even more out of character.[26]

Implications of Religious Terrorism for Use of WMD

In recent years, however, these long-standing assumptions have increasingly been called into question by terrorist attacks that have either involved a weapon of mass destruction or caused large numbers of fatalities. Three incidents in particular (discussed in chapter 5) have generated heightened concern that terrorism may be entering a period of increased violence and bloodshed. They are:

• the March 1995 nerve gas attack on the Tokyo subway system;
• the bombing a month later of the Alfred P. Murrah Federal Building in Oklahoma City;
• the 1993 bombing of New York City's World Trade Center.

The connecting thread (although not necessarily the sole motivating factor) linking these otherwise unrelated incidents is religion. Indeed, in addition to these examples, some of the most serious terrorist acts – either in lethality or in their political implications – of the years 1995–7 have similarly had a salient religious element.

As the three incidents listed above demonstrate, the more 'traditional' and familiar types of ideological, ethno-nationalist and separatist organizations which dominated terrorism from the 1960s to the 1990s – and upon which analysts like Jenkins based many of their most fundamental judgements about terrorists and their behaviour – have now been joined by a variety of rather different terrorist entities with arguably less comprehensible nationalist or ideological motivations. Many in this 'new generation' of terrorist groups not only espouse far more amorphous religious and millenarian aims but are themselves less cohesive organizational bodies, with a more diffuse structure and membership. Even more disturbing is that in some instances their aims go far beyond the establishment of a theocracy amenable to their specific deity (e.g. the creation of an Iranian-style Islamic republic in Algeria, Egypt or Saudi Arabia) to embrace mystical, almost transcendental, and divinely inspired imperatives or a vehemently anti-government form of populism reflecting far-fetched conspiracy notions based on a volatile mixture of seditious, racial and religious dicta. In this respect, the emergence of obscure, idiosyncratic millenarian movements (such as the Japanese Aum Shinrikyo religious sect, which committed the March 1995 nerve gas attack on the Tokyo underground, and the militantly anti-government Christian white supremacist militias that have surfaced in the United States, implicated in the Oklahoma City bombing) alongside zealously nationalist religious groups (such as the Islamic extremists who carried out the World Trade Center bombing, the Algerian GIA and the Lebanese Hezbollah, with its links to various shadowy Egyptian and Saudi extremist groups) represents a very different and potentially far more lethal threat than the more familiar, 'traditional' terrorist groups.

Indeed, while some observers point optimistically to the decline in the number of international terrorist incidents during the 1990s as an especially noteworthy and salutary development in the struggle against terrorism, at the same time the proportion of persons killed in terrorist incidents has paradoxically – and alarmingly – increased. According to the RAND–St Andrews Chronology, a record 484 international terrorist incidents were recorded in 1991, the year of the Gulf War, followed by 343 incidents in 1992, 360 in 1993 and 353 in 1994, falling to 278 incidents in 1995 (the last calendar year for which complete statistics are available). But while terrorists were becoming less active, they were also becoming more lethal. For example, at least one person was killed in 29 per cent of terrorist incidents in 1995: the highest ratio of fatalities to incidents recorded in the Chronology since 1968, and an increase of 2 per cent over the previous year's record figure.[27] By comparison, only 17 per cent of international terrorist incidents in the 1970s killed anyone, and just 19 per cent in the 1980s. Whether this development represents an enduring trend or not remains unclear. It nonetheless provides evidence for the assertion that international terrorism is more lethal today than it has been in the past and therefore raises the question: why this is so?

Among the various factors that account for terrorism's increasing lethality (including the terrorist's perennial quest for attention; the increased prevalence of state sponsorship and the greater resources thereby accorded terrorists; developments in terrorist weaponry, which is getting smaller, more easy to conceal and more powerful; and the increasing sophistication of professional terrorism), the most significant is perhaps the dramatic proliferation of terrorist groups motivated by a religious imperative. This suggestion is borne out by the pattern of international terrorism during 1995. As previously noted, although religious terrorists committed only 25 per cent of the recorded international terrorist incidents in 1995, they were responsible for 58 per cent of the total number of fatalities recorded that year. Looking at the data from another perspective, those attacks that caused the greatest numbers of deaths in 1995 (incidents that killed eight or more persons) were all perpetrated by religious terrorists.

We have already noted that since the mid-1980s it has been religious terrorists or members of either mainstream religious movements or smaller 'cults' in the United States and Israel who have come closest to crossing the threshold of terrorist use of WMD, or evidence the traits and tactical abilities required to carry out such attacks. Three incidents reported in 1995 involved persons with connections to various American Christian white supremacist organizations who plotted to obtain deadly toxins and contaminants. In March, two members of the

Minnesota Patriots Council, a so-called 'militia' organization, were convicted of stockpiling enough ricin to kill at least 129 persons,[28] allegedly as part of a plan to murder IRS agents, US marshals and local deputy sheriffs. According to the FBI, ricin is ranked the third most toxic known substance, behind only plutonium and botulism: a minute amount can kill in minutes if inhaled, ingested or absorbed through the skin. Two months later, a man described as a certified microbiologist – who also had links with the Idaho-based Aryan Nations – was able to order a quantity of bubonic plague agent through the mail from a Maryland chemical supply firm. He had obtained three vials of *Yersinia pestis* – a bacterium credited with having wiped out one-third of the population of fourteenth-century Europe. In addition to the bacterium, police also found in his home a dozen M-1 carbines, smoke grenades, blasting caps – and white supremacist literature.[29] Finally, in December of that year, an Arkansas resident with reputed ties to white supremacist 'survivalist' groups in that state was arrested at his farm on charges of having attempted to smuggle 130 grams of ricin into the United States from Canada. In addition to the ricin, Canadian customs officials had discovered in the man's car four guns and more than 20,000 rounds of ammunition. When US authorities searched the man's Arkansas farm they found copies of the (commercially available) *Poisoner's Handbook*, which explains how to extract ricin from castor beans, and *Silent Death*, which describes how to use toxic compounds to poison people.[30]

The potentially catastrophic casualties that might have resulted in any of these cases, alongside the consequences in Tokyo had the Aum sect's nerve gas attack reached its true killing potential, the American white supremacists' plot to poison water supplies and the indications that Prime Minister Rabin's assassination in Israel was to be but a prelude to a campaign of mass murder designed to disrupt the peace process, illustrate the deadly potential of religious (or religious-inspired) terrorists' obsessions. Indeed, the Aum sect's nerve gas attack on the Tokyo subway arguably crossed an important psychological threshold so far as terrorist use and potential use of WMD is concerned: for this incident clearly demonstrated that it is possible to execute a successful chemical terrorist attack, and may conceivably have raised the stakes for terrorists everywhere. Terrorist groups in the future may well feel driven to emulate or surpass the Tokyo incident, either in levels of death and destruction caused or in the use of a non-conventional weapon of mass destruction in order to ensure the same, if not greater, media coverage and public attention as the 1995 attack generated.

The proliferation of religious terrorism also raises a number of other disquieting possibilities and consequences, given that the members of many of these groups, sects and cults are what might be described as 'amateur' terrorists in contrast to the relatively small number of 'professionals' who have dominated terrorism in the past. Previously, terrorism was not just a matter of having the will and motivation to act, but of having the capability to do so – the requisite training, access to weaponry and operational knowledge. These were not necessarily readily available, and were generally acquired through training undertaken in camps known to be run either by other terrorist organizations or in concert with the terrorists' state sponsors. Today, however, information on the means and methods of terrorism can be easily obtained at bookstores, from mail-order publishers, on CD-ROM or even over the Internet. In February 1997, for example, British newspapers reported that the IRA had launched a massive propaganda campaign over the Internet, including detailed instructions on how to make and use Molotov cocktails 'to maximum effect' in riots and various 'pointers' on counter-intelligence, crafting false identities, forging documents and creating disguises.[31] Using such commercially published or otherwise readily accessible bomb-making manuals and operational guides to poisons, assassinations and chemical and biological weapons fabrication (e.g. the detailed, step-by-step, 98-page *Terrorist's Handbook* 'published' by 'Chaos Industries and Gunzenbombz Pyro-Technologies', which has been widely available for downloading from various Internet sites for at least two years), the 'amateur' terrorist can be just as deadly and destructive as his more 'professional' counterpart.

Terrorism has thus arguably become accessible to anyone with a grievance, an agenda, a purpose or any idiosyncratic combination of the above. The 'Unabomber' – who, as described in chapter 6, dispatched home-made bombs, made from ordinary materials, through the post allegedly from a remote cabin in the Montana hinterland – is a particularly pertinent case in point; further illustrations, with especial regard to WMD, are provided by the three incidents in 1995 noted above, involving persons with connections to US white supremacist organizations. We have also seen that the intention of the bombers of the World

Trade Center in 1993 is believed to have been to bring down one of the 110-storey twin towers on top of the other and to release into the damaged tower a toxic cloud of sodium cyanide that allegedly would have killed any surviviors of the initial blast. According to the judge who presided over the bombers' trial, had they succeeded, the sodium cyanide in the bomb would have been 'sucked into the north tower', thus killing everyone there.[32] By comparison, there is no evidence that the secular or 'professional' terrorists of the past – the persons once considered to be the world's arch-terrorists, such as the Carloses, Abu Nidals and Abul Abbases – ever contemplated, much less attempted, the complete destruction of a high-rise office building packed with people, let alone further enhancing such an attack by deploying a chemical weapon.

Not only is the information necessary to undertake WMD attacks relatively easily accessible, but the availability of critical *matériel* may already have been facilitated by the proliferation of fissile materials from the former Soviet Union and the putative illicit market in nuclear materials that is reportedly emerging in Eastern and Central Europe. While much of the material believed to be on offer in this black market cannot be classified as strategic nuclear material (SNM), that is, suitable for use in the construction of a fissionable explosive device, such highly toxic radioactive agents could be paired with conventional explosives and turned into a crude, non-fissionable atomic bomb (known as a 'dirty' bomb). For example, a combination fertilizer truck-bomb with radioactive agents could have not only destroyed one of the World Trade Center's towers, but also rendered a considerable chunk of prime real estate in one of the world's financial nerve centres indefinitely unusable because of radioactive contamination. The prospect not only of the resulting disruption to commerce, but of the attendant publicity and enhanced coercive power of terrorists armed with such 'dirty' bombs (arguably a more credible risk than terrorist acquisition of fissile nuclear weapons), is deeply disturbing.

The growth of religious terrorism and its emergence in recent years as a driving force behind the increasing lethality of international terrorism shatters some of our most basic assumptions about terrorists and the violence they commit. It also raises serious questions about the continued relevance of much of the conventional wisdom on terrorism – particularly as it pertains to potential future terrorist use of WMD.

In the past, most analyses of the possibility of mass indiscriminate killing involving chemical, biological, radiological or nuclear terrorism tended to discount it, for reasons surveyed above. Few terrorists, it was argued, know anything about the technical intricacies of either developing or dispersing such weapons. Political, moral and practical considerations were also perceived as important restraints on terrorist use of such weapons. Terrorists, we assured ourselves, wanted more people watching than dead. Therefore we believed that terrorists had little interest in and still less to gain from killing wantonly and indiscriminately.

While some of these arguments may still have force in respect of most secular terrorists, incidents like the nerve gas attack on the Tokyo subway and the World Trade Center and Oklahoma City bombings in particular – alongside some of the other attacks perpetrated by religious terrorists and additional plots that went awry – appear to render them dangerously anachronistic. In sum, compelling new motives, notably those associated with religious terrorism, coupled with increased access to critical information and key components, notably involving WMD, leading to enhanced terrorist capabilities, could portend an even bloodier and more destructive era of violence ahead than any we have seen before.

A Disquieting Trajectory

Events in Kenya and Tanzania, Afghanistan and the Sudan in August 1998 demonstrate clearly that terrorism is – and will remain – one of the main threats to international security as we approach the twenty-first century. The tragic embassy bombings in Nairobi and Dar es Salaam underscore with particular force that terrorism is among the most fluid and dynamic of political phenomena: one constantly evolving into new and ever more dangerous forms in order to evade existing security procedures and surmount the defensive barriers placed in its path. At the same time, the dramatic American cruise missile attacks on terrorist training camps in Afghanistan and a pharmaceutical factory alleged to be manufacturing chemical weapons in the Sudan serve as timely reminders of how difficult and complex a problem terrorism is and how governmental responses must accordingly be both innovative and multi-faceted if they are to achieve any demonstrable effects. Any government's ability to craft an effective response to terrorist attack and provocation will inevitably depend on its ability fully to understand the fundamental changes that distinguish today's terrorists from their predecessors. Only in this way can the array of required countermeasures be first identified and then brought to bear with genuinely positive results.

The two embassy attacks conform to an emerging trend in international terrorism: the infliction of mass, indiscriminate casualties by enigmatic adversaries striking far beyond terrorism's traditional operational theatres in Europe and the Middle East. As we have seen, terrorism was formerly practised by distinct organizational entities with established chains of command and a defined set of political, social or economic objectives. These groups also often issued communiqués taking credit for – and explaining in great detail – their actions.[33] Hence, however disagreeable or distasteful their aims and motivations may have been, their ideology and intentions – albeit politically radical and personally fanatical – were at least comprehensible.

Most significantly, however, these more familiar terrorist groups engaged in highly selective and mostly discriminate acts of violence directed against a comparatively narrow range of targets. Moreover, only rarely did these groups venture outside their self-proclaimed operational area (in the main, their own or neighbouring countries, established international centres, or global crossroads of diplomacy and commerce) to carry out attacks: Palestinian and Lebanese terrorists frequently operated in Europe, and on occasion the IRA might strike in Germany or the ETA in France. Thus, for nearly three decades, the locus of *international* terrorism remained firmly entrenched in Europe and the Middle East. Only occasionally did it spill over into Asia and Latin America; Africa remained almost untouched.

Finally, these groups were often numerically small. According to the US Department of Defense, neither the Japanese Red Army nor the Red Army Faction ever numbered more than twenty to thirty hardcore members. The Red Brigades were only slightly larger, with a total of fewer than fifty to seventy-five dedicated terrorists. Even the IRA and ETA were unlikely to be able to call on the violent services of more than two hundred to four hundred activists, while the feared Abu Nidal Organization was limited to some five hundred men-at-arms at any given time.[34]

The two embassy attacks diverged dramatically from these established patterns. First, rather than attempting either to limit casualties or to strike specifically at the citizens of their self-proclaimed enemy state, the bombers were clearly prepared to inflict random, widespread collateral casualties among the hundreds of Kenyan and Tanzanian embassy employees and ordinary passers-by in pursuit of their objective.

Second, the bombings occurred in a region of the world that had hitherto remained – mercifully – outside the maelstrom of international terrorism. Indeed, the masterminds behind the attacks probably regarded Kenya and Tanzania as irresistibly attractive operational environments for precisely this reason. Both countries, they doubtless believed, were unschooled in the vast array of counterterrorist measures routinely deployed in other parts of the world and were therefore unattuned to the need for eternal vigilance against the transnational terrorist threats so prevalent elsewhere. This factor alone must send disquieting reverberations to other parts of the globe as yet unaffected by international terrorism. *No* country can any longer feel completely secure. In 1992 and again in 1994, Argentina – another state located in a part of the world traditionally outside the ambit of international terrorism – became tragically enmeshed in far-distant struggles with the massive truck bombings of the Israeli embassy in Buenos Aires and, two years later, of a Jewish community centre in the same city.

Third, the bombings themselves do not appear to have been undertaken by a specific existing or identifiable terrorist organization. Instead, the Kenyan and Tanzanian attacks are believed to have been financed by a millionaire Saudi Arabian dissident, Osama bin Laden, as part of his worldwide campaign against the United States. In the months before the bombings, bin Laden not only publicly declared war on the United States because of its support for Israel and the presence of American military forces in Saudi Arabia, but had issued a *fatwa*, thereby endowing his calls for violence with an incontrovertible theological as well as political justification. In the wake of this edict, an estimated four to five thousand individuals scattered throughout the Muslim world are reported to have pledged their loyalty to bin Laden and are allegedly prepared to follow his summons to battle.

Fourth, in contrast to the explicit, intelligible demands of the familiar, predominantly secular terrorist groups, most of which in the past claimed credit for and explained their violent acts, no credible claim of responsibility for the embassy bombings has ever been issued. To date, the only information that has come to light has been in the form of a vague message justifying the bombings in terms of defending the Muslim holy places in Mecca and Medina and promising to 'pursue US forces and strike at US interests everywhere'.[35] The resurgence of terrorism motivated by a religious imperative could hardly be more palpable.

Finally, this type of indiscriminate attack by an enigmatic adversary, accompanied by hazy claims and broad demands, is typical of a pattern of international terrorism observed increasingly in recent years, whereby an *ad hoc* gathering of like-minded individuals appears to be brought together for a specific mission – sometimes only a one-off – for which they emerge from obscurity and after which they are meant to vanish as suddenly into thin air. This trend represents a very different threat from that posed by the more familiar, traditional terrorist adversaries – and one potentially far more lethal.

The absence of any publicly identified central command authority may play a critical role in removing any inhibitions on the terrorists' intention to inflict widespread, indiscriminate casualties. Further, the anonymity intrinsic to this type of operation, coupled with the lack of a discernible organizational structure with a distinguishable command chain behind the attackers (as was common to terrorist groups in the past), is deliberately designed both to thwart easy identification and to facilitate the perpetrators' escape and evasion of detection. The main evidence linking bin Laden to the embassy bombings came in the first instance from a Palestinian or Jordanian man arrested in Pakistan, who arrived from Kenya on the day of the explosions travelling on a false Yemeni passport. Had it not been for a fortuitously alert immigration official in Karachi, even this tenuous connection might never have materialized.

These new types of adversaries impose new limits on the means and measures that the United States and other similarly afflicted nations can bring to bear in countering them. The so-called 'privatization' of terrorism, encapsulated by bin Laden's allegedly pivotal role in funding and supporting anti-American terrorism worldwide and the East

Africa bombings in particular, raises a new battery of problems that are certain to make combating terrorism even more difficult than it has been in the past.

In this particular case, less than two weeks after the embassy attacks the Clinton administration dramatically decided to act on the confession extracted by Pakistani authorities from the bin Laden follower they had arrested, backed up by corroborative information from America's intelligence agencies. The result was the coordinated cruise missile attacks launched against terrorist targets in Afghanistan and what was alleged to be a chemical weapons factory in the Sudan – attacks mounted, the President and his advisers strenuously claimed, to pre-empt impending further terrorist outrages.

With this operation, America's struggle against terrorism crossed a new threshold. It was not, of course, the first time that the United States had used military force in response to terrorist provocation. In April 1986 US warplanes had bombed Libya in retaliation for the country's role in the bombing of a West Berlin discothèque frequented by US sevicemen; and in June 1993 American cruise missiles destroyed Saddam Hussein's secret service headquarters in Baghdad after an Iraqi plot to assassinate former President Bush on a visit to Kuwait was thwarted.

The more recent air strikes, however, differed from these previous incidents in one critical respect. The attacks on Libya and Iraq were targeted at the governments of sovereign nations that had been *directly* implicated in the terrorist activities of which they were accused. In the 1998 cruise missile raids, however, the US strikes were aimed at neither Afghanistan nor the Sudan itself: instead, the Clinton administration had singled out a private individual, bin Laden, as the provocation for, and target of, the missile attacks, evidencing little regard for either the two countries' ruling governments or their international rights as bona fide members of the United Nations.

Further, the US government justified the missile attacks not on retaliatory grounds – as in the Libyan and Iraqi cases – but in terms of the right to self-defence contained in Article 51 of the UN Charter. This was a critical distinction for the United States to have made. For, whereas simple reprisal is not considered a legitimate reason for resort to force in international law, the right to self-defence, under the UN Charter, permits a country legitimately to take military action to pre-empt an attack that is perceived to be imminent. And only a day before the US strikes bin Laden himself had declared publicly that his followers were poised to launch new attacks against American citizens and targets worldwide.

Given these circumstances and this explicitly voiced threat, was it reasonable to expect a country that had already been victim to two massive terrorist attacks to sit back passively and await yet another? Indeed, might not continued inaction have been construed by the terrorists as confirmation that they could proceed with impunity, thereby encouraging further attack? Accordingly, the United States decided to act by targeting the sites in Afghanistan on the grounds that they were used by bin Laden and his followers to train terrorists and therefore presumably as bases from which to mount attacks. The Khartoum factory was targeted somewhat more controversially, on the basis of intelligence of bin Laden's previous financial investment in that facility alongside his acknowledged interest in acquiring chemical weapons. Significantly, both military operations were portentously heralded by Secretary of State Madeleine Albright as the first blow in 'the war of the future', thereby promising further – even continued – American offensive action, as needed.[36] Never before had the US struggle against terrorism been so specifically couched in such terms – no doubt in order to send a powerful deterrent message to bin Laden, his followers and any countries that might be providing them with sanctuary and support.

Over the months since the cruise missile attacks, the US response has been debated – and decried – with increasing fervour. But even while the legitimacy of the American attacks remains an issue of intense and often polemical debate, one thing is clear: a new era of terrorism has begun, with the potential to inflict injury, death and destruction on a scale greater than ever before. The challenge the US and other governments face is to avoid the fate of the apocryphal German generals who, on the eve of the First World War, prepared to fight the last war – a comfortably familiar conflict that they were serenely confident they could again win. No country today facing the threat of terrorism, with the fear of terrorist use of weapons of mass destruction, can afford similarly to rest on laurels won in previous conflicts or on ephemeral successes.

In countering and deterring these future terrorist threats, the most urgent and pressing need is continually to improve intelligence capabilities. Just as terrorism itself is dynamic and constantly evolving, so too must governmental capabilities and responses improve and adapt. In no area is this more critical than in the realm of HUMINT – human intelligence. Clearly, the controversy that has raged over whether the Sudanese factory was actually manufacturing the chemical precursors to VX nerve gas is testimony to the need for up-to-date, completely accurate intelligence of a type obtainable only from reliable, on-the-spot agents and sources.

Success in the struggle against terrorism will to a large extent depend also on continued, and continually strengthened, international cooperation – as evident in the helpful assistance provided by Kenyan, Tanzanian and Pakistani authorities to the FBI and other American investigators. While this is an especially positive and welcome development, like much counterterrorist activity it is inherently reactive in nature and, in the case of the embassy bombings, akin to closing the barn door after the horse has escaped. In the future, therefore, if governments are effectively to prevent and pre-empt other such attacks, increased and strengthened multinational intelligence sharing and law enforcement cooperation on a more regular and systematic basis will be critical. Given the transnational dimension of many of these threats – for example, bin Laden's alleged complementary global financial and terror networks; the Aum Shinrikyo sect's activities not only in Japan but in Russia and Australia; and the network of Algerian Islamic extremists operating across Europe as well as in Algeria itself – any response that is to yield results will have to involve enhanced binational and multinational intelligence exchange, cooperation over extradition, the enactment of more formal accords and treaties both between individual countries and on a more comprehensive basis, and the coordination of national policies to monitor, prevent, pre-empt and judicially resolve terrorist acts. The UN resolution passed in December 1997 that defined indiscriminate attacks on civilians, such as those caused by bombings, as terrorist acts is clearly a step in the right direction.

At the same time, perhaps the most sobering realization that arises from addressing the phenomenon of terrorism is that the threat and the problems that fuel it can never be eradicated completely. Their complexity, diversity and often idiosyncratic characteristics mean that there is no magic bullet, no single solution to be found and applied *pari passu*. This conclusion, however, reinforces the need for creative solutions if not to solve, then at least to ameliorate both the underlying causes and the violent manifestations. Only in this way will the international community be able prudently, effectively and productively to marshal its resources where and against whom they will have the greatest positive effect.

In sum, the emergence of this new breed of terrorist adversary means that nothing less than a sea-change in our thinking about terrorism and the policies required to counter it will be required. Too often in the past we have lulled ourselves into believing that terrorism was among the least serious or complex of security issues. We cannot afford to go on making this mistake.

A Ray of Hope?

Only eight days after the embassy attacks, news of yet another terrorist tragedy flashed around the world. At eight minutes past three on a busy Saturday afternoon in downtown Omagh, Northern Ireland, a massive car bomb exploded. Some 300 pounds of home-made explosives had been packed into a stolen red Vauxhall Cavalier that the bombers had strategically parked amid the crowds of shoppers and passers-by out for a stroll in the mild August weather on the town's Market Street. Twenty-nine people were killed and 250 injured. Eleven children and twelve women were among the dead in what was desribed as the deadliest attack in nearly thirty years of sectarian violence in the province. The shock and horror were all the more profound given that the IRA had recently declared its second ceasefire in four years, thus prompting many on both sides of the seectarian divide to dare to believe – once again – that the 'troubles' might finally have ended. Like the tragic deaths the previous month of three brothers, aged eleven, nine and seven, who perished in the firebombing of a Catholic housing estate in Ballymoney, Country Antrim, by suspected Loyalist paramilitaries, the carnage at Omagh seemed to bring everyone sharply to their senses. The opprobrium from both sides that was being heaped upon the landmark Good Friday accord suddenly stopped. The tenuous and painstakingly achieved peace was on the verge of being squandered. A precious, fragile opportunity was about to disintegrate.

As leaders of movements with constituencies not entirely dissimilar to those of non-violent, legitimate political parties, the hard men commanding the IRA and its renegade Republican splinter groups, as well as their Protestant counterparts controlling the various Loyalist paramilitary groups, arguably had no choice but to respond to the popular outcry for peace and normality that had been behind both the original 1994 ceasefires and the Good Friday agreement. Regardless of whether any of these men or their organizations believe that a lasting peace is actually attainable, they have nonetheless been repeatedly forced by popular pressure at least to allow the process of seeking it to go forward – if only to retain their bases of support.

The deaths at Omagh and Ballymoney, however, are salutary reminders of how easily progress can be reversed and how even great achievements, worthy of the Nobel Prize, and be cruelly vitiated. They also provide additional proof – were any needed – that the hard men on both sides have neither gone away nor gone soft. The daily regimen of punishment beatings still meted out by paramilitary 'enforcers' to adolescent car thieves and other petty criminals, the continued extortion and blackmail of businesses in the province, and the unabated intimidation of jurors and witnesses in criminal court cases demonstrate how far Northern Ireland still has to go to realize the promise of peace and normality that its people so ardently desire. Here as everywhere, the struggle against terrorism is far from over.

Notes

Chapter 1

1   *The Oxford English Dictionary, Compact Edition* (Oxford: Oxford University Press, 1971), p. 3268, col. 216.
2   Ibid.
3   David Rapoport, 'Terrorism', in Mary Hawkesworth and Maurice Kogan (eds), *Routledge Encyclopedia of Government and Politics*, vol. 2 (London: Routledge, 1992), p. 1061.
4   Quoted in R. R. Palmer, *The Age of the Democratic Revolution*, vol. 2: *The Struggle* (Princeton, NJ: Princeton University Press, 1970), p. 126.
5   Quoted ibid., p. 124.
6   Walter Laqueur, *The Age of Terrorism* (Boston: Little, Brown, 1987), p. 11.
7   Quoted in *OED, Compact Edition*, p. 3268, col. 216.
8   It should be noted that the phrase itself was popularized by Paul Brousse, the French physician turned anarchist, in the newspaper he founded and edited, *L'Avant-Garde*. See David Stafford, *From Anarchism to Reformism: A Study of the Political Activities of Paul Brousse within the First International and the French Socialist Movement 1870–90* (Toronto: University of Toronto Press, 1971), pp. 76–88, 123–4. The text of the article may be found on pp. 256–9.
9   Quoted in George Woodcock (ed.), *The Anarchist Reader* (Glasgow: Fontana, 1977), pp. 43–4.

10Interestingly, the group was staunchly opposed to terrorism in democratic, open societies such as the United States. In 1881, for example, the executive committee of Narodnaya Volya publicly denounced for this reason the alleged anarchist political motive behind the assassination that year of US President James Garfield. As Grant Wardlaw explains, Narodnaya Volya believed that terrorism could only be justified in extreme circumstances and denounced all such actions in countries which permitted 'normal political activity': see *Political Terrorism: Theory, Tactics, and Counter-measures* (Cambridge: Cambridge University Press, 1990), p. 23.

11Lavrov quoted in Zeev Ivianksi, 'Fathers and Sons: A Study of Jewish Involvement in the Revolutionary Movement and Terrorism in Tsarist Russia', *Terrorism and Political Violence*, vol. 1, no. 2 (April 1989), p. 146.

12The successor group active in 1905 is detailed above. In 1887 another group – which included Vladimir Lenin's older brother – attempted to assassinate Alexander III. They too were arrested and hanged. See Vera Broido, *Apostles into Terrorists: Women and the Revolutionary Movement in the Russia of Alexander II* (London: Maurice Temple Smith, 1977), pp. 198–203.

13The anarchist, it should be noted, was neither necessarily nor exclusively violent. Indeed, many remained simply intellectuals, advocating freedom of all types, while abjuring and condemning the use of violence.

14Quoted in James Joll, *The Anarchists* (Boston and Toronto: Little, Brown, 1964), p. 145.

15For example, in addition to McKinley, anarchists attempted to assassinate the German Kaiser in 1878 and murdered the president of Italy in 1894, King Umberto I of Italy in 1900, Empress Elizabeth of Austria-Hungary in 1898, and the prime ministers of Spain in 1897 and 1912, and were implicated in the 1886 Haymarket Square bombing in Chicago and in other incidents such as François-Claudius Ravachol's bombings of Paris's boulevard St Germain in 1892, and Emile Henry's bombing of the Café Terminus in 1894.

16As Joll recounts: 'The violence of this propaganda and the explicit incitement contained in pamphlets like [Johann] Most's ... *Science of Revolutionary Warfare* ("a manual of instruction in the use and preparation of Nitro-glycerine, Dynamite, Gun-cotton, Fulminating Mercury, Bombs, Fuses, Poisons, etc.") all contributed to the anarchists' being held responsible for any violent disturbances': *The Anarchists*, p. 141.

17 Kachig Toloyan, 'Martyrdom as Legitimacy: Terrorism, Religion and Symbolic Appropriation in the Armenian Diaspora', in Paul Wilkinson and A. M. Stewart (eds), *Contemporary Research on Terrorism* (Aberdeen: Aberdeen University Press, 1987), pp. 90–1.

18 See Roland Gaucher, *Les Terroristes* (Paris: Editions Albin Michel, 1965), pp. 181–9.

19 The second is Hitler's 'Final Solution' involving the Jews, and the third Pol Pot's reign of terror in Cambodia after 1975.

20 Laurence Lafore, *The Long Fuse: An Interpretation of the Origins of World War I* (London: Weidenfeld & Nicolson, 1966), p. 180.

21 Ibid.

22 The names of both the Black Hand and Dmitrievich were again invoked in July 1997 in threats issued against British peacekeeping forces stationed in Bosnia as part of the NATO-led Stabilization Force, SFOR.

23 Imanuel Geiss (ed.), *July 1914: The Outbreak of the First World War* (New York: W. W. Norton, 1967), p. 52.

24 Ibid., pp. 52–3. See also Vladimir Dedijer, *The Road to Sarajevo* (London: MacGibbon & Kee, 1967), pp. 393–5.

25 Quoted in Laqueur, *The Age of Terrorism*, p. 66.

26 Quoted in Alan Bullock, *Hitler: A Study in Tyranny* (New York: Harper, 1958), pp. 239–40.

27 Robert Conquest, *The Great Terror* (Harmondsworth: Penguin, 1971), p. 14.

28 Robert C. Tucker, *Stalin in Power: The Revolution from Above, 1928–1941* (New York and London: W. W. Norton, 1990), p. 271.

29 Yassir Arafat, 'Address to the UN General Assembly (November 13, 1974)', in Walter Laqueur (ed.), *The Israel–Arab Reader: A Documentary History of the Middle East Conflict* (New York: Bantam, 1976), p. 510.

30 Claire Sterling, *The Terror Network: The Secret War of International Terrorism* (New York: Holt, Rinehart & Winston,

1981). See also Ray S. Cline and Yonah Alexander, *Terrorism: The Soviet Connection* (New York: Crane Russak, 1984); and, by far the least polemical of this genre, Roberta Goren (ed. Jillian Becker), *The Soviet Union and Terrorism* (London: Allen & Unwin, 1984).

31   See e.g. Brian Michael Jenkins, *New Modes of Conflict* (Santa Monica, CA: RAND Corporation, R-3009-DNA, June 1983), pp. 13–14; Brian Michael Jenkins, *International Terrorism: The Other World War* (Santa Monica, CA: RAND Corporation, R-3302-AF, November 1985), pp. 19–20; David C. Martin and John Walcott, *Best Laid Plans: The Inside Story of America's War Against Terrorism* (New York: Harper & Row, 1988), p. 46.

32   The term was first coined by the French criminologist and expert on insurgency, Xavier Raufer, in 1991.

33   Rachel Ehrenfeld, *Narco-terrorism* (New York: Basic Books, 1990), pp. ix, xiii.

34   Two particularly informative discussions about the myth of 'narco-terrorism' and the political baggage the term carried with it can be found in Grant Wardlaw, 'Linkages Between the Illegal Drugs Traffic and Terrorism', *Conflict Quarterly*, vol. 8, no. 3 (Summer 1988), pp. 5–26, and Abraham H. Miller and Nicholas A. Damask, 'The Dual Myths of "Narco-terrorism": How Myths Drive Policy', *Terrorism and Political Violence*, vol. 8, no. 1 (Spring 1996), pp. 114–31.

35   Peter Lupsha, 'Gray Area Phenomenon: New Threats and Policy Dilemmas', unpublished paper quoted by Ambassador Edwin G. Corr, 'Introduction', in Max G. Manwaring (ed.), *Gray Area Phenomena: Confronting the New World Disorder* (Boulder, CO: Westview, 1993), p. xiii.

36   Xavier Raufer, 'Gray Areas: A New Security Threat', *Political Warfare*, no. 19 (Spring 1992), p. 1.

37   Bruce Hoffman, 'Low-intensity Conflict: Terrorism and Guerrilla Warfare in the Coming Decades', in Lawrence Howard (ed.), *Terrorism: Roots, Impact, Responses* (New York: Praeger, 1992), p. 140.

38   See e.g. John [Johann] Most, 'Advice for Terrorists', in Walter Laqueur and Yonah Alexander (eds), *The Terrorism Reader* (New York: Meridian, 1987), pp. 100–9; David Rapoport, 'The Politics of

Atrocity', in Yonah Alexander and Seymour Maxwell Finger (eds), *Terrorism: Interdisciplinary Perspectives* (New York: John Jay Press, 1977), p. 46.

39 See e.g. the treatises written by two group members: Nikolai Morozov, 'The Terrorist Struggle', and G. Tarnovski, 'Terrorism and Routine', in Laqueur and Alexander (eds), *The Terrorism Reader*, pp. 72–9; also Broido, *Apostles into Terrorists*, p. 180.

40 Rapoport, 'The Politics of Atrocity', p. 46; Joseph Heller, *The Stern Gang: Ideology, Politics and Terror 1940–1949* (London: Frank Cass, 1995), pp. 104, 115, 125.

41 Martha Crenshaw, *Terrorism and International Cooperation*, Occasional Paper Series 11 (New York: Institute for East–West Security Studies, 1989), p. 5.

42 Carlos Marighela (trans. John Butt and Rosemary Sheed), *For the Liberation of Brazil* (Harmondsworth: Penguin, 1971), pp. 62, 89.

43 Quoted in Julian Nundy, 'Wounded Jackal Defends Record of Family Values', *Independent* (London), 31 August 1994.

44 Quoted in Hala Jaber, *Hezbollah: Born with a Vengeance* (New York: Columbia University Press, 1997), p. 130.

45 Konrad Kellen, *On Terrorists and Terrorism* (Santa Monica, CA: RAND Corporation, N-1942-RC, December 1982), p. 10.

46 Quoted in Alison Jamieson, *Terrorism* (Hove, E. Sussex: Wayland Publishers, 1991), p. 33.

47 See e.g. Crenshaw, *Terrorism and International Cooperation*, p. 5; Brian Michael Jenkins, *The Study of Terrorism: Definitional Problems* (Santa Monica, CA: RAND Corporation, P-6563, December 1980), p. 10; Gary Sick, 'The Political Underpinnings of Terrorism', in Charles W. Kegley Jr (ed.), *International Terrorism: Characteristics, Causes, Controls* (New York: St Martin's Press, 1990), p. 52; Paul Wilkinson, 'Terrorism', in Michael Foley (ed.), *Ideas that Shape Politics* (Manchester: Manchester University Press, 1994), p. 189.

48 Jenkins, *The Study of Terrorism*, p. 10.

49 Quoted in Harris O. Schoenberg, *A Mandate for Terror: The United Nations and the PLO* (New York: Shapolsky Books, 1989), p. 71.

50 Quoted in Frederick J. Hacker, *Crusaders, Criminals, Crazies: Terror and Terrorism in Our Time* (New York: W. W. Norton, 1976), p. 174.

51 Quoted in Schoenberg, *A Mandate for Terror*, pp. 75–6.

52   Quoted in Hacker, *Crusaders, Criminals, Crazies*, p. 274.

53   Quoted in Abraham D. Sofaer, 'Terrorism and the Law', *Foreign Affairs*, vol. 64, no. 5 (Summer 1986), p. 904.

54   Quoted in Albert Parry, *Terrorism: From Robespierre to Arafat* (New York: Vanguard, 1976), p. 552.

55   North Atlantic Assembly Papers, Sub-Committee on Terrorism, *Terrorism* (Brussels: International Secretariat, January 1989), p. 34.

56   Jenkins, *The Study of Terrorism*, p. 2.

57   A brief discussion of this dichotomy may be found in 'What is Terrorism?', *The Economist* (London), 2 March 1996, pp. 23–5.

58   Quoted in Sofaer, 'Terrorism and the Law', p. 904.

59   Alex P. Schmid, Albert J. Jongman et al., *Political Terrorism: A New Guide to Actors, Authors, Concepts, Data Bases, Theories, and Literature* (New Brunswick, NJ: Transaction Books, 1988), p. 12.

60   Quoted in Christopher Dobson, *Black September: Its Short, Violent History* (London: Robert Hale, 1974, 1975), pp. 62–3.

61   'Arab Leaders Join World in Assailing Terrorists' Attack', *Los Angeles Times*, 19 December 1973.

62   'The Arab Terrorists', *New York Times*, 18 December 1973.

63   Juan de Onis, 'Guerrilla Unit Attacks Cairo Proposal', *New York Times*, 21 June 1973.

64   John K. Cooley, 'New Arab Unity Hits Palestinian Guerrillas', *Christian Science Monitor* (Boston), 19 September 1973; Joseph Fitchett, 'Guerrillas Seeking Leverage', *Christian Science Monitor*, 27 November 1973.

65   'Syrian Clampdown on Fatah Guerrillas Told', *Los Angeles Times*, 20 September 1973.

66   Jonathan C. Randal, 'Guerrillas Fear Trade-off of Interests', *Washington Post*, 12 October 1973; Jim Hoagland, 'Palestinian Guerrillas Say They Reject Cease-fire', *Washington Post*, 23 October 1973.

67   Rapoport, 'The Politics of Atrocity', p. 46.

68   '30 More Slain By "Terrorists" Near Algiers', *International Herald Tribune* (Paris), 15 April 1997.

69   James F. Clarity, 'Obscure Doctor Again Faces Sinn Fein Chief', *International Herald Tribune* (Paris), 15 April 1997.

70   'In Our Pages: 100, 75 and 50 Years Ago – 1947: Zionists' Suicide', *International Herald Tribune* (Paris), 22 April 1997.

71 '39 Killed in Jerusalem Headquarters', *The Times* (London), 23 July 1946; '41 Dead, 53 Injured, 52 Missing, in Terrorist Attack on Secretariat', *Palestine Post* (Jerusalem), 23 July 1946.

72 Rapoport, 'The Politics of Atrocity', p. 46.

73 Office of the Coordinator for Counterterrorism, *Patterns of Global Terrorism 1996*, US Department of State Publication 10433 (Washington, DC: State Department, April 1997), p. vi.

74 Terrorist Research and Analytical Center, National Security Division, Federal Bureau of Investigation, *Terrorism in the United States 1995* (Washington, DC: US Department of Justice, 1996), p. ii.

75 United States Departments of the Army and the Air Force, *Military Operations in Low Intensity Conflict*, Field Manual 100-20/Air Force Pamphlet 3-20 (Washington, DC: Headquarters, Departments of the Army and the Air Force, 1990), p. 3-1.

76 Brian M. Jenkins, 'International Terrorism: A New Mode of Conflict', in David Carlton and Carlo Schaerf (eds), *International Terrorism and World Security* (London: Croom Helm, 1975), p. 16.

77 Alex P. Schmid, *Political Terrorism: A Research Guide* (New Brunswick, NJ: Transaction Books, 1984), p. x.

78 Schmid, Jongman et al., *Political Terrorism*, p. 1.

79 Walter Laqueur, *Terrorism* (London: Weidenfeld & Nicolson, 1977), p. 7; Laqueur, *The Age of Terrorism*, pp. 11, 142–56.

80 The 'study of terrorism', Laqueur further argued, 'can manage with a minimum of theory'. Quoted in Schmid, Jongman et al., *Political Terrorism*, p. 3.

81 Schmid, Jongman et al., *Political Terrorism*, p. 6.

82 As Laqueur notes, 'The distinction is of more than academic importance; there have been guerrilla units of ten thousand men and women but an urban terrorist unit seldom, if ever, comprises more than a few people and urban terrorist "movements" rarely consist of more than a few hundred members.' See Walter Laqueur, *Guerrilla: A Historical and Critical Study* (Boston and Toronto: Little, Brown, 1976), p. xi.

83 Central Intelligence Agency, *Guide to the Analysis of Insurgency* (Washington, DC: US Government Printing Office, no date), p. 2.

84 Kellen, *On Terrorists and Terrorism*, p. 9.

85 Ibid., p. 10.

Chapter 2

1   B. H. Liddell Hart, *History of the Second World War* (New York: Paragon Books, 1979), p. 233.

2   See e.g. General George Grivas's observations concerning the impact of these promises on post-war Greek-Cypriot nationalist aspirations, in Charles Foley (ed.), *The Memoirs of General Grivas* (London: Longmans, 1964), p. 12.

3   David Thomson, *Europe since Napoleon* (Harmondsworth: Penguin, 1978), p. 778.

4   Text of the 'Joint Declaration by the President and the Prime Minister, August 12, 1941' in Winston S. Churchill, *The Second World War*, vol. 3: *The Grand Alliance* (London: The Reprint Society, 1956), p. 352.

5   Winston S. Churchill, *The Second World War*, vol. 4: *The Hinge of Fate* (London: The Reprint Society, 1956), p. 705.

6   Quoted in Alistair Horne, *A Savage War of Peace: Algeria 1954–1962* (Harmondsworth: Penguin, 1977), p. 42.

7   Quoted in Foley (ed.), *The Memoirs of General Grivas*, p. 13.

8   Menachem Begin, *The Revolt: Story of the Irgun* (Jerusalem: Steimatzky, 1977), p. 52.

9   Quoted in Bruce Hoffman, 'Jewish Terrorist Activities and the British Government in Palestine 1939 to 1947', unpublished D.Phil thesis, Oxford University, 1986, pp. 327–8.

10   Begin, *The Revolt*, pp. 52–4.

11   Ibid., p. 56.

12   Carlos Marighela (trans. John Butt and Rosemary Sheed), *For the Liberation of Brazil* (Harmondsworth: Penguin, 1971), pp. 61–97.

13   Begin, *The Revolt*, p. 52.

14   *Hansard*, House of Commons, vol. 441, col. 2342 (Oliver Stanley), 12 August 1947.

15   Begin, *The Revolt*, pp. 54–5.

16   See texts of 80th Congress, House Joint Resolution 196, introduced by Andrew Somers on 15 May 1947, and Senate Resolution 149, introduced by Warren Magnusson et al. on 17 July 1947, in Isaac Zaar, *Rescue and Liberation: America's Part in the Birth of Israel* (New York: Bloch, 1954), pp. 230, 243; House Joint

Resolution 237, introduced by Somers on 11 July 1947, quoted in Hoffman, 'Jewish Terrorist Activities', p. 370.

17 Quoted in Michael J. Cohen, *Palestine and the Great Powers, 1945–1948* (Princeton, NJ: Princeton University Press, 1982), p. 250.

18 Elizabeth Monroe, 'Mr Bevin's "Arab Policy"', in Albert Hourani (ed.), St Antony's Papers no. 11, *Middle Eastern Affairs No. 2* (London: Chatto & Windus, 1961), p. 34.

19 For details of UNSCOP's visit and deliberations, see Jorge Garcia-Granados, *The Birth of Israel: The Drama as I Saw It* (New York: Knopf, 1948). Garcia-Granados was the Guatemalan representative on the committee.

20 The special committee issued its report on 31 August 1947 and unanimously recommended that Palestine should be granted its independence. See 'Summary of the Report of UNSCOP', in Walter Laqueur (ed.), *The Israel–Arab Reader: A Documentary History of the Middle East Conflict* (New York: Bantam, 1976), pp. 108–12.

21 Creech-Jones Papers (Rhodes House, Oxford), Boxes 32/3 and 32/6, Letters, Creech-Jones to Munro [*sic*], 23 October, 30 November 1961.

22 'Only Thus' was the Irgun's motto. See 'Speech of the Commander-in-Chief of the Irgun Zvai Le'umi, 15 May 1948', in Eli Tavin and Yonah Alexander (eds), *Psychological Warfare and Propaganda: Irgun Documentation* (Wilmington, DE: Scholarly Resources, 1982), pp. 240–1.

23 Foley (ed.), *The Memoirs of General Grivas*, p. 47.

24 Quoted in Horne, *A Savage War of Peace*, p. 95.

25 Foley (ed.), *The Memoirs of General Grivas*, p. 208.

26 Quoted in Horne, *A Savage War of Peace*, p. 95.

27 General Grivas (trans. A. A. Pallis), *Guerrilla Warfare and Eoka's Struggle* (London: Longmans, 1964), p. 19.

28 Appendix 1 in Foley (ed.), *The Memoirs of General Grivas*, p. 204.

29 Foley (ed.), *The Memoirs of General Grivas*, p. 31.

30 Grivas, *Guerrilla Warfare*, p. 19.

31 Ibid., p. 38.

32 Foley (ed.), *The Memoirs of General Grivas*, p. 53.

33 Ibid., pp. 56–7; Michael Dewar, *Brush Fire Wars: Minor Campaigns*

of the British Army since 1945 (New York: St Martin's Press, 1984), p. 80.

34   Foley (ed.), *The Memoirs of General Grivas*, p. 71.

35   Charles Foley and W. I. Scobie, *The Struggle for Cyprus* (Stanford, CA: Hoover Institution Press, 1975), p. 160.

36   Quoted in Alan Hart, *Arafat: A Political Biography. The Definitive Biography Written in Co-operation with Yasser Arafat* (London: Sidgwick & Jackson, 1994), pp. 112–13. See also John K. Cooley, *Green March, Black September: The Story of the Palestinian Arabs* (London: Frank Cass, 1973), p. 91; David Hirst, *The Gun and the Olive Branch* (London: Futura, 1977), pp. 273, 276, 306–7; Edgar O'Ballance, *Arab Guerilla Power* (London: Faber, 1974), pp. 23, 26; Zeev Schiff and Raphael Rothstein, *Fedayeen: The Story of the Palestinian Guerrillas* (London: Valentine, Mitchell, 1972), pp. 8, 60.

37   Nelson Mandela, *Long Walk to Freedom* (London: Abacus, 1994), pp. 326, 355.

38   Quoted in Roland Gaucher, *Les Terroristes* (Paris: Editions Albin Michel, 1965), p. 262.

39   Quoted in Horne, *A Savage War of Peace*, p. 186.

40   Quoted ibid., p. 194.

41   Quoted in George Armstrong Kelly, *Lost Soldiers: The French Army and Empire in Crisis, 1947–1962* (Cambridge, MA: MIT Press, 1965), p. 201.

Chapter 3

1   Quoted in Alex P. Schmid and Janny de Graaf, *Violence as Communication: Insurgent Terrorism and the Western News Media* (London and Beverly Hills, CA: Sage, 1982), p. 32.

2   Between 1968 and 1980, Palestinian groups were responsible for 331 incidents compared with the 170 incidents attributed to the next most active group, the anti-Castro Cuban terrorist movements, and Irish and Turkish groups in third position with 115 incidents each (RAND–St Andrews Chronology of International Terrorist Incidents: see note 12 below).

3   Quoted in David Hirst, *The Gun and the Olive Branch* (London: Futura, 1977), p. 304.

4   Quoted in Schmid and de Graaf, *Violence as Communication*, p. 30.

5   Abu Iyad with Eric Rouleau (trans. Linda Butler Koseoglu), *My Home, My Land: A Narrative of the Palestinian Struggle* (New York: Times Books, 1981), pp. 111–12.

6   John K. Cooley, *Green March, Black September: The Story of the Palestinian Arabs* (London: Frank Cass, 1973), p. 126; Hirst, *The Gun and the Olive Branch*, p. 311. The American ABC network alone had 400 broadcast staff present. See James W. Hoge, 'The Media and Terrorism', in Abraham Miller (ed.), *Terrorism: The Media and the Law* (New York: Transnational, 1982), p. 96.

7   Peter Taylor, *States of Terror: Democracy and Political Violence* (London: Penguin, 1993), p. 8.

8   Guy R. Sanan, 'Olympic Security 1972–1996: Threat, Response, and International Cooperation', unpublished Ph.D. thesis, St Andrews University, 1997, p. 77.

9   Quoted in Christopher Dobson and Ronald Payne, *The Carlos Complex: A Study in Terror* (London: Coronet/Hodder & Stoughton, 1978), pp. 17–18.

10   *Al-Sayad* (Beirut), 13 September 1972, quoted ibid., p. 102. The same communiqué, attributed to George Habash, is quoted in part in Taylor, *States of Terror*, p. 8

11   Schmid and de Graaf, *Violence as Communication*, p. 31.

12   The RAND–St Andrews University Chronology of International Terrorism includes a computerized database of international terrorist incidents that have occurred worldwide from 1968 to the present. The Chronology has been continuously maintained since 1972, first by the renowned American think-tank, the RAND Corporation, in Santa Monica, California, and since 1994 by the Centre for the Study of Terrorism and Political Violence at St Andrews University, Scotland. The incidents in this chronology are concerned with *international terrorism*, defined here as incidents in which terrorists go abroad to strike their targets, select victims or targets that have connections with a foreign state (e.g. diplomats, foreign businessmen, offices of foreign corporations), or create international incidents by attacking airline passengers, personnel and equipment. It excludes violence carried out by terrorists within their own country against their own nationals, and terrorism perpetrated by governments against their own citizens. It

should also be emphasized that the data contained in the Chronology are intended to be illustrative only and do not purport or claim to be a definitive listing of every international terrorist incident that has occurred everywhere since 1968. Its value, accordingly, is as a means of identifying terrorist trends and projecting likely future terrorist patterns.

13   'Interview with ASALA', *Panorama Magazine* (Milan), 1 September 1980, pp. 62–5.

14   Armenian Secret Army for the Liberation of Armenia, *The Reality* (ASALA, no date), p. 4; repr. as 'Booklet Giving History of ASALA's Existence Gives New Insight Into the Revolutionary Movement', *The Armenian Reporter* (New York), 10 January 1985.

15   Moorad Mooradian, 'Terrorists Speak: Interviews with ASALA Members', unpublished paper, no date, pp. 15–16.

16   'Armenians Turning to Terrorism', *Los Angeles Times*, 25 January 1981.

17   'The Portrait of an Armenian Terrorist Leader', *Le Matin* (Paris), quoted in 'French Paper Provides Information on ASALA Leader Hagopian', *Mamara* (Istanbul), 16 January 1985.

18   Gerard Chaliand and Yves Ternon (trans. Tony Berrett), *The Armenians: From Genocide to Resistance* (London: Zed, 1983), p. 6.

19   Andrew Corsun, *Research Papers on Terrorism – Armenian Terrorism: 1975–1980* (Washington, DC: Office of Security Threat Analysis Group, US Department of State, 1982), p. 1.

20   Mark Armen Aryanian and John Z. Ayanian, 'Armenian Political Violence on American Network News: An Analysis of Content', *Armenian Review*, vol. 40, no. 1-157 (Spring 1987), p. 28.

21   Alex P. Schmid and Janny de Graaf, *Insurgent Terrorism and the Western News Media: An Exploratory Analysis with a Dutch Case Study* (Leiden: Center for the Study of Social Conflicts (COMT), Dutch State University, The Netherlands, November 1980), quoted in Brian Michael Jenkins, *The Psychological Implications of Media-covered Terrorism* (Santa Monica, CA: RAND Corporation, P-6627, June 1981), p. 7.

22   'The Palestinians of the 1990s', *Foreign Report* (London), no. 2202, 2 April 1992.

23   Quoted in I. Fetscher and G. Rohrmoser, *Analysen zum Terrorismus (Analyses on the Subject of Terrorism)*, vol. 1: *Ideologien und*

Strategien (*Ideologies and Strategies*) (Bonn: Westdeutscher Verlag, 1981), p. 301.

24   Christoph Wackerngel, 'Transcript of a Talk by Christoph Wackerngel', 14 September 1995, unpublished, p. 1.

25   Eileen MacDonald, *Shoot the Women First* (New York: Random House, 1991), p. 210.

26   Michael 'Bommi' Baumann (trans. Helene Ellenbogen and Wayne Parker), *Terror or Love? Bommi Baumann's Own Story of His Life as a West German Urban Guerrilla* (New York: Grove Press, 1979), pp. 19–20. The book was originally published in Germany in 1971 under the title *Wie alles anfing* (*How It All Began*).

27   Klein had first gained notoriety for his role in the 1975 seizure of the OPEC ministers' meeting in Vienna masterminded by the infamous Carlos, 'The Jackal', the Venezuelan terrorist Ilich Ramirez Sanchez. Seriously wounded during the attack, in 1978 Klein broke with his former comrades and completely disavowed armed struggle as a means to achieve political change.

28   Quoted in Jean Marcel Bougereau, 'Memoirs of an International Terrorist: Conversations with Hans Joachim Klein', in *The German Guerrilla: Terror, Reaction, and Resistance* (Sanday, Orkney: Cienfuegos Press, no date), p. 12. See also the similar statements on pp. 9, 14, 15.

29   See especially 'CHANGE YOUR HATRED INTO ENERGY' (issued by the BLACK FRONT); 'SHALOM & NAPALM' (issued by the BLACK RATS, T.W.); and 'STATION TW', quoted in Baumann, *Terror or Love?*, pp. 56–7, 67–9. For the wider influence of the Vietnam War on German terrorism, see especially the communiqués claiming credit for the attempted assassination of the American commander-in-chief of NATO (and future secretary of state) General Alexander Haig in Obourg, Belgium, on 25 June 1979 and the 'Hunger Strike Declaration of 4 December 1984 by Imprisoned Members of the Red Army Faction', both quoted in Dennis Pluchinksy, 'Western Europe's Red Terrorists: The Fighting Communist Organizations', in Yonah Alexander and Dennis Pluchinsky, *Europe's Red Terrorists: The Fighting Communist Organizations* (London: Frank Cass, 1992), pp. 24, 62.

30   Quoted in Stefan Aust, *The Baader–Meinhof Group: The Inside Story of a Phenomenon* (London: Bodley Head, 1987), p. 366.

31   Baumann, *Terror or Love?*, p. 60. See also p. 59 and the 'SHALOM & NAPALM' communiqué on pp. 67–8.

32   Baumann, *Terror or Love?*, p. 55.

33   David C. Rapoport, 'The International World as Some Terrorists Have Seen It: A Look at a Century of Memoirs', *Journal of Strategic Studies*, vol. 10, no. 4 (December 1987), p. 45.

34   David Th. Schiller, 'From a National to an International Response', in H. H. Tucker (ed.), *Combating the Terrorists: Democratic Responses to Political Violence* (New York and Oxford: Facts on File, 1988), p. 188.

35   James Adams, *The Financing of Terror* (New York: Simon & Schuster, 1986), p. 49.

36   Ibid., p. 243.

37   Ibid., p. 104.

38   Iyad, *My Home, My Land*, p. 221.

39   Christopher Walker, '£194m "Missing" as Arafat Seeks Aid from Britain', *The Times* (London), 14 July 1997.

Chapter 4

1   Quoted in John Kifner, 'Israelis Investigate Far Right; May Crack Down on Speech', *New York Times*, 8 November 1995.

2   *Oxford English Dictionary, Compact Edition* (Oxford: Oxford University Press, 1971), p. 3868, col. 87.

3   See David C. Rapoport, 'Fear and Trembling: Terrorism in Three Religious Traditions', *American Political Science Review*, vol. 78, no. 3 (September 1984), pp. 668–72; Walter Laqueur, *The Age of Terrorism* (Boston: Little, Brown, 1987), pp. 7–8.

4   *OED, Compact Edition*, p. 3311, col. 388.

5   Rapoport, 'Fear and Trembling', pp. 660–4. If one accepts that upwards of a million persons may have been murdered by the Thugs, then on average they killed 833.333 persons a year.

6   *OED, Compact Edition*, p. 125, col. 499.

7   Rapoport, 'Fear and Trembling', p. 659.

8   Numbers of active, *identifiable* terrorist groups from 1968 to the present are derived from the RAND–St Andrews University Chronology of International Terrorist Incidents.

9   Mark Juergensmeyer, 'Terror Mandated by God', *Terrorism and*

Political Violence, vol. 9, no. 2 (Summer 1997), p. 20.

10   Murray Sayle, 'Martyrdom Complex', *New Yorker*, 13 May 1996.

11   Nicholas D. Kristof, 'Japanese Cult Planned US Attack', *International Herald Tribune* (Paris), 24 March 1997; Robert Whymant, 'Cult Planned Gas Raids on America', *The Times* (London), 29 March 1997.

12   The hijackers' plans were foiled, however, after the French authorities learned of their intentions and ordered commandos to storm the aircraft after it had landed for refuelling in Marseilles.

13   Religious terrorists were responsible for 167 of the 287 fatalities in 1995 and committed 71 of that year's 278 incidents. See Bruce Hoffman and Donna Kim Hoffman, 'Chronology of International Terrorism 1995', *Terrorism and Political Violence*, vol. 8, no. 3 (Autumn 1996), pp. 87–127.

14   Ibid.

15   According to the RAND–St Andrews University Chronology of International Terrorist Incidents, between 1982 and 1989 Shi'a terrorist groups committed 247 terrorist incidents and were responsible for 1,057 deaths.

16   Imam Khomeini, *Islam and Revolution* (trans. Hamid Algar) (London: KPI, 1981), pp. 286–7.

17   Quoted in Amir Taheri, *Holy Terror: The Inside Story of Islamic Terrorism* (London: Sphere, 1987), pp. 7–8.

18   Hezbollah was the product of several splits within the Lebanese Shi'a movement. Its origins can be traced back to 1974, when a Lebanese Shi'a cleric, Imam Musa al-Sadr, who had studied in the Iranian holy city of Qom, organized the 'Movement of the Underprivileged' to advance Shi'a interests and improve the community's lowly socio-economic conditions. This movement was subsequently reorganized as the principal Shi'a political party in Lebanon, Amal, which formed its own militia during the civil war that racked Lebanon a year later. In 1979, however, al-Sadr vanished during a visit to Libya. The disappearance of the Imam created a vacuum within Amal that made the party fertile ground for Iranian influence, and rendered the movement susceptible to the fundamentalist call of the revolution which had brought Khomeini to power earlier that year. Nabih Berri, a lawyer, was appointed head of Amal the following year. Hussein Mussawi, the

person quoted above and the alleged mastermind behind the terrorist campaign against Libya to recover the Imam, was named as Berri's deputy and commander of the militia. A fanatical supporter of Khomeini, Mussawi sought to place Amal in the vanguard of a regional revolution based on the new Iranian Islamic Republic. Berri, on the other hand, clung to a moderate line and advocated a new deal for the Shi'a community within the confines of the existing Lebanese state structure. By this time, however, the radicalization of the Shi'a in Lebanon had gone far beyond the narrow nationalist and social aims of Amal. In 1981, Mussawi broke with Berri and founded his own organization, Islamic Amal. Shortly after, another faction split from Amal and under the leadership of Abbas Mussawi (a nephew of Hussein) and the 'spiritual guidance' of Shiekh Muhammed Hussein Fadlallah, it soon came to be known as the Hezbollah. Like Islamic Amal, Hezbollah embraced Khomeini's summons for a pan-Islamic revolt designed to turn Lebanon into an Iranian-style Islamic republic.

19 'Open Letter from the Party of God to the Disinherited of Lebanon and the World Revealing the Way and the Intentions which are their Own on the Occasion of the First Anniversary of Ragheb Harb, Symbol of the Islamic Resistance and Exemplary Martyr', issued by Hezbollah, Beirut, Lebanon, 16 February 1985.

20 Ayatollah Muhammed Hussein Fadl Allah (*sic*), 'Islam and Violence in Political Reality', *Middle East Insight*, vol. 4, nos. 4–5 (1986), pp. 4–13. See also the quote from Fadlallah's book *Invisible Armies* in Alison Jamieson, *Terrorism* (Hove, E. Sussex: Wayland, 1991), p. 33: 'We don't see ourselves as terrorists, because we don't believe in terrorism . . . We don't see resisting the occupier as a terrorist action. We see ourselves as *mujihadeen* who fight a Holy War for the people. Faith, whether religious or political, is all. To the individual terrorist, or supporter of terrorism, a murder can be an expression of the defence of freedom; a car-bomb which kills civilians can be a blow struck in a war of liberation; a kidnapping and murder can be a step towards justice. The intensity of conviction that justifies one man's justice at any price almost inevitably means that the freedom or justice of others will be ignored, or at worst trampled and destroyed.'

21   Quoted in Laura Marlowe, 'A Fiery Cleric's Defense of Jihad',
     Time (New York), 15 January 1996.

22   Quoted in draft copy of the *United States Department of Defense
     Commission on the Beirut International Airport (BIA) Terrorist Act
     of October 23, 1983* (known as 'The Long Commission' in refer-
     ence to its chairman, retired Admiral Robert L. J. Long, US Navy),
     p. 38.

23   Armed Islamic Group communiqué, containing a twelve-page
     interview with Antar Zouabri, September 1996.

24   Hamas was founded in 1987 by Sheikh Amad Ibrahim Yassin. Its
     estimated $70 million annual budget is derived mostly from contri-
     butions by Iran and Saudi Arabia, although Palestinians and Arabs
     in countries throughout the world (including the United States
     and Britain) also donate funds to the movement. In addition to its
     violent activities, Hamas also provides social services to Palestinian
     communities in the Gaza Strip and West Bank, including schools,
     medical assistance and related welfare activities. In this respect,
     Hamas is consciously emulating the success of both the PLO and
     Hezbollah in providing social services while simultaneously
     waging a violent terrorist campaign.

25   Quoted in ADL Special Background Report, *Hamas, Islamic Jihad
     and the Muslim Brotherhood: Islamic Extremists and the Terrorist
     Threat to America* (New York: Anti-Defamation League of B'nai
     B'rith, 1993), p. 4.

26   As Fathi Shiqaqi, the general secretary of the Jihad Movement,
     whom it is believed was assassinated by the Israeli secret services in
     Malta in 1995, once explained: 'Our struggle with the enemy in
     Palestine is meant to open every possible form of jihad, including
     suicide attacks. The enemy thought he had closed the Palestine file
     when he signed the Oslo Agreements and thus could eliminate us.
     That requires us to make a special effort to foil his plot. That is why
     suicide bombers are important.' Quoted in Rafi Yisra'eli,
     'Islamikaze: Suicide Terrorism Examined', *Nativ* (Tel Aviv),
     January–April 1997, p. 3.

27   Imad Saluji quoted in Mark Juergensmeyer, 'The Worldwide Rise
     of Religious Nationalism', *Journal of International Affairs*, vol. 50,
     no. 1 (Summer 1996), p. 1.

28   Quoted in Yisra'eli, 'Islamikaze', p. 3.

29 Quoted in ADL Special Background Report, *Hamas, Islamic Jihad and the Muslim Brotherhood*, p. 4.

30 Abdallah Shami interviewed on Israeli television Channel 1 on 9 December 1994, quoted in Yisra'eli, 'Islamikaze', p. 3.

31 'Wedded to Death in a Blaze of Glory – Profile: The Suicide Bomber', *Sunday Times* (London), 10 March 1996; Christopher Walker, 'Palestinian "Was Duped into Being Suicide Bomber"', *The Times* (London), 27 March 1997.

32 Yisra'eli, 'Islamikaze', p. 3.

33 Lance Corporal Eddie DiFranco, quoted in David C. Martin and John Walcott, *Best Laid Plans: The Inside Story of America's War against Terrorism* (New York: Harper & Row, 1988), p. 125.

34 The Israeli secret service reportedly planted a small bomb comprising an estimated two ounces of plastic explosive in a cellular phone used by Ayyash that was detonated by radio signal on 5 January 1996 when he answered a telephone call from his father. See Joel Greenberg, 'Slaying Blended Technology and Guile', *New York Times*, 10 January 1996; Serge Schmemann, 'Palestinian Believed to be Bombing Mastermind is Killed', *New York Times*, 6 January 1997.

35 'Hamas Issues Statement on Ayyash Killing', al-Quds Palestinian Radio in Arabic, 1755 GMT, 5 January 1996.

36 Quoted in Harvey W. Kushner, 'Suicide Bombers: Business as Usual', *Studies in Conflict and Terrorism*, vol. 19, no. 4 (October–December 1996), p. 335.

37 Kahane was assassinated in New York City in November 1990 by El Sayyid A. Nosair, one of the men convicted of conspiring to bomb the World Trade Center (while he was serving a prison term in connection with Kahane's assassination) as well as the follow-on plot to blow up bridges and tunnels linking New York with New Jersey in hopes of obtaining the Trade Center bombers' release.

38 See e.g. books such as *Never Again! A Program for Survival* (Los Angeles: Nash Publishing, 1971) and *They Must Go* (New York: Grosset & Dunlap, 1981), and pamphlets such as *Viewpoint Kahane: 'There Is No More Tal'* (no date) and *Uncomfortable Questions for Comfortable Jews* (no date).

39 His 'Rabbi Kahane Speaks' column was regularly featured in the American-Jewish newspaper, the *Jewish Press*.

40 Kahane, *Never Again!*, p. 110.

41 Ehud Sprinzak, 'Violence and Catastrophe in the Theology of Rabbi Meir Kahane: The Ideologization of Mimetic Desire', in Juergensmeyer (ed.), *Violence and the Sacred in the Modern World*, pp. 51, 64–6. In his book, written at the height of the Algerian war, Fanon, a psychiatrist, wrote of the 'liberating' effects of violence on the oppressed. See Frantz Fanon, *The Wretched of the Earth* (London: Penguin, 1990).

42 Quoted in Janet L. Dolgin, *Jewish Identity and the JDL* (Princeton, NJ: Princeton University Press, 1977), p. 69.

43 *New York Times*, 15 May 1980, quoted in Bruce Hoffman, 'The Jewish Defense League', *Terrorism, Violence and Insurgency Journal*, vol. 5, no. 1 (Summer 1984), p. 13.

44 Kahane speaking at the California State University at Northridge, California, March 1988 (attended by author).

45 Ibid.

46 Kahane, *They Must Go*, p. 272 (emphasis in original).

47 Ehud Sprinzak, *The Ascendance of Israel's Radical Right* (New York and Oxford: Oxford University Press, 1991), pp. 98–9.

48 Ehud Sprinzak, 'Fundamentalism, Terrorism, and Democracy: The Case of the Gush Emunim Underground', Wilson Center Occasional Paper no. 4 (Washington, DC: Smithsonian Institution, 1986), p. 11.

49 See Thomas L. Friedman, 'Jewish Terrorists Freed by Israel', *New York Times*, 9 December 1984; Grace Halsell, 'Why Bobby Brown of Brooklyn Wants to Blow Up Al Aqsa', *Arabia*, August 1984; Martin Merzer, 'Justice for All in Israel?', *Miami Herald*, 17 May 1985; 'Jail Term of Jewish Terrorist Reduced', *Jerusalem Post* (international edition), 12 October 1985. The information pertaining to the terrorists' desire to provoke a cataclysmic holy war between Muslims and Jews was verified by an American law enforcement officer, involved with the investigation of Jewish terrorist incidents in the United States and knowledgeable about the Jerusalem incident, in conversation with the author.

50 Sprinzak, 'Fundamentalism, Terrorism, and Democracy', pp. 11–13.

51 Quoted in Joel Greenberg, 'Israeli Police Question Two Rabbis in Rabin Assassination', *New York Times*, 22 November 1995.

52   Quoted in Christopher Walker, 'Rabin Killer "Trained by Shin Bet"', *The Times* (London), 21 November 1995.

53   Quoted in Marie Colvin, 'Rabbi Calls for Suicide Bombings', *Sunday Times* (London), 13 April 1997.

54   The assault came at the end of a 51-day stand-off between the Branch Davidian cult, led by the Reverend David Koresh, and agents of both the Bureau of Alcohol, Tobacco and Firearms (BATF) and the FBI. The crisis began when BATF agents attempted to arrest Koresh and some of his followers on charges of illegal possession of firearms (specifically of converting single-shot AR-15 assault rifles into full automatic machine-guns). There had also been reports of the cult's bizarre sexual practices and abuse of its members' children that had prompted increased law enforcement interest in the Davidians' Mount Carmel compound. Koresh believed that he was God's special, messianic messenger, sent to earth, he claimed, to 'reveal the hidden meaning of the entire biblical prophetic corpus'. Through his charismatic and persuasive personality, Koresh inculcated in his followers a sense of imminent redemption and apocalyptic visions that culminated in the deaths of Koresh and his followers on 19 April 1993. See James D. Tabor and Eugene V. Gallagher, *Why Waco? Cults and the Battle for Religious Freedom in America* (Berkeley, CA: University of California Press, 1995).

55   In 1992, one US marshal was killed attempting to arrest Randy Weaver for the sale of illegal sawn-off shotguns. Weaver's son was shot to death in the initial confrontation and his wife was subsequently killed by an FBI sniper before the tense stand-off was defused six days later. The incident became a *cause célèbre* for the militias and other extremist groups and is widely believed to have 'lit the fuse' for the 1995 Oklahoma City bombing.

56   Quoted in Associated Press, 'McVeigh Aimed to Spark Revolt, Ex-Buddy Says', *International Herald Tribune* (Paris), 13 May 1997.

57   Quoted in Keith Schneider, 'Fearing a Conspiracy, Some Heed a Call to Arms', *New York Times*, 14 November 1994.

58   Quoted in Jo Thomas, 'Militias Hold a Congress, and Not a Gun is Seen', *New York Times*, 1 November 1994.

59   The US Anti-Defamation League of B'nai B'rith, one of the most authoritative of the groups monitoring the militia phenomenon,

puts the number of active members at a considerably lower figure of 15,000 persons in forty states (see Anti-Defamation League of B'nai B'rith, *ADL Special Report: The Militia Movement in America* (New York: Anti-Defamation League of B'nai B'rith, 1995), p. 1); while the Southern Poverty Law Center reports some 809 militia organizations that have been active in all fifty states plus the District of Columbia (see *False Patriots: The Threat of Antigovernment Extremists* (Montgomery, AL: Southern Poverty Law Center, 1996), pp. 58–68). Meanwhile, another authority, Paul de Armond, the director of the Washington State grassroots community organization, The Public Good, claims that the total number of militia members plus other Americans involved in the wider Christian white supremacist movement exceeds five million (see Paul de Armond, 'The Anti-democratic Movement – More than Militias', June, August 1995 on http://www.nwcitizen.com/publicgood.

60 There is reportedly also a 'bridge' faction, believed to consist of extreme right-wing Mormons associated with the racist (but not anti-semitic) splinter of the far-right Libertarian Party, known as the Constitution Party, attempting to reconcile these two factions. I am indebted to Paul de Armond, of The Public Good in Bellingham, Washington State, for drawing my attention to these critical distinctions and providing me with information on these groups.

61 Quoted in David Harrison, 'Jackboot Stamp of the New Right', *Observer* (London), 23 April 1995.

62 See John Carlin, 'DIY Apocalypse', *Independent* (London), 30 April 1995; Timothy Egan, 'Trying to Explain Contacts with Paramilitary Groups', *New York Times*, 2 May 1995.

63 Quoted in John Carlin, '"We Need Blood to Cleanse Us"', *Independent* (London), 2 May 1995.

64 Gritz's millenarian preparatory plans suffered a grievous setback when he was arrested on kidnapping charges in Connecticut involving his part in an ugly child-custody battle.

65 Personal communication between the author and Paul de Armond, chairman of The Public Good, Bellingham, Washington State, 25 July 1995.

66 The group was itself also involved in a week-long siege with law enforcement authorities that was resolved peacefully despite

threats by the militia to 'wage an Alamo-style fight to the death': Sam Howe Verhovek, 'Showdown at the "Republic of Texas" Ends in Surrender', *International Herald Tribune* (Paris), 5 May 1997.

67 Quoted in Harrison, 'Jackboot Stamp of the New Right'.

68 The group's name is believed to be derived from the so-called 'Operation American Viper' – a 68-page 'war plan' cum strategy document that is circulated among US militias inciting them to revolution and guerrilla war against the 'global conspiracy' orchestrated by the US federal government and the United Nations in league with international bankers, Jews and others. See Steven A. Holmes, 'US Charges 12 in Arizona Plot to Blow Up Government Office', *New York Times*, 2 July 1996.

69 James Brooke in *New York Times*: 'Agents Seize Arsenal of Rifles and Bomb Making Material in Arizona Militia Inquiry', 3 July 1996, 'Volatile Mix in Viper Militia: Hatred Plus a Love for Guns', 4 July 1996 and 'As Trial Nears For Militia, Some Charges Are Dropped', 9 October 1996.

70 McVeigh, however, claims that he used 5,400 pounds (108 50-pound bags) of ammonium nitrate that he bought for $540. He paid about $3,000 for the racing fuel. See James Brooke, 'Newspaper Says McVeigh Described Role in Bombing', *New York Times*, 1 March 1997.

71 Quoted in Tim Kelsey, 'The Oklahoma Suspect Awaits Day of Reckoning', *Sunday Times* (London), 21 April 1996.

72 See James Corcoran, *Bitter Harvest: The Birth of Paramilitary Terrorism in the Heartland* (New York: Penguin, 1995), passim.

73 Quoted in Flo Conway and Jim Siegelman, 'Identity and the Militia', *Arkansas Democrat-Gazette* (Little Rock), 3 December 1995.

74 Quoted in Kelsey, 'The Oklahoma Suspect Awaits Day of Reckoning'.

75 *This is Aryan Nations*, brochure distributed by the Aryan Nations (no date). This document can also be accessed from the World-Wide Web at http://www.stormfront.org/aryan_nations/platform.html.

76 Aryan Nations, *Calling Our Nation*, no. 53 (no date), p. 2. This document can also be accessed from the World-Wide Web at http://www.stormfront.org/aryan_nations/platform.html.

77 'To Our New People', Open Letter from Richard G. Butler, Pastor, Aryan Nations (no date).

78 *This is Aryan Nations*, brochure distributed by the Aryan Nations (no date).

79 *Washington Post*, 26 December 1984, quoted in Bruce Hoffman, *Terrorism in the United States and the Potential Threat to Nuclear Facilities* (Santa Monica, CA: RAND Corporation, R-3351-DOE, January 1986), p. 42.

80 Roy B. Masker, 'An All White Nation? – Why Not?', Aryan Nations, *Calling Our Nation*, no. 53, p. 23.

81 See Rodney Bowers, 'White Radicals Charged with Sedition', *Arkansas Gazette* (Little Rock), 25 April 1987.

82 Joseph M. Melnachak, 'A Chronicle of Hate: A Brief History of the Radical Right in America', *Terrorism, Violence and Insurgency Report*, vol. 6, no. 4 (no date), pp. 41–2. This was also confirmed to the author by an FBI agent present at the raid.

83 Andrew MacDonald, *The Turner Diaries* (Arlington, VA: The National Alliance/National Vanguard Books, 1985). For a biography of MacDonald/Pierce see Michael Janofsky, 'One Man's Journey from Academia to Extremism', *New York Times*, 5 July 1995.

84 *New York Times*, 27 December 1984, quoted in Hoffman, *Terrorism in the United States*, p. 42.

85 McVeigh, quoted in interviews with Patrick E. Cole, '"I'm Just Like Anyone Else"', *Time* (New York), 15 April 1996, and Kelsey, 'The Oklahoma Suspect Awaits Day of Reckoning'.

86 Quoted in Conway and Siegelman, 'Identity and the Militia'.

87 Quoted in Anti-Defamation League of B'nai B'rith, *Hate Groups in America: A Record of Bigotry and Violence* (New York: Anti-Defamation League of B'nai B'rith, 1982), p. 52.

88 Quoted ibid., pp. 51, 53.

89 Carlin, 'DIY Apocalypse'.

90 Paul de Armond, 'Christian Patriots at War with the State', The Public Good home page at http://www.nwcitizen.com/public-good.

91 Among the congregants of Peters' church in Laporte, Colorado, were members of the 1980s terrorist group 'The Order': Jeffrey Kaplan, 'Right-wing Violence in North America', *Terrorism and*

Political Violence, vol. 7, no. 1 (Spring 1995), p. 54; Conway and Siegelman, 'Identity and the Militia'.

92   See Morris Dees with James Corcoran, *Gathering Storm: America's Militia Threat* (New York: HarperCollins, 1996), pp. 1–2 and passim; Paul de Armond, 'Leaderless Resistance: The Two-pronged Movement Consolidates under Identity', The Public Good home page at http://www.nwcitizen.com/publicgood.

93   Louis Beam, *Leaderless Resistance* (text from Cyberspace Minuteman BBS (312) 275-6326), quoted in Tom Burghardt, 'Leaderless Resistance and the Oklahoma City Bombing', The Public Good home page at http://www.nwcitizen.com/public-good.

94   *Field Manual Section 1: Principles Justifying the Arming and Organizing of a Militia* (Wisconsin: The Free Militia, 1994), p. 78, quoted ibid.

95   Quoted in de Armond, 'Leaderless Resistance'.

96   Quoted in James Ridgeway, 'Arms and the Men: Are Far Right Militia Cells Using Robbery to Fund Their Cause?', *Village Voice* (New York), 9 May 1995.

97   Ibid.; James Brooke, 'Arrests Add to Idaho's Reputation as a Magnet for Supremacists', *New York Times*, 27 October 1996; Loretta J. Ross, 'Using the Bible to Justify Killing', *Baltimore Sun*, 8 August 1994; personal communication between Paul de Armond and the author, August 1997.

98   Quoted in 'Klanwatch, a Project of the Southern Poverty Law Center', *Intelligence Report* (Montgomery, AL), no. 84 (November 1996), pp. 1, 4.

99   Similarly, although not invoking the Phineas Priesthood name, a group calling itself the 'Army of God' claimed credit in April 1997 for two unsolved bombings in Atlanta that have wounded a total of twelve persons. The first explosion occurred outside an abortion clinic in January, the second outside a gay night-club.

100 Quoted in Ross, 'Using the Bible to Justify Killing'.

101 'Spokane Robbery Document' on The Public Good home page at http://www.nwcitizen.com/publicgood.

102 Leonard Doyle, 'US Militias Show Way for British Fascists', *Independent* (London), 27 April 1995.

103 Personal communication with Paul de Armond, April 1996.

104 Quoted in Mary Thornton, 'Oregon Guru Disavows Rajneeshism, Vows to Survive Investigations', *Washington Post*, 20 October 1985; Peter H. King, 'Guru Revels in Revelation of a "Paradise" Defiled', *Los Angeles Times*, 22 September 1985.

105 Quoted in David E. Kaplan and Andrew Marshall, *The Cult at the End of the World: The Incredible Story of Aum* (London: Hutchinson, 1996), pp. 7–12.

106 Shoichi Okawa, 'Aum Shinrikyo', at http://www.guardian.co.uk/cults/a-z-cults/a_cults.html.

107 Kaplan and Marshall, *The Cult at the End of the World*, p. 18.

108 Andrew Pollack, 'Japanese Sect May Struggle to Get By Without its Leader', *New York Times*, 17 May 1995; Alessandra Stanley, 'Russians Shut Down Branch of Japanese Sect', *New York Times*, 30 March 1995.

109 William J. Broad, 'Seismic Blast: Bomb or Quake?', *New York Times*, 23 January 1997.

110 Quoted in James Walsh, 'Shoko Asahara: The Making of a Messiah', *Time* (New York), 3 April 1995.

111 Quoted in National Police Agency, 'Aum Shinrikyo: An Alarming Report on the Terrorist Group's Organization and Activities', *Shoten* (Tokyo), no. 252 (1995), p. 6.

112 Quoted in Kaplan and Marshall, *The Cult at the End of the World*, pp. 16–17.

113 Quoted in Nicholas D. Kristof with Sheryl WuDunn, 'The Seer among the Blind: Japanese Sect Leader's Rise', *New York Times*, 26 March 1995.

114 Quoted in James K. Campbell, 'Excerpts from Research Study "Weapons of Mass Destruction and Terrorism: Proliferation by Non-State Actors"', p. 14, paper presented at International Conference on Aviation Safety and Security in the 21st Century, White House Commission on Aviation Safety and Security and George Washington University, Washington, DC, 13–15 January 1997.

115 See David Van Biema, 'Prophet of Poison', *Time* (New York), 3 April 1995.

116 Quoted in Juergensmeyer, 'The Worldwide Rise of Religious Nationalism', p. 17.

117 Quoted in Kaplan and Marshall, *The Cult at the End of the World*, p. 85.

118 Broad, 'Seismic Blast: Bomb or Quake?'.
119 Okawa, 'Aum Shinrikyo'.
120 Richard Lloyd Parry, 'Sect's Poisons "Could Kill 4.2m"', *Independent on Sunday* (London), 26 March 1995; Andrew Pollack, 'Japanese Police Say They Found Germ-War Material at Cult Site', *New York Times*, 29 March 1995.
121 Following an outbreak of Ebola in Zaire in 1992, Asahara and forty followers travelled to that country ostensibly on a humanitarian aid mission: Associated Press and Agence France-Presse, 'Cult "Studied Deadly Ebola Virus"', *New York Times*, 25 April 1995. See also Kaplan and Marshall, *The Cult at the End of the World*, pp. 96–7.
122 National Police Agency, 'Aum Shinrikyo', p. 11.
123 Reuters, 'Tokyo Cult Leader Said to Have Made Gas Confession', *The Times* (London), 5 October 1995.
124 Jonathan Annells and James Adams, 'Did Terrorists Kill with Deadly Nerve Gas Test?', *Sunday Times* (London), 19 March 1995. Interestingly, this news account was published only a day before the nerve gas attack on the Tokyo underground took place.
125 Kevin Sullivan, 'Japan Cult Survives While Guru Is Jailed', *Washington Post*, 28 September 1997.

Chapter 5

1 Frederick J. Hacker, *Crusaders, Criminals, Crazies: Terror and Terrorism in Our Time* (New York: W. W. Norton, 1976), p. xi.
2 Quoted in Gerald McKnight, *The Mind of the Terrorist* (London: Michael Joseph, 1974), p. 168.
3 Brian Michael Jenkins, 'International Terrorism: A New Mode of Conflict' in David Carlton and Carlo Schaerf (eds), *International Terrorism and World Security* (London: Croom Helm, 1975), p. 16.
4 J. Bowyer Bell, 'Terrorist Scripts and Live-action Spectaculars', *Columbia Journalism Review*, vol. 17, no. 1 (1978), p. 50.
5 Tony Atwater, 'Network Evening News Coverage of the TWA Hostage Crisis', *Terrorism and the News Media Research Project* (Boston: Emerson College, no date), p. 5.
6 Ibid., p. 7.
7 John Dillin, 'NBC News President Defends, but Revises, Terrorism

Coverage', *Christian Science Monitor* (Boston), 5 August 1985.

8   ABC dispatched forty people, NBC sent twenty-five and CBS twenty. See Roderick Townley and John Weisman, 'The Reporters' Rat Race – Danger, Chaos and Rumors of Payoffs', *TV Guide* (Radnor, PA), 21 September 1985.

9   Atwater, 'Network Evening News Coverage of the TWA Hostage Crisis', p. 6.

10   Eleanor Randolph, 'Networks Turn Eye on Themselves', *Washington Post*, 30 June 1985.

11   Quoted in Fred Barnes, 'Shiite Spin Control', *The New Republic* (Washington, DC), 15, 22 July 1985, p. 12.

12   Quoted in Edwin Diamond, 'The Coverage Itself – Why it Turned into "Terrorvision"', *TV Guide* (Radnor, PA), 21 September 1985, p. 13.

13   Quoted ibid., p. 10.

14   Quoted in A. P. Schmid, 'Terrorism and the Media: The Ethics of Publicity', *Terrorism and Political Violence*, vol. 1, no. 4 (October 1989), p. 564.

15   Joseph Fromm, 'TV: Does it Box in [the] President in a Crisis?', *US News and World Report* (Washington, DC), 5 July 1985.

16   Walter Mears, quoted in Randolph, 'Networks Turn Eye on Themselves'.

17   Quoted in Walter Laqueur, *The Age of Terrorism* (Boston: Little, Brown, 1987), p. 125.

18   Diamond, 'The Coverage Itself', pp. 10, 12.

19   As part of the deal, West German television was forced to broadcast footage of each of the five freed terrorists being released and boarding the aircraft that would take them to freedom, as well as present communiqués prepared by the Second of June terrorist group: Daniel Schorr, 'The Encouragement of Violence', in Benjamin Netanyahu (ed.), *Terrorism: How The West Can Win* (New York: Avon, 1986), p. 114.

20   Notes from the International Seminar on Terrorism and the Mass Media held in Sicily, 3–5 April 1981; archival material in the RAND–St Andrews Terrorism Database, Centre for the Study of Terrorism and Political Violence, St Andrews University, Scotland.

21   Henry McDonald, 'How the BBC Dances to an IRA Tune', *Sunday Times* (London), 19 January 1997.

22 Followed by Israel, France, Britain, Germany, the former Soviet Union/Russia, Turkey, Cuba, Spain and Iran: RAND–St Andrews University Chronology of International Terrorism.

23 Including the geographical scope and diversity of America's overseas commercial interests, its numerous military bases on foreign soil and the United States' stature as the leader of the free world during the Cold War and as the lone remaining superpower today.

24 Quoted in Laqueur, *The Age of Terrorism*, p. 125.

25 Grant Wardlaw, *Political Terrorism: Theory, Tactics, and Counter-measures* (Cambridge: Cambridge Univeresity Press, 1990), p. 80.

26 Ibid.

27 Jeffrey Z. Rubin and Nehemia Friedland, 'Theater of Terror', *Psychology Today*, vol. 20, no. 3 (March 1986), p. 24.

28 Barnes, 'Shiite Spin Control', p. 10.

29 David C. Martin and John Walcott, *Best Laid Plans: The Inside Story of America's War against Terrorism* (New York: Harper & Row, 1988), p. 189.

30 Garrick Utley, 'The Shrinking of Foreign News', *Foreign Affairs*, vol. 76, no. 2 (March–April 1997), p. 6.

31 Quoted in James Adams, 'The Role of the Media', in Robert L. Pfaltzgraff Jr and Richard H. Schultz Jr (eds), *Ethnic Conflict and Regional Instability: Implications for US Policy and Army Roles and Missions* (Carlisle, PA: US Army Strategic Studies Institute, 1994), p. 163.

32 Utley, 'The Shrinking of Foreign News', p. 2.

33 Ibid., p. 6.

34 T. E. Pattern and R. D. McClure, *The Unseeing Eye: The Myth of Television Power in National Elections* (New York: G. P. Putnam's Sons, 1976), quoted in Sandra Wurth-Hough, 'Network News Coverage of Terrorism: The Early Years', *Terrorism*, vol. 6, no. 3 (Summer 1983), p. 410.

35 Tom Shales, 'America's Ordeal by Television', *Washington Post*, 2 July 1985.

36 Burns W. Roper, *Public Perceptions of Television and Other Mass Media: A Twenty Year Review, 1959–1978* (New York: The Roper Organization, Inc., 1979), pp. 1–5, quoted in Mark Armen Aryanian and John Z. Ayanian, 'Armenian Political Violence on

American Network News: An Analysis of Content', *Armenian Review*, vol. 40, no. 1-157 (Spring 1987), p. 16.

37   See Aryanian and Ayanian, 'Armenian Political Violence on American Network News', pp. 28–9.

38   Adams, 'The Role of the Media', p. 162.

39   Ibid., p. 166.

40   Neil Hickey, 'Terrorism and Television', *TV Guide* (Radnor, PA), 31 July 1976, p. 6.

41   Schmid, 'Terrorism and the Media', p. 559.

42   In addition to Kissinger and Brzezinksi, mentioned above, the US Attorney-General at the time, Edward Meese, Secretary of Defense Caspar Weinberger and the US State Department Legal Adviser Abraham D. Sofaer also called for greater press restraint in the aftermath of the TWA hostage crisis.

43   See e.g. the discussions in Yonah Alexander and Richard Latter (eds), *Terrorism and the Media* (McLean, VA: Brassey's, 1990), passim, and Netanyahu (ed.), *Terrorism: How The West Can Win*, pp. 109–29, 229–39.

44   Laqueur, *The Age of Terrorism*, p. 121.

45   Quoted in R. W. Apple Jr, 'Meese Suggests Press Code on Terrorism', *New York Times*, 18 July 1985.

46   Paul Wilkinson, 'Terrorism and Propaganda', in Alexander and Latter (eds), *Terrorism and the Media*, p. 30.

47   Margaret Thatcher, quoted in Karen DeYoung, 'US Considering Talks on Hijacking Coverage', *Washington Post*, 18 July 1985.

48   Netanyahu (ed.), *Terrorism: How The West Can Win*, p. 109.

49   Ibid.

50   Perhaps the most far-reaching legislation enacted in this respect was the ban imposed by Britain between 1988 and 1994 on the broadcast of all interviews with terrorists or their supporters. According to the home secretary at the time the ban was introduced, Douglas Hurd, this extreme measure was not an attempt to impose censorship of the media but simply to deny members of the IRA, Sinn Fein and other paramilitary groups 'this easy platform for those who use it to propagate terrorism' (*Guardian* (London), 20 October 1988). Its effects, however, were perhaps more farcical than efficacious. Although the terrorists or spokespersons themselves were prevented from appearing on air,

their statements were nonetheless still broadcast: by actors 'standing in' for the proscribed individuals, in essence, reading scripts prepared by the terrorists. The result went beyond even the obvious circumvention and dilution of the legislation's intent, but mocked the government – completely destroying its efforts to control the dissemination of terrorist views. For a contrasting view, see the analysis in Shane Kingston, 'Terrorism, the Media, and the Northern Ireland Conflict', *Studies in Conflict and Terrorism*, vol. 18, no. 3 (July–September 1995), pp. 203–32.

51 Lawrence K. Grossman, 'Television and Terrorism: A Common Sense Approach', *TVI Report* (Beverly Hills, CA), vol. 6, no. 4 (1986), p. 3.

52 Laqueur, *The Age of Terrorism*, p. 127.

53 Theo Downes-LeGuin and Bruce Hoffman, *The Impact of Terrorism on Public Opinion, 1988 to 1989* (Santa Monica, CA: RAND Corporation, MR-225-FF/RC, 1993), p. 16.

54 It should be noted, however, that a small percentage of the respondents who expressed relevant ethnic identification with a specific group was found to have slightly more ambivalent attitudes (mainly Jewish Americans and Irish Americans respectively with regard to the Jewish Defense League and IRA): ibid., p. 16.

55 Konrad Kellen, quoted ibid.

56 Philip Geyelin, 'NBC: How to Protect a Terrorist', *Washington Post*, 19 May 1986.

57 Quoted ibid. See also the editorial by Mortimer B. Zuckerman, the chairman and editor-in-chief of *US News and World Report*, 'Playing the Terrorists' Game', *US News and World Report* (Washington, DC), 9 June 1986.

58 As John O'Sullivan of the London *Daily Telegraph* remarked in a 1985 interview, 'We mishandle [terrorists] because . . . we treat them in effect as politicians rather than . . . criminals': 'Do Terrorists Need Television, TV Guide Asks', United Press International, 18 February 1985.

59 Quoted in Sir John Hermon, 'The Police, the Media, and the Reporting of Terrorism', in Alexander and Latter (eds), *Terrorism and the Media*, p. 39.

60 See Martin and Walcott, *Best Laid Plans*, p. 188–92.

61 Abraham D. Sofaer, quoted in DeYoung, 'US Considering Talks on Hijacking Coverage'.

62 Quoted in Diamond, 'The Coverage Itself'.

63 Margaret Genovese, 'Terrorism: Newspapers Grapple with the Extraordinary Challenges of Covering Worldwide Terrorist Incidents', *Presstime* (New York), August 1986.

64 Grossman, 'Television and Terrorism', p. 1.

65 Donald Bremner, 'Media Given Mixed Reviews on Terrorism', *Los Angeles Times*, 26 September 1986.

66 Quoted in Fromm, 'TV: Does it Box in [the] President in a Crisis?'.

67 Quoted in Barnes, 'Shiite Spin Control', p. 12.

68 Quoted in Fromm, 'TV: Does it Box in [the] President in a Crisis?'.

69 Patrick Clawson, 'Why We Need More but Better Coverage of Terrorism', *Orbis*, vol. 80, no. 4 (Winter 1987), p. 702. It should be noted, however, that Sir Geoffrey Jackson, the British ambassador to Uruguay, who was kidnapped by the Tupamaros in 1971 and held for eight months, maintains that the absence of media publicity was critical in the terrorists' decision to release him.

70 Martin and Walcott, *Best Laid Plans*, p. 191.

71 'Public Support Adams Talks', *Sunday Times* (London), 18 February 1996.

72 Downes-LeGuin and Hoffman, *The Impact of Terrorism on Public Opinion, 1988 to 1989*, pp. 14–15. Information on dog bites provided courtesy of Dr Andrew Rowan, researcher at Tufts University, Medford, Massachusetts.

73 See David Rapoport, 'Terrorism', in Mary Hawkesworth and Maurice Kogan (eds), *Routledge Encyclopedia of Government and Politics*, vol. 2 (London: Routledge, 1992), p. 1073.

74 Graham Norton, 'The Terrorist and the Traveller: A Gulf Aftermath Assessment', *The World Today* (London), May 1991, p. 81.

75 Desmond Balmer, 'US Tourists React to Terrorism Fear', *New York Daily News*, 2 March 1986.

76 Stuart I. Feiler, 'Terrorism: Is Tourism Really the Target?', *Hotel and Restaurants International*, October 1986.

77 Survey conducted by the US Travel Data Center (a national non-profit travel and tourism trade organization) cited in Harvey J. Iglarsh, 'Fear of Flying: Its Economic Costs', *Terrorism*, vol. 10, no. 1 (Winter 1987), p. 46.

78   Feiler, 'Terrorism: Is Tourism Really the Target?'.

79   Ralph Blumenthal, 'Peak Season of American Travel to Europe Ends Showing Little Recovery', *New York Times*, 14 September 1986.

80   Norton, 'The Terrorist and the Traveller', p. 81.

81   ABC News/*Washington Post* poll, cited in 'Views on National Security', *National Journal* (Washington, DC), 25 October 1986.

82   Norton, 'The Terrorist and the Traveller', p. 81.

83   Quoted in Martin and Walcott, *Best Laid Plans*, p. 191.

84   Quoted in Fromm, 'TV: Does it Box in [the] President in a Crisis?'.

85   Adams, 'The Role of the Media', pp. 164–5.

86   Thomas Plate and William Tuohy, 'Los Angeles Times Interview: John Major – Even Under Fire, Britain's Prime Minister Holds His Own', *Los Angeles Times*, 20 June 1993.

87   Tom Squiteri, 'US: Return Our Men', *USA Today* (Washington, DC), 6 October 1993.

88   B. Drummond Ayres Jr, 'The Somalia Mission: Voices', *New York Times*, 9 October 1993.

89   Everett Carl Ladd, 'US Public and Somalia', *Christian Science Monitor* (Boston), 15 October 1993.

90   American Broadcasting Companies, Inc., *Nightline* (ABC, 11.30 p.m. ET), 7 October 1993.

91   Cited in Benjamin C. Schwarz, *Casualties, Public Opinion and US Military Intervention: Implications for US Regional Deterrence Strategies* (Santa Monica, CA: RAND Corporation, MR-431-A/AF, 1994), p. 24.

92   Quoted in Fromm, 'TV: Does it Box in [the] President in a Crisis?'.

93   See 'Khaled Tribute', *The Times* (London), 3 September 1997; Christopher Walker, 'Arabs Are Convinced Car Crash was a Murder Plot', *The Times* (London), 4 September 1997.

94   See 'Unabomber Manifesto', *Washington Post*, 19 September 1995.

95   David Rapoport, 'Editorial: The Media and Terrorism; Implications of the Unabomber Case', *Terrorism and Political Violence*, vol. 8, no. 1 (Spring 1996), p. viii.

Chapter 6

1 Peter H. Merkl, 'Prologue', in Peter H. Merkl (ed.), *Political Violence and Terror* (Berkeley, CA: University of California Press, 1986), p. 8.

2 Quoted in Peter Neuhauser, 'The Mind of a German Terrorist', *Encounter*, vol. 51, no. 3 (September 1978), p. 81.

3 Quoted in Richard Drake, *The Aldo Moro Murder Case* (Cambridge, MA, and London: Harvard University Press, 1995), pp. 118–19.

4 On the night of 10 November 1938, German stormtroopers destroyed virtually every synagogue in Germany and set fire to some 7,000 Jewish businesses. About 30,000 Jews were arrested and thrown into concentration camps. The event takes its name – *Kristallnacht* – from the broken plate-glass windows of the Jewish-owned stores.

5 Neuhauser, 'The Mind of a German Terrorist', pp. 83–4.

6 Baumann's vignette, like the previously discussed 1972 Munich Olympics operation, again underscores how even attacks that fail to achieve their ostensible objective (the successful detonation of a bomb and attendant damage and destruction caused) can nonetheless still fulfil a terrorist group's immediate objectives and therefore just as effectively serve its wider intentions.

7 Quoted in Alison Jamieson, *The Heart Attacked: Terrorism and Conflict in the Italian State* (London and New York: Marion Boyars, 1989), p. 89.

8 Patrizio Peci, *Io, l'infame* (*I, The Scoundrel*) (Milan: Arnoldo Mondadori, 1983), p. 46.

9 'RAF Philosophy', in *The German Guerrilla: Terror, Reaction, and Resistance*, pp. 98–9.

10 Quoted in Eileen MacDonald, *Shoot the Women First* (New York: Random House, 1991), p. 11.

11 Quoted in Peter Taylor, *Provos: The IRA and Sinn Fein* (London: Bloomsbury, 1997), p. 201.

12 David McKittrick, *Despatches from Belfast* (Belfast: Blackstaff Press, 1989), p. 77.

13 Patrick Bishop and Eamonn Mallie, *The Provisional IRA* (London: Corgi, 1989), p. 387.

14   Robert W. White, 'The Irish Republican Army: An Assessment of
      Sectarianism', *Terrorism and Political Violence*, vol. 9, no. 1 (Spring
      1997), p. 44.

15   'But Basques aren't Irish', *The Economist* (London), 20 July
      1996.

16   Quoted in Gerald McKnight, *The Mind of the Terrorist* (London:
      Michael Joseph), p. 26.

17   Quoted in Christopher Dobson, *Black September: Its Short, Violent
      History* (London: Robert Hale, 1974, 1975), p. 95.

18   Quoted in McKnight, *The Mind of the Terrorist*, p. 26.

19   Quoted in Howell Raines, 'With Latest Bomb, IRA Injures its Own
      Cause', *New York Times*, 15 November 1987.

20   Eamon Collins, with Mick McGovern, *Killing Rage* (London:
      Granta, 1997), p. 296.

21   Quoted in MacDonald, *Shoot the Women First*, p. 5.

22   See, for example, the compelling autobiographical account of
      the German neo-Nazi Ingo Hasselbach, with Tom Reiss, *Führer-
      Ex: Memoirs of a Former Neo-Nazi* (London: Chatto & Windus,
      1996).

23   Quoted in Bill Buford, *Among the Thugs* (London: Mandarin,
      1992), p. 154.

24   Hasselbach, *Führer-Ex*, p. 119.

25   Ibid., pp. 274–5.

26   Quoted in McKnight, *The Mind of the Terrorist*, p. 179.

27   Ayla H. Schbley, 'Religious Terrorists: What They Aren't Going to
      Tell Us', *Terrorism*, vol. 13, no. 3 (Summer 1990), p. 240.

28   Quoted in Agence France-Presse, 'Bomber "Wanted to Kill Jews"',
      The Times (London), 15 October 1997.

29   Islamic Group in Egypt, 'Statement on US Sentencing of Sheikh
      Rahman', 19 January 1996.

30   Leila Khaled, *My People Shall Live: The Autobiography of a
      Revolutionary* (London: Hodder & Stoughton, 1973), p. 209.

31   Quoted in Jamieson, *The Heart Attacked*, p. 271.

32   Peci, *Io, l'infame*, p. 46.

33   David Rapoport, 'Terrorism', in Mary Hawkesworth and Maurice
      Kogan (eds), *Routledge Encyclopedia of Government and Politics*,
      vol. 2 (London: Routledge, 1992), p. 1067.

34   Quoted in Bonnie Cordes, 'When Terrorists Do the Talking:

Reflections on Terrorist Literature', *Journal of Strategic Studies*, vol. 10, no. 4 (December 1987), p. 155.

35 Quoted in 'Inside the Red Brigades', *Newsweek* (New York), 15 May 1978.

36 Abu Iyad with Eric Rouleau (trans. Linda Butler Koseoglu), *My Home, My Land: A Narrative of the Palestinian Struggle* (New York: Times Books, 1981), p. 226.

37 Quoted in David Blundy, 'Inside the IRA', *Sunday Times* (London), 3 July 1977.

38 Quoted in M. L. R. Smith, *Fighting For Ireland? The Military Strategy of the Irish Republican Movement* (London and New York: Routledge, 1995), p. 224.

39 Quoted in Patricia G. Steinhoff, 'Portrait of a Terrorist: An Interview with Kozo Okamoto', *Asian Survey*, vol. 16, no. 9 (September 1976), pp. 844–5.

40 Quoted in I. Fetscher and G. Rohrmoser, *Analysen zum Terrorismus* (*Analyses on the Subject of Terrorism*), vol. 1: *Ideologien und Strategien* (*Ideologies and Strategies*) (Bonn: Westdeutscher Verlag, 1981), p. 327.

41 Gudrun Ensslin, 'Statement of 19 January 1976', in Red Army Faction, *Texte der RAF* (*RAF Texts*) (Malmö, Sweden: Verlag Bo Cavefors, 1977), p. 345.

42 Jane Alpert, *Growing Up Underground* (New York: William Morrow, 1981), pp. 141, 175.

43 Michael 'Bommi' Baumann (trans. Helene Ellenbogen and Wayne Parker), *Terror or Love? Bommi Baumann's Own Story of His Life as a West German Urban Guerrilla* (New York: Grove Press, 1979), p. 49.

44 Anonymous, 'Notes for the First Analysis of the Phenomenon of Terrorism of the Right', unpublished study commissioned by the Italian secret services, no date, p. 2.

45 Franco Ferracuti and Francesco Bruno, 'Psychiatric Aspects of Terrorism in Italy', unpublished study commissioned by the Italian secret services, no date, pp. 18, 20.

46 Susan Stern, *With the Weathermen: The Personal Journey of a Revolutionary Woman* (Garden City, NY: Doubleday, 1975), p. 90. Alpert, in her memoir, describes similar discussions and frustrations giving way to action. See *Growing Up Underground*, pp. 140–1, 155.

47 'RAF Philosophy', in *The German Guerrilla*, pp. 99–100. Alpert similarly recalls how her lover and fellow terrorist, Sam Melville, quickly passed the point where he was fed up with talk and ready for action. 'Sam, after a few days, dispensed with theorizing and got down to what interested him: hideouts, disguises, dynamite, plastique, secret communiqués.' See Alpert, *Growing Up Underground*, p. 155.

48 Menachem Begin, *The Revolt: Story of the Irgun* (Jerusalem: Steimatzky, 1977), p. 46.

49 Khaled, *My People Shall Live*, p. 110.

50 Quoted in Peter Taylor, *States of Terror: Democracy and Political Violence* (London: Penguin, 1993), p. 159.

51 Hasselbach, *Führer-Ex*, p. 272.

52 Patrick Seale, *Abu Nidal: A Gun For Hire* (New York: Random House, 1992), p. 57.

53 Collins, *Killing Rage*, p. 177.

54 Quoted in Michael Seufert, 'Dissension among the Terrorists: Killing People is Wrong', *Encounter*, vol. 51, no. 3 (September 1978), p. 84.

55 Neuhauser, 'The Mind of a German Terrorist', pp. 82–3. Heckler & Koch is a leading German weapons manufacturer, producing 'top of the line' hand-guns, sub-machine guns and other small arms.

56 Quoted in Stefan Aust, *The Baader–Meinhof Group: The Inside Story of a Phenomenon* (London: Bodley Head, 1987), p. 97.

57 Quoted in Jillian Becker, *Hitler's Children: The Story of the Baader–Meinhof Gang* (London: Panther Books, 1978), p. 90.

58 Quoted ibid., p. 244.

59 Observation of Dr Sue Ellen Moran, a RAND consultant, in April 1985.

60 Neuhauser, 'The Mind of a German Terrorist', p. 85.

61 Stern, *With the Weathermen*, p. 41.

62 Collins, *Killing Rage*, p. 363.

63 Quoted in Taylor, *States of Terror*, p. 125.

64 Quoted in MacDonald, *Shoot the Women First*, p. 198.

65 Quoted in McKnight, *The Mind of the Terrorist*, p. 180.

66 Klein specifically recalls that when the German news magazine *Der Spiegel* serialized a book about Carlos written by an English journalist – presumably Colin Smith's *Carlos: Portrait of a Terrorist*

(London: André Deutsch, 1976) – he 'kept all the articles and had them translated': Jean Marcel Bougereau, 'An Interview with Hans Joachim Klein', in *The German Guerrilla*, p. 38.

67 Quoted ibid., p. 36.

68 James Bone and Alan Road, 'Terror by Degree', *The Times Magazine* (London), 18 October 1997.

69 See e.g. David Hearst, 'Publicity Key Element of Strategy', *Guardian* (London), 31 July 1990; David Pallister, 'Provos Seek to "Play Havoc with British Nerves and Lifestyle"', *Guardian* (London), 31 July 1990.

70 Quoted in Bougereau, 'An Interview with Hans Joachim Klein', pp. 12, 39.

71 Quoted in James Brooke, 'Newspaper Says McVeigh Described Role in Bombing', *New York Times*, 1 March 1997.

72 Quoted in Oriana Fallaci, 'Interview with George Habash', *Life Magazine* (New York), 12 June 1970.

73 Collins, *Killing Rage*, pp. 65–6.

74 Quoted in 'Bombs Blast a Message of Hate', *Life Magazine* (New York), 27 March 1970.

75 See Frederick Kempe, 'Deadly Survivors: The Cold War is Over but Leftist Terrorists in Germany Fight On', *Wall Street Journal*, 27 December 1991.

76 Quoted in Adrian Bridge, 'German Police Search for Red Army Faction Killers', *Independent* (London), 6 April 1991.

77 Quoted in Kempe, 'Deadly Survivors'.

78 Quoted in Edward Gorman, 'How to Stop the IRA', *The Times* (London), 11 January 1992.

79 Quoted in William E. Schmidt, 'Protestant Gunmen Are Stepping Up the Violence in Northern Ireland', *New York Times*, 29 October 1991.

80 'Terrorists Killed by their Own Devices', *Independent* (London), 20 February 1996.

81 Quoted in Ian Graham, 'Official: IRA Using "Bigger, Better" Bombs', London Press Association, 23 January 1992.

82 Quoted in Edward Gorman, 'Bomb Disposers Mark 21 Years in Ulster', *The Times* (London), 7 November 1992.

83 See e.g. Maria McGuire, *To Take Arms: A Year in the Provisional IRA* (London: Macmillan, 1973), p. 62.

84   Quoted in 'Outrage Not a Reason for Inaction', *Manchester Guardian, International Edition*, 21 October 1984.

85   Interview, North Armagh, Northern Ireland, August 1992.

86   C. Wright Mills, *The Power Elite* (London and New York: Oxford University Press, 1956), p. 171.

87   Quoted in 'Don't Spoil the Party', *The Economist* (London), 13 July 1996.

Chapter 7

1   This list of state sponsors of terrorism was mandated by the Export Administration Act of 1979 to identify and report to Congress 'countries that have repeatedly provided state support for international terrorism'. See Office of the Coordinator for Counterterrorism, *Patterns of Global Terrorism 1996*, Publication 10433 (Washington, DC: US Department of State, April 1997), p. v.

2   Patrick Seale, *Abu Nidal: A Gun For Hire* (New York: Random House, 1992), pp. 202–5.

3   Quoted in Magnus Ranstorp, *Hizb'allah in Lebanon: The Politics of the Western Hostage Crisis* (Basingstoke and London: Macmillan, 1997), p. 38.

4   The sharpened tip of the umbrella contained ricin, a poison derived from castor beans that is ranked third in toxicity behind only plutonium (which is used in thermonuclear weapons) and botulism. Before he died, Markov told doctors that a man had bumped into him on Westminister Bridge and had casually apologized for poking Markov with his umbrella. Traces of the poisoned pellet concealed in the umbrella were discovered in Markov's thigh. See Christopher Andrew and Oleg Gordievsky, *KGB: The Inside Story* (New York: HarperCollins, 1990), pp. 64–5.

5   Michael Binyon and Michael Theodoulou, 'Bounty on Rushdie Raised to $2.5m', *The Times* (London), 13 February 1997. The bounty had previously been raised to $2 million in 1992. See Reuters, '$2 Million Reward for Death of Rushdie Repeated by Iran', *New York Times*, 18 June 1992.

6   For the most detailed accounts of the plot to kill the Pope, who as a staunch Polish nationalist, head of the Roman Catholic Church and ardent proponent of civil liberties and religious freedoms had

supposedly incurred the unswerving enmity of the Kremlin, see Paul B. Henze, *The Plot to Kill the Pope* (New York: Charles Scribner's Sons, 1983), passim; Claire Sterling, *The Time of the Assassins* (New York: Holt, Rinehart & Winston, 1983), passim. For a different interpretation, see Ugur Mumcu, *Papa-Mafya-Agca* (*Pope, Mafia, Agca*) (Ankara: Tekin Yayinevi, 1984), passim.

7 Unpublished 'Discussion Paper on Preventing Terrorism: US Government Prevention Capabilities', 23 July 1996, p. 6.

8 See Karen Gardela and Bruce Hoffman, *The RAND Chronology of International Terrorism for 1987* (Santa Monica, CA: RAND Corporation, R-4006-RC, 1991), p. 7.

9 See 'IRA: The Libyan Connection', *The Economist* (London), 31 March 1990. See also James Adams and Liam Clarke, 'War Without End', *Sunday Times* (London), 17 June 1990; Edward Gorman, 'Libyan Arms Shipments Allow IRA to Maintain Campaign of Violence', *The Times* (London), 7 March 1991; Robert Cottrell, 'French Court Told of Huge Libyan Arms Run by IRA', *Independent* (London), 8 January 1991; David McKittrick, 'Voyage into Business of Terror', *Independent* (London), 12 January 1991.

10 See Karen Gardela and Bruce Hoffman, *The RAND Chronology of International Terrorism for 1986* (Santa Monica, CA: The RAND Corporation, R-3890-RC, 1990), p. 6.

11 Office of the Coordinator for Counterterrorism, *Patterns of Global Terrorism 1996*, p. 25.

12 A 193-count federal grand jury indictment presented in Washington, DC, charged the two Libyans, Abdel Basset Ali al-Megrahi and Lamen Khalifa Fhimah, with specifically executing the bombing of Pan Am 103 by placing a suitcase containing the bomb on board a flight originating in Malta that would be subsequently transferred to the ill-fated Pan Am aircraft. See United States District Court for the District of Columbia, *United States of America* v. *Abdel Basset Ali al-Megrahi and Lamen Khalifa Fhimah*, 14 November 1991.

13 Office of the Coordinator for Counterterrorism, *Patterns of Global Terrorism 1996*, pp. 23–4.

14 Robin Wright, 'Iran Supplies Lebanese Radicals Through Syria, US Aides Say', *International Herald Tribune* (Paris), 14–15 December 1996.

15   Douglas Jehl, 'Iran Tells the Europeans That It Doesn't Back Terrorism', *New York Times*, 8 March 1996.

16   William Drozdiak, 'EU Recalls Envoys as Iran is Found Guilty of Terror', *International Herald Tribune* (Paris), 11 April 1997.

17   Quoted in Tom Rhodes, 'Sanctions on Iran "a Failure"', *The Times* (London), 13 October 1995.

18   The remaining questions regarding the PFLP-GC and Syria's involvement in the Pan Am flight 103 bombing are documented in Roy Rowan, 'Pan Am 103: Why Did They Die?', *Time*, 27 April 1992. See also David Hoffman, 'Reports Renew Suspicions of Iran, Syria Bomb Link', *Washington Post*, 26 April 1992; Kathy Evans and Richard Norton-Taylor, 'Spain Checks Syrian Link to Lockerbie', *The Times* (London), 6 June 1992; David Twersky, 'The Risks of Cozying Up to Syria', *New York Times*, 28 July 1992.

19   Office of the Coordinator for Counterterrorism, *Patterns of Global Terrorism 1996*, p. 26.

20   Irving Soloway, Chief, Private Sector Liaison Staff, US Department of State, in his presentation at the Annual Overseas Security Advisory Council Briefing, US Department of State, Washington, DC, 20 November 1991. Discussion with US State Department officials, December 1992.

21   Brian Michael Jenkins, *International Terrorism: The Other World War* (Santa Monica, CA: RAND Corporation, R-3302-AF, November 1985), p. 12.

22   Radiological terrorism involves *contamination* with readily available radioactive materials, for instance those used in medicine and commerce, as compared with nuclear terrorism, which implies an explosion caused by the chain reaction created by fissionable materials.

23   From time to time additional reports have surfaced, for example, that in 1979 RAF terrorists were being trained at Palestinian camps in Lebanon in the use of bacteriological weapons and earlier threats by the group to poison water supplies in twenty German towns if three radical lawyers were not permitted to defend an imprisoned RAF member; su spicions that in 1986 terrorists in India may have contemplated poisoning drinking water tanks there; and the letters sent to Western embassies by

Tamil guerrillas in 1986 claiming to have poisoned Sri Lankan tea with potassium cyanide.

24 Admittedly, these are only those incidents or plots that we *definitely* know about and that have also been reported in open, published sources.

25 Brian Michael Jenkins, *The Likelihood of Nuclear Terrorism* (Santa Monica, CA: RAND Corporation, P-7119, July 1985), p. 6.

26 Brian Michael Jenkins, *Will Terrorists Go Nuclear?* (Santa Monica, CA: RAND Corporation, P-5541, November 1975), pp. 6–7.

27 Terrorist trends for 1994 provide a particularly good illustration of this development not only in terms of the previous record-setting percentage of fatalities to incidents, but also in that the total of 423 fatalities recorded that year was the fifth highest annual figure in the Chronology since 1968 (RAND–St Andrews Chronology of International Terrorist Incidents).

28 Associated Press, 'Man Accused of Possessing Lethal Toxin Hangs Himself', *Los Angeles Times*, 24 December 1995.

29 Karl Vick, 'Man Gets Hands on Bubonic Plague Germs, But That's No Crime', *Washington Post*, 30 December 1995.

30 Associated Press, 'Man Accused of Possessing Lethal Toxin Hangs Himself'; John Kifner, 'Antiterrorism Law Used in Poison Smuggling Case', *New York Times*, 23 December 1995 and 'Man Arrested in Poison Case Kills Himself in Jail Cell', *New York Times*, 24 December 1995.

31 'IRA Bomb-making Guide on Internet', *Sunday Times* (London), 9 February 1997.

32 Tom Hays and Larry Neumeister, 'Trade Center Bombers Get Life in Prison', Associated Press, 25 May 1994; Richard Bernstein, 'Chemist Can't Pinpoint Bomb Contents at Trial', *New York Times*, 21 January 1994. See also Matthew L. Wald, 'Figuring What it Would Take to Take Down a Tower', *New York Times*, 21 March 1993.

Bibliography

Adams, James. *The Financing of Terror.* New York, Simon & Schuster, 1986.

Adams, James. 'The Role of the Media', in Robert L. Pfaltzgraff Jr and Richard H. Schultz Jr (eds), *Ethnic Conflict and Regional Instability: Implications for US Policy and Army Roles and Missions.* Carlisle, PA, US Army Strategic Studies Institute, 1994.

Adams, James. *Secret Armies: Inside the American, Soviet and European Special Forces.* New York, Atlantic Monthly Press, 1987.

Adams, James and Clarke, Liam. 'War Without End', *Sunday Times* (London), 17 June 1990.

Agence France-Presse. 'Bomber "Wanted to Kill Jews"', *The Times* (London), 15 October 1997.

Alden, Robert. 'Terrorism Issue Taken up at UN', *New York Times*, 10 November 1972.

Alexander, Yonah and Latter, Richard (eds). *Terrorism and the Media.* McLean, VA, Brassey's, 1990.

Allen-Mills, Tony. 'McVeigh Trial Leaves Militia Riddle Unsolved', *Sunday Times* (London), 15 June 1997.

Allen-Mills, Tony. 'Real-life Rambo Meets his Match in Schoolyard', *Sunday Times* (London), 6 October 1996.

Allison, Graham T. et al. *Avoiding Nuclear Anarchy: Containing the Threat of Loose Russian Nuclear Weapons and Fissile Material.* Cambridge, MA, MIT Press, 1996.

Alpert, Jane. *Growing Up Underground.* New York, William Morrow, 1981.

Ambler, John Steward. *The French Army in Politics 1945–1962.* Columbus, OH: Ohio State University Press, 1966.

American Broadcasting Companies, Inc. *Nightline* (ABC, 11.30 p.m. ET), 7 October 1993.

Andrew, Christopher and Gordievsky, Oleg. *KGB: The Inside Story.* New York, HarperCollins, 1990.

Annells, Jonathan and Adams, James. 'Did Terrorists Kill with Deadly Nerve Gas Test?', *Sunday Times* (London), 19 March 1995.

Anonymous. 'Notes for the First Analysis of the Phenomenon of Terrorism of the Right'. Unpublished study commissioned by the Italian secret services, no date.

Anti-Defamation League of B'nai B'rith. *ADL Special Background Report: Hamas, Islamic Jihad and the Muslim Brotherhood: Islamic Extremists and the Terrorist Threat to America.* New York, Anti-Defamation League of B'nai B'rith, 1993.

Anti-Defamation League of B'nai B'rith. *ADL Special Report: The Militia Movement in America.* New York, Anti-Defamation League of B'nai B'rith, 1995.

Anti-Defamation League of B'nai B'rith. *Hate Groups in America: A Record of Bigotry and Violence.* New York, Anti-Defamation League of B'nai B'rith, 1982.

Apple, Jr, R. W. 'Meese Suggests Press Code on Terrorism', *New York Times*, 18 July 1985.

'Arab Leaders Join World in Assailing Terrorists' Attack', *Los Angeles Times*, 19 December 1973.

Armed Islamic Group. Communiqué, containing a twelve-page interview with Antar Zouabri, September 1996.

Armenian Secret Army for the Liberation of Armenia. *The Reality.* The Armenian Secret Army for the Liberation of Armenia, no date.

'Armenians Turning to Terrorism', *Los Angeles Times*, 25 January 1981.

Armond, Paul de. 'Christian Patriots at War with the State', The Public Good home page at http://www.nwcitizen.com/publicgood.

Armond, Paul de. 'Leaderless Resistance: The Two-pronged Movement Consolidates under Identity', The Public Good home page at http://www.nwcitizen.com/publicgood.

Armond, Paul de. 'The Anti-democratic Movement – More than Militias', August 1995, The Public Good home page at http://www.nwcitizen.com/publicgood.

Arnold, Guy, et al. *Revolutionary and Dissident Movements*. Harlow, Longman, 1991.

Aryan Nations. *Calling Our Nation*, no. 53 (no date) at http://www.stormfront.org/aryan_nations/platform.html.

Aryanian, Mark Armen and Ayanian, John Z. 'Armenian Political Violence on American Network News: An Analysis of Content', *Armenian Review*, vol. 40, no. 1-157 (Spring 1987).

Asprey, Robert B. *War in the Shadows: The Guerrilla in History*, vol. 2. New York, Doubleday, 1975.

Associated Press. 'McVeigh Aimed to Spark Revolt, Ex-Buddy Says', *International Herald Tribune* (Paris), 13 May 1997.

Associated Press. 'Man Accused of Possessing Lethal Toxin Hangs Himself', *Los Angeles Times*, 24 December 1995.

Associated Press and Agence France-Presse. 'Cult "Studied Deadly Ebola Virus"', *New York Times*, 25 April 1995.

Aston, Clive C. *A Contemporary Crisis: Political Hostage-taking and the Experience of Western Europe*. Westport, CT, and London, Greenwood Press, 1982.

Atwater, Tony. 'Network Evening News Coverage of the TWA Hostage Crisis', *Terrorism and the News Media Research Project*. Boston, Emerson College, no date.

Aust, Stefan. *The Baader–Meinhof Group: The Inside Story of a Phenomenon*. London, Bodley Head, 1987.

Ayres, Jr, B. Drummond. 'The Somalia Mission: Voices', *New York Times*, 9 October 1993.

Balmer, Desmond. 'US Tourists React to Terrorism Fear', *New York Daily News*, 2 March 1986.

Barber, Noel. *The War of the Running Dogs: How Malaya Defeated the Communist Guerrillas 1948–60*. London, Fontana, 1972.

Barkun, Michael. 'Millenarian Aspects of "White Supremacist" Movements', *Terrorism and Political Violence*, vol. 1, no. 4 (October 1989).

Barkun, Michael. 'Millenarian Groups and Law Enforcement Agencies: The Lessons of Waco', *Terrorism and Political Violence*, vol. 6, no. 1 (Spring 1994).

Barkun, Michael. 'Racist Apocalypse: Millennialism on the Far Right', *American Studies*, vol. 31 (1990).

Barnaby, Frank. 'Nuclear Accidents Waiting to Happen', *The World*

Today (London), vol. 52, no. 4 (April 1996).

Barnes, Fred. 'Shiite Spin Control', *The New Republic* (Washington, DC), 15, 22 July 1985.

Bauer, Yehuda. *From Diplomacy to Resistance: A History of Jewish Palestine 1939–1945*. New York, Atheneum, 1973.

Baumann, Michael 'Bommi' (trans. Helene Ellenbogen and Wayne Parker). *Terror or Love? Bommi Baumann's Own Story of His Life as a West German Urban Guerrilla*. New York, Grove Press, 1979.

Becker, Jillian. *Hitler's Children: The Story of the Baader–Meinhof Gang*. London, Panther Books, 1978.

Begin, Menachem. *The Revolt: Story of the Irgun*. Jerusalem, Steimatzky, 1977.

Begin, Menachem. *White Nights: The Story of a Prisoner in Russia*. Jerusalem, Steimatzky, 1977.

Bell, J. Bowyer. *A Time of Terror: How Democratic Societies Respond to Revolutionary Violence*. New York, Basic Books, 1978.

Bell, J. Bowyer. *Terror Out of Zion: The Violent and Deadly Shock Troops of Israeli Independence, 1929–1949*. New York, St Martin's Press, 1977.

Bell, J. Bowyer. 'Terrorist Scripts and Live-action Spectaculars', *Columbia Journalism Review*, vol. 17, no. 1 (1978).

Bell, J. Bowyer. *The Secret Army: The IRA, 1916–1979*. Dublin, Poolbeg, 1989.

Bennett, Will. 'Simple Bombs Improved but Lack Accuracy', *Independent* (London), 8 February 1991.

Bennett, Will. 'Terrorists Keep Changing Tactics to Elude Security Forces', *Independent* (London), 17 December 1991.

Bernstein, Richard. 'Chemist Can't Pinpoint Bomb Contents at Trial', *New York Times*, 21 January 1994.

Binyon, Michael and Theodoulou, Michael. 'Bounty on Rushdie Raised to $2.5m', *The Times* (London), 13 February 1997.

Bishop, Patrick and Mallie, Eamonn. *The Provisional IRA*. London, Heinemann, 1987; pb Corgi, 1989.

Blumenthal, Ralph. 'Peak Season of American Travel to Europe Ends Showing Little Recovery', *New York Times*, 14 September 1986.

Blundy, David. 'Inside the IRA', *Sunday Times* (London), 3 July 1977.

'Bombs Blast a Message of Hate', *Life Magazine* (New York), 27 March 1970.

Bone, James and Road, Alan. 'Terror by Degree', *The Times Magazine* (London), 18 October 1997.

'Booklet Giving History of ASALA's Existence Gives New Insight into the Revolutionary Movement', *The Armenian Reporter* (New York), 10 January 1985.

Bougereau, Jean Marcel, 'Memoirs of an International Terrorist: Conversations with Hans Joachim Klein', in *The German Guerrilla: Terror, Reaction, and Resistance.* Sanday, Orkney, Cienfuegos Press, no date.

Bowers, Rodney. 'White Radicals Charged with Sedition', *Arkansas Gazette* (Little Rock, ARK), 25 April 1987.

Bremner, Donald. 'Media Given Mixed Reviews on Terrorism', *Los Angeles Times*, 26 September 1986.

Bridge, Adrian. 'German Police Search for Red Army Faction Killers', *Independent* (London), 6 April 1991.

Brinton, Crane. *The Anatomy of Revolution.* New York, Vintage, 1965.

British Broadcasting Corporation. 'Bosnia Serb "Black Hand" Group Threatens to Kill Peace Force', *BBC Summary of World Broadcasts*, 17 July 1997.

British Broadcasting Corporation. 'Leaflet in Banja Luka Vows Revenge on British Forces "Soon"', *BBC Summary of World Broadcasts*, 19 July 1997.

Broad, William J. 'Seismic Blast: Bomb or Quake?', *New York Times*, 23 January 1997.

Broido, Vera. *Apostles into Terrorists: Women and the Revolutionary Movement in the Russia of Alexander II.* London, Maurice Temple Smith, 1977.

Brooke, James. 'Agents Seize Arsenal of Rifles and Bomb Making Material in Arizona Militia Inquiry', *New York Times*, 3 July 1996.

Brooke, James. 'Armed Group under Siege has Sown Anger and Hate', *New York Times*, 31 March 1996.

Brooke, James. 'Arrests Add to Idaho's Reputation as a Magnet for Supremacists', *New York Times*, 27 October 1996.

Brooke, James. 'As Trial Nears for Militia, Some Charges are Dropped', *New York Times*, 9 October 1996.

Brooke, James. 'Newspaper Says McVeigh Described Role in Bombing', *New York Times*, 1 March 1997.

Brooke, James. 'Volatile Mix in Viper Militia: Hatred Plus a Love for Guns', *New York Times*, 4 July 1996.

Buford, Bill. *Among the Thugs*. London, Mandarin, 1992.

Bullock, Alan. *Hitler: A Study in Tyranny*. New York, Harper, 1958.

Burghardt, Tom. 'Leaderless Resistance and the Oklahoma City Bombing', The Public Good home page at http://www.nwcitizen.com/publicgood.

'But Basques aren't Irish', *The Economist* (London), 20 July 1996.

Butler, Reverend Richard G. 'To Our New People', Aryan Nations (no place, no date).

Byford-Jones, W. *Grivas and the Story of EOKA*. London, Robert Hale, 1959.

Campbell, James K. 'Excerpts from Research Study "Weapons of Mass Destruction and Terrorism: Proliferation by Non-State Actors"', *Terrorism and Political Violence*, vol. 9, no. 2 (Summer 1997).

Carlin, John. 'DIY Apocalypse', *Independent* (London), 30 April 1995.

Carlin, John. '"We need blood to cleanse us"', *Independent* (London), 2 May 1995.

Carr, Caleb. 'Terrorism as Warfare: The Lessons of Military History', *World Policy Journal*, vol. 13, no. 4 (Winter 1996–7).

Carruthers, Susan L. *Winning Hearts and Minds: British Governments, the Media and Colonial Counter-Insurgency 1944–1960*. London and New York, Leicester University Press, 1995.

Carver, Michael. *War since 1945*. London, Weidenfeld & Nicolson, 1980.

Central Intelligence Agency. *Guide to the Analysis of Insurgency*. Washington, DC, US Government Printing Office, no date.

Chaliand, Gerard and Ternon, Yves (trans. Tony Berrett), *The Armenians: From Genocide to Resistance*. London, Zed, 1983.

Churchill, Winston S. *The Second World War*, vol. 3: *The Grand Alliance*. London, The Reprint Society, 1956.

Churchill, Winston S. *The Second World War*, vol. 4: *The Hinge of Fate*. London, The Reprint Society, 1956.

Clarity, James F. 'Obscure Doctor Again Faces Sinn Fein Chief', *International Herald Tribune* (Paris), 15 April 1997.

Clarke, Thurston. *By Blood and Fire: The Attack on the King David Hotel*. New York, G. P. Putnam's Sons, 1981.

Clawson, Patrick. 'Why We Need More but Better Coverage of Terrorism', *Orbis*, vol. 80, no. 4 (Winter 1987).

Cline, Ray S. and Alexander, Yonah. *Terrorism: The Soviet Connection*. New York, Crane Russak, 1984.

Cohen, Michael J. *Palestine and the Great Powers, 1945–1948*. Princeton, NJ, Princeton University Press, 1982.

Cohen-Almagor, Raphael. 'Vigilant Jewish Fundamentalism: From the JDL to Kach (or "Shalom Jews, Shalom Dogs")', *Terror and Political Violence*, vol. 4, no. 1 (Spring 1992).

Cole, Patrick E. '"I'm Just Like Anyone Else"', *Time* (New York), 15 April 1996.

Collins, Eamon with McGovern, Mick. *Killing Rage*. London, Granta, 1997.

Colvin, Marie. 'Rabbi Calls for Suicide Bombings', *Sunday Times* (London), 13 April 1997.

Colvin, Marie and Goldberg, Andy. 'Israel on Alert for Wave of "Sleeper" Bombers', *Sunday Times* (London), 10 March 1996.

Conquest, Robert. *The Great Terror*. Harmondsworth, Penguin, 1971.

Conway, Flo and Siegelman, Jim. 'Identity and the Militia', *Arkansas Democrat-Gazette* (Little Rock), 3 December 1995.

Cooley, John K. *Green March, Black September: The Story of the Palestinian Arabs*. London, Frank Cass, 1973.

Cooley, John K. 'New Arab Unity Hits Palestinian Guerrillas', *Christian Science Monitor* (Boston), 19 September 1973.

Corbett, Robert. *Guerrilla Warfare from 1939 to the Present Day*. London, Orbis, 1986.

Corcoran, James. *Bitter Harvest: The Birth of Paramilitary Terrorism in the Heartland*. New York, Penguin, 1995.

Cordes, Bonnie. 'When Terrorists do the Talking: Reflections on Terrorist Literature', *Journal of Strategic Studies*, vol. 10, no. 4 (December 1987).

Corr, Ambassador Edwin G. 'Introduction', in Max G. Manwaring (ed.). *Gray Area Phenomena: Confronting the New World Disorder*. Boulder, CO, Westview Press, 1993.

Corsun, Andrew. *Research Papers on Terrorism – Armenian Terrorism: 1975–1980*. Washington, DC, Office of Security Threat Analysis Group, US Department of State, 1982.

Cottrell, Robert. 'French Court Told of Huge Libyan Arms Run by IRA', *Independent* (London), 8 January 1991.

Cowell, Alan. 'Berlin Court Says Top Iran Leaders Ordered

Killings', *New York Times*, 11 April 1997.

Cowell, Alan. 'Two More Held in Rabin Slaying; Israeli Police See a Conspiracy', *New York Times*, 10 November 1995.

Craig, Gordon. *Germany, 1866–1945.* Oxford, Clarendon Press, 1978.

Creech-Jones Papers, Boxes 32/3 and 32/6, Letters, Creech-Jones to Munro [*sic*], 23 October and 30 November 1961. Rhodes House, Oxford.

Crenshaw, Martha. *Terrorism and International Cooperation.* Occasional Paper Series no. 11. New York, Institute for East–West Security Studies, 1989.

Davis, Uri, Mack, Andrew and Yuval-Davis, Ira. 'Introduction', in Uri Davis, Andrew Mack and Ira Yuval-Davis (eds). *Israel and the Palestinians.* London, Ithaca Press, 1975.

Dedijer, Vladimir. *The Road to Sarajevo.* London, MacGibbon & Kee, 1967.

Dees, Morris with Corcoran, James. *Gathering Storm: America's Militia Threat.* New York, HarperCollins, 1996.

Dettmer, Jamie and Gorman, Edward. 'Seven Dead in IRA "Human" Bomb Attacks', *The Times* (London), 25 October 1990.

Dewar, Michael. *Brush Fire Wars: Minor Campaigns of the British Army since 1945.* New York, St Martin's Press, 1984.

DeYoung, Karen. 'US Considering Talks on Hijacking Coverage', *Washington Post*, 18 July 1985.

Diamond, Edwin. 'The Coverage Itself – Why it Turned into "Terrorvision"', *TV Guide* (Radnor, PA), 21 September 1985.

Dillin, John. 'NBC News President Defends, but Revises, Terrorism Coverage', *Christian Science Monitor* (Boston), 5 August 1985.

'Discussion Paper on Preventing Terrorism: US Government Prevention Capabilities', 23 July 1996.

'Do Terrorists Need Television, TV Guide Asks', United Press International, 18 February 1985.

Dobson, Christopher. *Black September: Its Short, Violent History.* London, Robert Hale, 1974, 1975.

Dobson, Christopher and Payne, Ronald. *Terror! The West Strikes Back.* London and Basingstoke, Macmillan, 1982.

Dobson, Christopher and Payne, Ronald. *The Carlos Complex: A Study in Terror.* London, Coronet/Hodder & Stoughton, 1978.

Dolgin, Janet L. *Jewish Identity and the JDL.* Princeton, NJ, Princeton University Press, 1977.

'Don't Spoil the Party', *The Economist* (London), 13 July 1996.

Downes-LeGuin, Theo and Hoffman, Bruce. *The Impact of Terrorism on Public Opinion, 1988 to 1989.* MR-225-FF/RC. Santa Monica, CA, RAND Corporation, 1993.

Doyle, Leonard. 'US Militias Show Way for British Fascists', *Independent* (London), 27 April 1995.

Drake, Richard. *The Aldo Moro Murder Case.* Cambridge, MA, and London, Harvard University Press, 1995.

Drozdiak, William. 'EU Recalls Envoys as Iran is Found Guilty of Terror', *International Herald Tribune* (Paris), 11 April 1997.

Dunn, Ross and Rhodes, Tom. 'The Stalking Assassin Who Killed Rabin at Third Try', *The Times* (London), 6 November 1995.

Eddy, Paul. 'Cover Story: True Detective Stories', *Sunday Times Magazine* (London), 10 August 1997.

Egan, Timothy. 'Trying to Explain Contacts with Paramilitary Groups', *New York Times*, 2 May 1995.

Ehrenfeld, Rachel. *Narco-terrorism.* New York, Basic Books, 1990.

Eickelman, Dale F. 'Trans-state Islam and Security' in Hoeber Rudolph, Susanne and Piscatori, James (eds). *Transnational Religion and Fading States.* Boulder, CO, Westview, 1996.

Ensslin, Gudrun. 'Statement of 19 January 1976', in Red Army Faction, *Texte der RAF* (*RAF Texts*). Malmö, Sweden, Verlag Bo Cavefors, 1977.

Evans, Kathy and Norton-Taylor, Richard. 'Spain Checks Syrian Link to Lockerbie', *The Times* (London), 6 June 1992.

Fadl Allah, Ayatollah Muhammed Hussein, 'Islam and Violence in Political Reality', *Middle East Insight*, vol. 4, nos 4–5 (1986).

Fallaci, Oriana. 'Interview with George Habash', *Life Magazine* (New York), 12 June 1970.

Fanon, Frantz. *The Wretched of the Earth.* London, Penguin, 1990.

Feiler, Stuart I. 'Terrorism: Is Tourism Really the Target?', *Hotel and Restaurants International*, October 1986.

Ferracuti, Franco and Bruno, Francesco. 'Psychiatric Aspects of Terrorism in Italy'. Unpublished study commissioned by the Italian secret services, no date.

Fetscher I. and Rohrmoser, G. *Analysen zum Terrorismus* (*Analyses on the Subject of Terrorism*), vol. 1: *Ideologien und Strategien* (*Ideologies and Strategies*). Bonn, Westdeutscher Verlag, 1981.

Fiskhoff, Sue. 'Gentle, Kind and Full of Religious Fervor', *Jerusalem*

Post, 27 February 1994.

Fitchett, Joseph. 'Guerrillas Seeking Leverage', *Christian Science Monitor*, 27 November 1973.

Foley, Charles. *Island in Revolt*. London, Longmans, 1962.

Foley, Charles (ed.). *The Memoirs of General Grivas*. London, Longmans, 1964.

Foley, Charles and Scobie, W. I. *The Struggle for Cyprus*. Stanford, CA, Hoover Institution Press, 1975.

'41 Dead, 53 Injured, 52 Missing, in Terrorist Attack on Secretariat', *Palestine Post* (Jerusalem), 23 July 1946.

'French Paper Provides Information on ASALA Leader Hagopian', *Mamara* (Istanbul), 16 January 1985.

Friedman, Thomas L. 'Jewish Terrorists Freed by Israel', *New York Times*, 9 December 1984.

Fromm, Joseph. 'TV: Does it Box in [the] President in a Crisis?', *US News and World Report* (Washington, DC), 5 July 1985.

Garcia-Granados, Jorge. *The Birth of Israel: The Drama as I Saw it*. New York, Knopf, 1948.

Gardela, Karen and Hoffman, Bruce. *The RAND Chronology of International Terrorism for 1986*. R–3890–RC. Santa Monica, CA, RAND Corporation, 1990.

Gardela, Karen, and Hoffman, Bruce. *The RAND Chronology of International Terrorism for 1987*. R–4006–RC. Santa Monica, CA, RAND Corporation, 1991.

Gaucher, Roland. *Les Terroristes*. Paris, Editions Albin Michel, 1965.

Geiss, Imanuel (ed.). *July 1914: The Outbreak of the First World War*. New York, W. W. Norton, 1967.

Genovese, Margaret. 'Terrorism: Newspapers Grapple with the Extraordinary Challenges of Covering Worldwide Terrorist Incidents', *Presstime* (New York), August 1986.

Geyelin, Philip. 'NBC: How to Protect a Terrorist', *Washington Post*, 19 May 1986.

Goren, Roberta (ed. Jillian Becker). *The Soviet Union and Terrorism*. London, Allen & Unwin, 1984.

Gorman, Edward. 'Bomb Disposers Mark 21 years in Ulster', *The Times* (London), 7 November 1992.

Gorman, Edward. 'How to Stop the IRA', *The Times* (London), 11 January 1992.

Gorman, Edward. 'Libyan Arms Shipments Allow IRA to Maintain Campaign of Violence', *The Times* (London), 7 March 1991.

Graham, Ian. 'Official: IRA Using "Bigger, Better" Bombs', London Press Association, 23 January 1992.

Greenberg, Joel. 'Israeli Police Question Two Rabbis in Rabin Assassination', *New York Times*, 22 November 1995.

Greenberg, Joel. 'Slaying Blended Technology and Guile', *New York Times*, 10 January 1996.

Grivas, General (trans. A. A. Pallis). *Guerrilla Warfare and Eoka's Struggle.* London, Longmans, 1964.

Grossman, Lawrence K. 'Television and Terrorism: A Common Sense Approach', *TVI Report* (Beverly Hills, CA), vol. 6, no. 4 (1986).

Hacker, Frederick J. *Crusaders, Criminals, Crazies: Terror and Terrorism in Our Time.* New York, W.W. Norton, 1976.

Halsell, Grace. 'Why Bobby Brown of Brooklyn Wants to Blow Up Al Aqsa', *Arabia*, August 1984.

'Hamas Issues Statement on 'Ayyash Killing', al-Quds Palestinian Radio in Arabic, 1755 GMT, 5 January 1996.

Hansard, 5th series, Parliamentary Debates. London, House of Commons.

Harrison, David. 'Jackboot Stamp of the New Right', *Observer* (London), 23 April 1995.

Hart, Alan. *Arafat: A Political Biography. The Definitive Biography Written in Co-operation with Yasser Arafat.* London: Sidgwick & Jackson, 1994.

Hasselbach, Ingo with Reiss, Tom. *Führer-Ex: Memoirs of a Former Neo-Nazi.* London, Chatto & Windus, 1996.

Hays, Tom and Neumeister, Larry. 'Trade Center Bombers Get Life in Prison', Associated Press, 25 May 1994.

Hearst, David. ' "Human Bomb" Fails to Explode', *Guardian* (London), 24 November 1990.

Hearst, David. 'IRA Mines Gap in Army Security', *Guardian* (London), 10 April 1990.

Hearst, David. 'Publicity Key Element of Strategy', *Guardian* (London), 31 July 1990.

Hedges, Chris and Greenberg, Joel. 'West Bank Massacre: Before Killing, a Final Prayer and a Final Taunt', *New York Times*, 28 February 1994.

Heggoy, Alf Andrew. *Insurgency and Counterinsurgency in Algeria*. Bloomington, ID, Indiana University Press, 1972.

Heller, Joseph. *The Stern Gang: Ideology, Politics and Terror 1940–1949*. London, Frank Cass, 1995.

Henze, Paul B. *The Plot to Kill the Pope*. New York, Charles Scribner's Sons, 1983.

Hermon, Sir John. 'The Police, the Media, and the Reporting of Terrorism', in Yonah Alexander and Richard Latter (eds), *Terrorism and the Media*. McLean, VA, Brassey's, 1990.

Hezbollah. 'Open Letter from the Party of God to the Disinherited of Lebanon and the World Revealing the Way and the Intentions which are their Own on the Occasion of the First Anniversary of Ragheb Harb, Symbol of the Islamic Resistance and Exemplary Martyr', Beirut, Lebanon, 16 February 1985.

Hickey, Neil. 'Terrorism and Television', *TV Guide* (Radnor, PA), 31 July 1976.

Hirst, David. *The Gun and the Olive Branch*. London, Futura, 1977.

Hoagland, Jim. 'Palestinian Guerrillas Say They Reject Cease-fire', *Washington Post*, 23 October 1973.

Hodson, Peregrine. 'Japanese Disband Aum Cult', *The Times* (London), 15 December 1995.

Hoffman, Bruce. 'Creatures of the Cold War: The JRA', *Jane's Intelligence Review*, vol. 9, no. 2 (February 1997).

Hoffman, Bruce. '"Holy Terror": The Implications of Terrorism Motivated by a Religious Imperative', *Studies in Conflict and Terrorism*, vol. 18, no. 4 (Winter 1995).

Hoffman, Bruce. 'Jewish Terrorist Activities and the British Government in Palestine 1939 to 1947'. Unpublished D.Phil. thesis, Oxford University, 1986.

Hoffman, Bruce. 'Low-intensity Conflict: Terrorism and Guerrilla Warfare in the Coming Decades', in Lawrence Howard (ed.), *Terrorism: Roots, Impact, Responses*. New York, Praeger, 1992.

Hoffman, Bruce. 'Recent Trends and Future Prospects of Iranian Sponsored International Terrorism', in Yonah Alexander (ed.), *Middle Eastern Terrorism: Current Threats and Future Prospects*. New York and Toronto, G. K. Hall, 1994.

Hoffman, Bruce. *Recent Trends and Future Prospects of Terrorism in the*

United States. R-3618. Santa Monica, CA, RAND Corporation, April 1986.

Hoffman, Bruce. 'Right-wing Terrorism in Europe', *Conflict*, vol. 5, no. 3 (Fall 1984).

Hoffman, Bruce. 'Right-wing Terrorism in Europe since 1980', *Orbis*, vol. 28, no. 1 (Spring 1984).

Hoffman, Bruce. *Right-wing Terrorism in Germany.* Research Report no. 13. London, Institute of Jewish Affairs, December 1986.

Hoffman, Bruce. 'Right-wing Terrorism in the United States', *Violence, Aggression, Terrorism Journal*, vol. 1, no. 1 (Winter 1987).

Hoffman, Bruce. *Terrorism in the United States and the Potential Threat to Nuclear Facilities.* R-3351-DOE. Santa Monica, CA, RAND Corporation, January 1986.

Hoffman, Bruce. 'The Bombing of the King David Hotel', *Midstream*, vol. 29, no. 7 (August/September 1983).

Hoffman, Bruce. 'The Contrasting Ethical Foundations of Terrorism in the 1980s', *Terrorism and Political Violence*, vol. 1, no. 3 (July 1989).

Hoffman, Bruce. 'The Jewish Defense League', *Terrorism, Violence and Insurgency Journal*, vol. 5, no. 1 (Summer 1984).

Hoffman, Bruce and Hoffman, Donna Kim. 'Chronology of International Terrorism 1995', *Terrorism and Political Violence*, vol. 8, no. 3 (Autumn 1996).

Hoffman, David. 'Reports Renew Suspicions of Iran, Syria Bomb Link', *Washington Post*, 26 April 1992.

Hoge, James W. 'The Media and Terrorism', in Abraham Miller (ed.), *Terrorism: The Media and the Law.* New York, Transnational, 1982.

Holmes, Steven A. 'US Charges 12 in Arizona Plot to Blow Up Government Office', *New York Times*, 2 July 1996.

Horne, Alistair. *A Savage War of Peace: Algeria 1954–1962.* Harmondsworth, Penguin, 1977.

Hurwitz, Harry. *Menachem Begin.* Johannesburg, Jewish Herald, 1977.

Hyams, Edward. *Terrorists and Terrorism.* New York, St Martin's Press, 1974.

Ibrahim, Youssef M. 'Muslim Edicts Take on New Force', *New York Times*, 12 February 1995.

Iglarsh, Harvey J. 'Fear of Flying: Its Economic Costs' *Terrorism*, vol. 10, no. 1 (Winter 1987).

'In our Pages: 100, 75 and 50 Years Ago – 1947: Zionists' Suicide',

International Herald Tribune (Paris), 22 April 1997.

'Inside the Red Brigades', *Newsweek* (New York), 15 May 1978.

Institute for Palestine Studies, International Studies Section. *Who is Menachem Begin? A Documentary Sketch*. Beirut, Institute for Palestine Studies, 1977.

'Interview with ASALA', *Panorama Magazine* (Milan), 1 September 1980.

'IRA: The Libyan Connection', *The Economist* (London), 31 March 1990.

'IRA Bomb-making Guide on Internet', *Sunday Times* (London), 9 February 1997.

Islamic Group in Egypt. 'Statement on US Sentencing of Sheikh Rahman', 19 January 1996.

'Israelis Discover Mass Murder Plot', *Sunday Times* (London), 26 November 1995.

Ivianksi, Zeev. 'Fathers and Sons: A Study of Jewish Involvement in the Revolutionary Movement and Terrorism in Tsarist Russia', *Terrorism and Political Violence*, vol. 1, no. 2 (April 1989).

Ivianski, Zeev. 'Sources of Inspiration for Revolutionary Terrorism: The Bakunin–Nechayev Alliance', *Conflict Quarterly*, vol. 8, no. 3 (Summer 1988).

Iwanski, Len. 'All 16 Remaining Freemen Surrender Peacefully', Associated Press, 14 June 1996.

Iyad, Abu with Rouleau, Eric (trans. Linda Butler Koseoglu). *My Home, My Land: A Narrative of the Palestinian Struggle*. New York, Times Books, 1981.

Jaber, Hala. *Hezbollah: Born with a Vengeance*. New York, Columbia University Press, 1997.

'Jail Term of Jewish Terrorist Reduced', *Jerusalem Post* (international edition), 12 October 1985.

Jamieson, Alison. *The Heart Attacked: Terrorism and Conflict in the Italian State*. London and New York, Marion Boyars, 1989.

Jamieson, Alison. *Terrorism*. Hove, E. Sussex, Wayland, 1991.

Janke, Peter. *Guerrilla and Terrorist Organisations: A World Directory and Bibliography*. New York, Macmillan, 1983.

Janofsky, Michael. 'For Aryan Congress Stridency and Scrutiny', *New York Times*, 23 July 1995.

Janofsky, Michael. 'One Man's Journey from Academia to Extremism', *New York Times*, 5 July 1995.

Jehl, Douglas. 'Iran Tells the Europeans That It Doesn't Back Terrorism', *New York Times*, 8 March 1996.

Jenkins, Brian Michael. 'International Terrorism: A New Mode of Conflict', in David Carlton and Carlo Schaerf (eds), *International Terrorism and World Security*. London, Croom Helm, 1975.

Jenkins, Brian Michael. *International Terrorism: The Other World War*. R-3302-AF. Santa Monica, CA, RAND Corporation, November 1985.

Jenkins, Brian Michael. *New Modes of Conflict*. R-3009-DNA. Santa Monica, CA, RAND Corporation, June 1983.

Jenkins, Brian Michael. *The Likelihood of Nuclear Terrorism*. P-7119. Santa Monica, CA, RAND Corporation, July 1985.

Jenkins, Brian Michael. *The Psychological Implications of Media-covered Terrorism*. P-6627. Santa Monica, CA, RAND Corporation, June 1981.

Jenkins, Brian Michael. *The Study of Terrorism: Definitional Problems*. P-6563. Santa Monica, CA, RAND Corporation, December 1980.

Jenkins, Brian Michael. *Will Terrorists Go Nuclear?*. P-5541. Santa Monica, CA, RAND Corporation, November 1975.

Johnston, David. 'Bomber is Called Killer Who is not on a Political Mission', *New York Times*, 6 November 1995.

Joll, James. *Europe since 1870: An International History*. New York, Harper & Row, 1973.

Joll, James. *The Anarchists*. Boston and Toronto, Little, Brown, 1964.

Jureidini, Paul A. *Case Studies in Insurgency and Revolutionary Warfare, Algeria 1954–1962*. Washington, DC, The American University, 1963.

Juergensmeyer, Mark. 'Terror Mandated by God', *Terrorism and Political Violence*, vol. 9, no. 2 (Summer 1997).

Juergensmeyer, Mark. *The New Cold War? Religious Nationalism Confronts the Secular State*. Berkeley, CA, University of California Press, 1993.

Juergensmeyer, Mark. 'The Worldwide Rise of Religious Nationalism', *Journal of International Affairs*, vol. 50, no. 1 (Summer 1996).

Juergensmeyer, Mark (ed.), *Violence and the Sacred in the Modern World*. London, Frank Cass, 1992.

Kahane, Rabbi Meir. *Never Again! A Program for Survival*. Los Angeles, Nash Publishing, 1971.

Kahane, Rabbi Meir. *They Must Go*. New York, Grosset & Dunlap, 1981.

Kaplan, David E. and Marshall, Andrew. *The Cult at the End of the World: The Incredible Story of Aum*. London, Hutchinson, 1996.

Kaplan, Jeffrey. 'Right-wing Violence in North America', *Terrorism and Political Violence*, vol. 7, no. 1 (Spring 1995).

Kedward, Roderick. *The Anarchists: The Men Who Shocked an Era*. London, BPC Unit 25, 1971.

Kellen, Konrad. *On Terrorists and Terrorism*. N-1942-RC. Santa Monica, CA, RAND Corporation, December 1982.

Kelly, George Armstrong. *Lost Soldiers: The French Army and Empire in Crisis, 1947–1962*. Cambridge, MA, MIT Press, 1965.

Kelsey, Tim. 'The Oklahoma Suspect Awaits Day of Reckoning', *Sunday Times* (London), 21 April 1996.

Kempe, Frederick. 'Deadly Survivors: The Cold War is over but Leftist Terrorists in Germany Fight On', *Wall Street Journal*, 27 December 1991.

Kenworthy, Tom. 'Peaceful End Sought to Siege of Montana "Freemen"', *Washington Post*, 30 March 1996.

Keppel, Gilles. *The Revenge of God: The Resurgence of Islam, Christianity and Judaism in the Modern World*. Cambridge, Polity Press, 1995.

Khaled, Leila. *My People Shall Live: The Autobiography of a Revolutionary*. London, Hodder & Stoughton, 1973.

'Khaled Tribute', *The Times* (London), 3 September 1997.

Khomeini, Imam (trans. Hamid Algar). *Islam and Revolution*. London, KPI, 1981.

Kifner, John. 'A Son of Israel: Rabin's Assassin', *New York Times*, 19 November 1995.

Kifner, John. 'Antiterrorism Law Used in Poison Smuggling Case', *New York Times*, 23 December 1995.

Kifner, John. 'Israelis Investigate Far Right: May Crack Down on Speech', *New York Times*, 8 November 1995.

Kifner, John. 'Man Arrested in Poison Case Kills Himself in Jail Cell', *New York Times*, 24 December 1995.

Kifner, John. 'Zeal of Rabin's Assassin Linked to Rabbis of the Religious Right', *New York Times*, 12 November 1995.

King, Peter H. 'Guru Revels in Revelation of a "Paradise" Defiled', *Los Angeles Times*, 22 September 1985.

Kingston, Shane. 'Terrorism, the Media, and the Northern Ireland Conflict', *Studies in Conflict and Terrorism*, vol. 18, no. 3 (July–September 1995).

Kitson, Frank. *Low-intensity Operations*. London, Faber, 1971.

Klanwatch, a Project of the Southern Poverty Law Center. *Intelligence Report* (Montgomery, AL), nos 84, 85 (November 1996, Winter 1997).

Knapp, Wilfrid. *A History of War and Peace 1939–1965*. London, Royal Institute of International Affairs and Oxford University Press, 1967.

Koust, Hal (ed.). *Cyprus, 1946–1968*. New York, Facts on File, 1970.

Kramer, Martin. 'Sacrifice and Fratricide in Shiite Lebanon', in Mark Juergensmeyer (ed.), *Violence and the Sacred in the Modern World*. London, Frank Cass, 1992.

Kristof, Nicholas D. 'In Shrine of Japan Cult, Police find Laboratory', *New York Times*, 27 March 1995.

Kristof, Nicholas D. 'Japanese Cult Planned US Attack', *International Herald Tribune* (Paris), 24 March 1997.

Kristof, Nicholas D. with WuDunn, Sheryl. 'The Seer among the Blind: Japanese Sect Leader's Rise', *New York Times*, 26 March 1995.

Kupperman, Robert H. and Trend, Darrel. *Terrorism: Threat, Reality, Response*. Stanford, CA, Hoover Institution Press, 1979.

Kushner, Harvey W. 'Suicide Bombers: Business as Usual', *Studies in Conflict and Terrorism*, vol. 19, no. 4 (October–December 1996).

Ladd, Everett Carl. 'US Public and Somalia', *Christian Science Monitor* (Boston), 15 October 1993.

Lafore, Lawrence. *The Long Fuse: An Interpretation of the Origins of World War I*. London, Weidenfeld & Nicolson, 1966.

Lapping, Brian. *End of Empire*. New York, St Martin's Press, 1985.

Laqueur, Walter. *Guerrilla: A Historical and Critical Study*. Boston and Toronto, Little, Brown, 1976.

Laqueur, Walter. 'Reflections on Terrorism', *Foreign Affairs*, vol. 65, no. 1 (Fall 1986).

Laqueur, Walter. *Terrorism*. London, Weidenfeld & Nicolson, 1977.

Laqueur, Walter. *The Age of Terrorism*. Boston, Little, Brown, 1987.

Laqueur, Walter (ed.). *The Israel–Arab Reader: A Documentary History of the Middle East Conflict*. New York, Bantam, 1976.

Laqueur, Walter and Alexander, Yonah (eds). *The Terrorism Reader*. New York, Meridian, 1987.

Leventhal, Paul and Alexander, Yonah (eds). *Nuclear Terrorism: Defining the Threat*. Washington, DC, Pergamon-Brassey's, 1986.

Lewis, Bernard. *The Assassins: A Radical Sect in Islam*. London, Al Saqi Books, 1985.

Liddell Hart, B. H. *History of the Second World War*. New York, Paragon Books, 1979.

Long, David E. *The Anatomy of Terrorism*. New York, Free Press, 1990.

Love, Kennett. *Suez: The Twice-Fought War*. New York and Toronto, McGraw-Hill, 1969.

Luttwak, Edward and Horowitz, Dan. *The Making of the Israeli Army*. New York, Penguin, 1975.

'Luxor Attackers Sought Cleric's Release in US: Tourists Stream Home', *International Herald Tribune* (Paris), 19 November 1997.

McCartney, C. A. *The Habsburg Empire 1790–1918*. London, Weidenfeld & Nicolson, 1969.

MacDonald, Andrew. *The Turner Diaries*. Arlington, VA, The National Alliance/National Vanguard Books, 1985.

MacDonald, Eileen. *Shoot the Women First*. New York, Random House, 1991.

McDonald, Henry. 'How the BBC Dances to an IRA Tune', *Sunday Times* (London), 19 January 1997.

McFadden, Robert D. 'Mail Bomber Links an End to Killings to his Manifesto', *New York Times*, 30 June 1995.

Mcgee, Jim and Stassen-Berger, Rachel. '5th Suspect Arrested in Bombing', *Washington Post*, 26 March 1993.

McGuire, Maria. *To Take Arms: A Year in the Provisional IRA*. London, Macmillan, 1973.

McKittrick, David. *Despatches from Belfast*. Belfast, Blackstaff Press, 1989.

McKittrick, David. 'Voyage into Business of Terror', *Independent* (London), 12 January 1991.

McKnight, Gerald. *The Mind of The Terrorist*. London, Michael Joseph, 1974.

Maddox, Browne. 'Texan Militia at War with US', *The Times* (London), 22 February 1997.

Mandela, Nelson. *Long Walk to Freedom*. London, Abacus, 1994.

Marcus, Raine. 'Amir: I Wanted to Kill Rabin', *Jerusalem Post*, 8 March 1996.

Marighela, Carlos (trans. John Butt and Rosemary Sheed). *For the Liberation of Brazil.* Harmondsworth, Penguin, 1971.

Marlowe, Laura. 'A Fiery Cleric's Defense of Jihad', *Time* (New York), 15 January 1996.

Martin, David C. and Walcott, John. *Best Laid Plans: The Inside Story of America's War against Terrorism.* New York, Harper & Row, 1988.

Masker, Roy B. 'An All White Nation? – Why Not?', Aryan Nations, *Calling Our Nation*, no. 53, no date.

Melnachak, Joseph M. 'A Chronicle of Hate: A Brief History of the Radical Right in America', *Terrorism, Violence and Insurgency Report*, vol. 6, no. 4, no date.

Merkl, Peter H. 'Prologue', in Peter H. Merkl (ed.), *Political Violence and Terror.* Berkeley, CA, University of California Press, 1986.

Merzer, Martin. 'Justice for All in Israel?', *Miami Herald*, 17 May 1985.

Mikolus, Edward F. *Transnational Terrorism: A Chronology of Events, 1968–1979.* Westport, CT, Greenwood Press, 1980.

Mikolus, Edward F., Sandler, Todd and Murdock, Jean M. *International Terrorism in the 1980s: A Chronology of Events.* Ames, Iowa State University Press, 1989.

Miller, Abraham H. and Damask, Nicholas A. 'The Dual Myths of "Narco-terrorism": How Myths Drive Policy', *Terrorism and Political Violence*, vol. 8, no. 1 (Spring 1996).

Miller, Reuben. 'Game Theory and Hostage-taking Incidents: A Case Study of the Munich Olympics', *Conflict Quarterly*, vol. 10, no. 1 (Winter 1990).

Mills, C. Wright. *The Power Elite.* London and New York, Oxford University Press, 1956.

Mitchell, Alison. 'Fingerprint Evidence Grows in World Trade Center Blast', *New York Times*, 20 May 1993.

Monroe, Elizabeth. 'Mr Bevin's "Arab Policy"', in Albert Hourani (ed.), St Antony's Papers no. 11: *Middle Eastern Affairs No. 2.* London, Chatto & Windus, 1961.

Mooradian, Moorad. 'Terrorists Speak: Interviews with ASALA Members', unpublished paper, no date.

Morris, Benny. *Israel's Border Wars 1949–1956: Arab Infiltration, Israeli Retaliation, and the Countdown to the Suez War.* Oxford, Clarendon Press, 1993.

Morris, Benny. *The Birth of the Palestinian Refugee Problem, 1947–1949.*

Cambridge, Cambridge University Press, 1987.

Mumcu, Ugur. *Papa-Mafya-Agca*. Ankara, Tekin Yayinevi, 1984.

National Archives and Record Service, United States Office of Strategic Services. RG 226 OSS R&A Report no. 2612, 'The Objectives and Activities of the Irgun Zvai Leumi', 13 October 1944; OSS Report XL 18461, 'Biographical Information – Menachem Begin', 11 September 1945.

National Police Agency. 'Aum Shinrikyo: An Alarming Report on the Terrorist Group's Organization and Activities', *Shoten* (Tokyo), no. 252 (1995).

Netanyahu, Benjamin (ed.). *Terrorism: How The West Can Win*. New York, Avon, 1986.

Neuhauser, Peter. 'The Mind of a German Terrorist', *Encounter*, vol. 51, no. 3 (September 1978).

Niv, David. *Ma'archot Ha-Irgun Ha-Zvai Ha-Leumi* (*Battle for Freedom: The Irgun Zvai Leumi*), vol. 3. Tel Aviv, Klausner Institute, 1975.

North Atlantic Assembly Papers, Sub-Committee on Terrorism. *Terrorism*. Brussels, International Secretariat, January 1989.

Norton, Graham. 'The Terrorist and the Traveller: A Gulf Aftermath Assessment', *The World Today* (London), May 1991.

Notes from the International Seminar on Terrorism and the Mass Media held in Sicily, 3–5 April 1981.

Nundy, Julian. 'Wounded Jackal Defends Record of Family Values', *Independent* (London), 31 August 1994.

O'Ballance, Edgar. *Arab Guerrilla Power*. London, Faber, 1974.

Office of the Coordinator for Counterterrorism. *Patterns of Global Terrorism 1996*. Publication 10433. Washington, DC, US Department of State, April 1997.

Okawa, Shoichi. 'Aum Shinrikyo', at http://www.guardian.co.uk/cults/a-z-cults/a_cults.html.

Onis, Juan de. 'Guerrilla Unit Attacks Cairo Proposal', *New York Times*, 21 June 1973.

'Outrage Not a Reason for Inaction', *Manchester Guardian, International Edition*, 21 October 1984.

Oxford English Dictionary, Compact Edition. Oxford, Oxford University Press, 1971.

Pallister, David. 'Provos Seek to "Play Havoc with British Nerves and Lifestyle"', *Guardian* (London), 31 July 1990.

Palmer, A. W. *A Dictionary of Modern History*. Harmondsworth, Penguin, 1962.

Palmer, R. R. *The Age of the Democratic Revolution*, vol. 2: *The Struggle*. Princeton, NJ, Princeton University Press, 1970.

Palmer, R. R. *The World of the French Revolution*. New York, Harper Torchbooks, 1971.

Palmer, R. R. *Twelve Who Ruled: The Year of the Terror in the French Revolution*. Princeton, NJ, Princeton University Press, 1973.

Pappe, Ilan. *The Making of the Arab–Israeli Conflict, 1947–1951*. London and New York, I. B. Tauris, 1994.

Parry, Albert. *Terrorism: From Robespierre to Arafat*. New York, Vanguard, 1976.

Parry, Richard Lloyd. 'Sect's Poisons "Could Kill 4.2m"', *Independent on Sunday* (London), 26 March 1995.

Peci, Patrizio. *Io, l'infame* (*I, the Scoundrel*). Milan, Arnoldo Mondadori, 1983.

Phillips, John and Prentice, Eve-Ann. 'Tehran Opponent is Shot Dead in Rome', *The Times* (London), 17 March 1994.

'Photoflash Bomb Threat to the Public', *The Scotsman* (Edinburgh), 16 March 1994.

Plate, Thomas and Tuohy, William. 'Los Angeles Times Interview: John Major – Even Under Fire, Britain's Prime Minister Holds His Own', *Los Angeles Times*, 20 June 1993.

Pluchinksy, Dennis. 'Western Europe's Red Terrorists: The Fighting Communist Organizations', in Yonah Alexander and Dennis Pluchinsky, *Europe's Red Terrorists: The Fighting Communist Organizations*. London, Frank Cass, 1992.

Pollack, Andrew. 'Earlier Victims' Horrors Revived', *New York Times*, 22 March 1995.

Pollack, Andrew. 'Japanese Police Say They Found Germ-War Material at Cult Site', *New York Times*, 29 March 1995.

Pollack, Andrew. 'Japanese Sect May Struggle to Get By Without its Leader', *New York Times*, 17 May 1995.

Potter, William C. 'Before the Deluge? Assessing the Threat of Nuclear Leakage from the Post-Soviet States', *Arms Control Today*, October 1995.

'Public Support Adams Talks', *Sunday Times* (London), 18 February 1996.

Purver, Ron. 'Chemical Terrorism in Japan'. Unpublished paper by the

Canadian Security Intelligence Service, Ottawa, Canada, June 1995.

Quandt, William B. 'Political and Military Dimensions of Contemporary Palestinian Nationalism', in William B. Quandt, Fuad Jabber and Ann Moseley Lesch, *The Politics of Palestinian Nationalism*. Berkeley, CA, University of California Press, 1974.

'RAF Philosophy', in *The German Guerrilla: Terror, Reaction, and Resistance*. Sanday, Orkney, Cienfuegos Press, no date.

Randal, Jonathan C. 'Guerrillas Fear Trade-off of Interests', *Washington Post*, 12 October 1973.

Randolph, Eleanor. 'Networks Turn Eye on Themselves', *Washington Post*, 30 June 1985.

Raines, Howell. 'With Latest Bomb, IRA Injures its Own Cause', *New York Times*, 15 November 1987.

Ranstorp, Magnus. *Hizb'allah in Lebanon: The Politics of the Western Hostage Crisis*. Basingstoke and London, Macmillan, 1997.

Rapoport, David C. 'Editorial: The Media and Terrorism; Implications of the Unabomber Case', *Terrorism and Political Violence*, vol. 8, no. 1 (Spring 1996).

Rapoport, David C. 'Fear and Trembling: Terrorism in Three Religious Traditions', *American Political Science Review*, vol. 78, no. 3 (September 1984).

Rapoport, David. 'Terrorism', in Mary Hawkesworth and Maurice Kogan (eds), *Routledge Encyclopedia of Government and Politics*, vol. 2. London, Routledge, 1992.

Rapoport, David C. 'The International World as Some Terrorists Have Seen It: A Look at a Century of Memoirs', *Journal of Strategic Studies*, vol. 10, no. 4 (December 1987).

Rapoport, David. 'The Politics of Atrocity', in Yonah Alexander and Seymour Maxwell Finger (eds), *Terrorism: Interdisciplinary Perspectives*. New York, John Jay Press, 1977.

Raufer, Xavier. 'Gray Areas: A New Security Threat', *Political Warfare*, no. 19 (Spring 1992).

Ravitch, Norman. 'The Armenian Massacre', *Encounter*, vol. 57, no. 6 (December 1981).

Reuters. 'Aum Cult Gas Cache', *International Herald Tribune* (Paris), 13 December 1996.

Reuters. 'Tokyo Cult Leader Said to Have Made Gas Confession', *The Times* (London), 5 October 1995.

Reuters. '$2 Million Reward for Death of Rushdie Repeated by Iran', *New York Times*, 18 June 1992.

Rhodes, Tom. 'Federal US Faces War with "Army of God"', *The Times* (London), 7 April 1997.

Rhodes, Tom. 'Sanctions on Iran "a Failure"', *The Times* (London), 13 October 1995.

Ridgeway, James. 'Arms and the Men: Are Far Right Militia Cells Using Robbery to Fund Their Cause?', *Village Voice* (New York), 9 May 1995.

Roberts, Brad (ed.). *Terrorism with Chemical and Biological Weapons: Calibrating Risks and Responses*. Alexandria, VA, Chemical and Biological Arms Control Institute, 1997.

Rose, David. 'Devices Reveal IRA Know-how', *Guardian* (London), 18 May 1990.

Ross, Loretta J. 'Anti-abortionists and White Supremacists Make Common Cause', *The Progressive* (New York), October 1994.

Ross, Loretta J. 'Using the Bible to Justify Killing', *Baltimore Sun*, 8 August 1994.

Rowan, Roy. 'Pan Am 103: Why Did They Die?', *Time* (New York), 27 April 1992.

Rubin, Jeffrey Z. and Friedland, Nehemia. 'Theater of Terror', *Psychology Today*, vol. 20, no. 3 (March 1986).

Sanan, Guy R. 'Olympic Security 1972–1996: Threat, Response, and International Cooperation'. Unpublished Ph.D. thesis, St Andrews University, 1997.

'Satanic Verses Publisher is Shot in Oslo Suburb', *The Times* (London), 12 October 1993.

Sayle, Murray. 'Martyrdom Complex', *New Yorker*, 13 May 1996.

Schbley, Ayla H. 'Religious Terrorists: What They Aren't Going to Tell Us', *Terrorism*, vol. 13, no. 3 (Summer 1990).

Schere, Peter. 'RAF Concentrates on New Target Spectrum', *Die Welt*, 18 December 1991.

Schiff, Zeev and Rothstein, Raphael. *Fedayeen: The Story of the Palestinian Guerrillas*. London, Valentine, Mitchell, 1972.

Schiller, David Th. 'From a National to an International Response', in H. H. Tucker (ed.), *Combating the Terrorists: Democratic Responses to Political Violence*. New York and Oxford, Facts on File, 1988.

Schmemann, Serge. 'Palestinian Believed to be Bombing Mastermind is Killed', *New York Times*, 6 January 1997.

Schmemann, Serge. 'Police Say Rabin Killer Led Sect that Laid Plans to Attack Arabs', *New York Times*, 11 November 1995.

Schmid, Alex P. *Political Terrorism: A Research Guide*. New Brunswick, NJ: Transaction Books, 1984.

Schmid, A. P. 'Terrorism and the Media: The Ethics of Publicity', *Terrorism and Political Violence*, vol. 1, no. 4 (October 1989).

Schmid, Alex P. and de Graaf, Janny. *Violence as Communication: Insurgent Terrorism and the Western News Media*. London and Beverly Hills, CA, Sage, 1982.

Schmid, Alex P., Jongman, Albert J. et al. *Political Terrorism: A New Guide to Actors, Authors, Concepts, Data Bases, Theories, and Literature*. New Brunswick, NJ, Transaction Books, 1988.

Schmidt, William E. 'Protestant Gunmen Are Stepping Up the Violence in Northern Ireland', *New York Times*, 29 October 1991.

Schneider, Keith. 'Fearing a Conspiracy, Some Heed a Call to Arms', *New York Times*, 14 November 1994.

Schoenberg, Harris O. *A Mandate for Terror: The United Nations and the PLO*. New York, Shapolsky Books, 1989.

Schorr, Daniel. 'The Encouragement of Violence', in Benjamin Netanyahu (ed.), *Terrorism: How The West Can Win*. New York, Avon, 1986.

Schwarz, Benjamin C. *Casualties, Public Opinion and US Military Intervention: Implications for US Regional Deterrence Strategies*. MR-431-A/AF. Santa Monica, CA, RAND Corporation, 1994.

Seale, Patrick. *Abu Nidal: A Gun for Hire*. New York, Random House, 1992.

Segev, Tom. *1949: The First Israelis*. New York, Free Press, 1986.

Seufert, Michael. 'Dissension among the Terrorists: Killing People is Wrong', *Encounter*, vol. 51, no. 3 (September 1978).

Shales, Tom. 'America's Ordeal by Television', *Washington Post*, 2 July 1985.

Shamir, Itzhak. *Summing Up: An Autobiography*. London, Weidenfeld & Nicolson, 1994.

Shannon, Don. 'Gromyko Indirectly Supports US in UN Drive against Terrorism', *Los Angeles Times*, 27 September 1972.

Sheridan, Michael. 'Iranians "Landing Gulf Infiltrators"', *Independent* (London), 8 April 1995.

Shirer, William L. *The Rise and Fall of the Third Reich: A History of Nazi*

Germany. New York, Simon & Schuster, 1960.

Sick, Gary. 'The Political Underpinnings of Terrorism', in Charles W. Kegley Jr (ed.), *International Terrorism: Characteristics, Causes, Controls*. New York, St Martin's Press, 1990.

Simon, Jeffrey D. *Terrorists and the Potential Use of Biological Weapons: A Discussion of Possibilities*. R–3771–AFMIC. Santa Monica, CA, RAND Corporation, December 1989.

Skierka, Volker. 'Modern Nazis: A More Devious Version', *Stuttgarter Zeitung* (Stuttgart), 12 December 1981.

Smith, Colin. *Carlos: Portrait of a Terrorist*. London, André Deutsch, 1976.

Smith, Dan, et al. *The State of War and Peace Atlas*. London, Penguin, 1997.

Smith, Michael. 'IRA Use of Radar Guns in Bombings Described', *Daily Telegraph* (London), 20 May 1991.

Smith, M. L. R. *Fighting For Ireland? The Military Strategy of the Irish Republican Movement*. London and New York, Routledge, 1995.

Sofaer, Abraham D. 'Terrorism and the Law', *Foreign Affairs*, vol. 64, no. 5 (Summer 1986).

Sofer, Sasson. *Begin: An Anatomy of Leadership*. Oxford, Blackwell, 1988.

Southern Poverty Law Center. *False Patriots: The Threat of Antigovernment Extremists*. Montgomery, AL, Southern Poverty Law Center, 1996.

'Spokane Robbery Document', The Public Good home page at http://www.nwcitizen.com/publicgood.

Sprinzak, Ehud. 'Fundamentalism, Terrorism, and Democracy: The Case of the Gush Emunim Underground', Wilson Center Occasional Paper no. 4. Washington, DC, Smithsonian Institution, 1986.

Sprinzak, Ehud. *The Ascendance of Israel's Radical Right*. New York and Oxford, Oxford University Press, 1991.

Sprinzak, Ehud. 'Violence and Catastrophe in the Theology of Rabbi Meir Kahane: The Ideologization of Mimetic Desire', in Mark Juergensmeyer (ed.), *Violence and the Sacred in the Modern World*. London, Frank Cass, 1992.

Squiteri, Tom. 'US: Return Our Men', *USA Today* (Washington, DC), 6 October 1993.

Stafford, David. *From Anarchism to Reformism: A Study of the Political Activities of Paul Brousse within the First International and the French Socialist Movement 1870–90*. Toronto, University of Toronto Press, 1971.

Stanley, Alessandra. 'Russians Shut Down Branch of Japanese Sect', *New York Times*, 30 March 1995.

Steinhoff, Patricia G. 'Portrait of a Terrorist: An Interview with Kozo Okamoto', *Asian Survey*, vol. 16, no. 9 (September 1976).

Sterling, Claire. *The Terror Network: The Secret War of International Terrorism*. New York, Holt, Rinehart & Winston, 1981.

Sterling, Claire. *The Time of the Assassins*. New York, Holt, Rinehart & Winston, 1983.

Stern, Susan. *With the Weathermen: The Personal Journey of a Revolutionary Woman*. Garden City, NY, Doubleday, 1975.

Straus, Julius. 'Serb Attack on British Base', *Daily Telegraph* (London), 18 July 1997.

Sullivan, Kevin. 'Japan Cult Survives While Guru Is Jailed', *Washington Post*, 28 September 1997.

Sunday Times Insight Team. *Siege! Princes Gate, London, April 30–May 5 1980*. London, Hamlyn, 1980.

Suro, Robert. 'FBI Walks a Fine Line in its Pursuit of Militia Extremists', *International Herald Tribune* (Paris), 12 November 1996.

Sverdlik, Alan. 'Georgia Militia Members Who Conspired against ATF Found Guilty', *Washington Post*, 7 November 1996.

Swain, Jon. 'Algeria Dies Death of a Thousand Cuts', *Sunday Times* (London), 6 April 1997.

'Syria to Remain on US Terrorism List', *The Times* (London), 17 February 1992.

'Syrian Clampdown on Fatah Guerrillas Told', *Los Angeles Times*, 20 September 1973.

Tabor, James D. 'Bible Scholar Claims Branch Davidian Disaster Could Have Been Avoided', *Religious Studies News* (Society of Biblical Literature/the American Academy of Religion), September 1995.

Tabor, James D. and Gallagher, Eugene V. *Why Waco? Cults and the Battle for Religious Freedom in America*. Berkeley, CA, University of California Press, 1995.

Taheri, Amir. *Holy Terror: The Inside Story of Islamic Terrorism.* London, Sphere, 1987.

Talbott, John. *The War without a Name: France in Algeria 1954–1962.* London and Boston, Faber, 1980.

Talmadge, Eric. 'Tokyo Police Avert Cyanide Catastrophe', *Sunday Times* (London), 7 May 1995.

Tavin, Eli and Alexander, Yonah (eds), *Psychological Warfare and Propaganda: Irgun Documentation.* Wilmington, DE, Scholarly Resources, 1982.

Taylor, Peter. *Provos: The IRA and Sinn Fein.* London, Bloomsbury, 1997.

Taylor, Peter. *States of Terror: Democracy and Political Violence.* London, Penguin, 1993.

Tendler, Stewart. 'A Crude and Lethal Weapon to Thwart the Security Forces', *The Times* (London), 8 February 1991.

Terrorist Research and Analytical Center, National Security Division, Federal Bureau of Investigation. *Terrorism in the United States 1995.* Washington, DC, US Department of Justice, 1996.

'Terrorists Killed by their Own Devices', *Independent* (London), 20 February 1996.

'The Arab Terrorists', *New York Times*, 18 December 1973.

'The Palestinians of the 1990s', *Foreign Report* (London), no. 2202, 2 April 1992.

'30 More Slain By "Terrorists" Near Algiers', *International Herald Tribune* (Paris), 15 April 1997.

'39 Killed in Jerusalem Headquarters', *The Times* (London), 23 July 1946.

This is Aryan Nations (no date), at http://stormfront.org/aryan_nations/platform.html.

Thomas, Jo. 'Militias Hold a Congress, and Not a Gun is Seen', *New York Times*, 1 November 1994.

Thomson, David. *Europe since Napoleon.* Harmondsworth, Penguin, 1978.

Thornton, Mary. 'Oregon Guru Disavows Rajneeshism, Vows to Survive Investigations', *Washington Post*, 20 October 1985.

Toloyan, Kachig. 'Martyrdom as Legitimacy: Terrorism, Religion and Symbolic Appropriation in the Armenian Diaspora', in Paul Wilkinson and A. M. Stewart (eds) *Contemporary Research on Terrorism.* Aberdeen, Aberdeen University Press, 1987.

Townley, Roderick and Weisman, John. 'The Reporters' Rat Race – Danger, Chaos and Rumors of Payoffs', *TV Guide* (Radnor, PA), 21 September 1985.

Traynor, Ian. '"Iran Terrorism" Trail Comes to Climax', *Guardian* (London), 10 April 1997.

Trinquier, Roger (trans. Daniel Lee). *Modern Warfare: A French View of Counterinsurgency*. New York and London, Praeger, 1964.

Tucker, Jonathan B. 'Chemical/Biological Terrorism: Coping with a New Threat', *Politics and the Life Sciences*, vol. 15, no. 2 (1997).

Tucker, Robert C. *Stalin in Power: The Revolution from Above, 1928–1941*. New York and London, W.W. Norton, 1990.

Twersky, David. 'The Risks of Cozying Up to Syria', *New York Times*, 28 July 1992.

'Unabomber Manifesto', *Washington Post*, 19 September 1995.

United States Department of Defense. *Terrorist Group Profiles*. Washington, DC, US Government Printing Office, 1988.

United States Department of Defense Commission on the Beirut International Airport (BIA) Terrorist Act of October 23, 1983, no date.

United States Department of State. *Libya's Continuing Responsibility for Terrorism*. Washington, DC, US Department of State, November 1991.

United States Department of State, Bureau of Public Affairs, Office of Public Communication. *Fact Sheet: Additional Information on the Bombing of Pan Am Flight 103*. Washington, DC, US Department of State, 15 November 1991.

United States Departments of the Army and the Air Force. *Military Operations in Low Intensity Conflict*, Field Manual 100-20/Air Force Pamphlet 3-20. Washington, DC, Headquarters, Departments of the Army and the Air Force, 1990.

United States District Court for the District of Columbia. *United States of America* v. *Abdel Basset Ali al-Megrahi and Lamen Khalifa Fhimah*, 14 November 1991.

Utley, Garrick. 'The Shrinking of Foreign News', *Foreign Affairs*, vol. 76, no. 2 (March/April 1997).

Van Biema, David. 'Prophet of Poison', *Time* (New York), 3 April 1995.

Verhovek, Sam Howe. 'Showdown at the "Republic of Texas" Ends in Surrender', *International Herald Tribune* (Paris), 5 May 1997.

Vick, Karl. 'Man Gets Hands on Bubonic Plague Germs, But That's No Crime', *Washington Post*, 30 December 1995.

Vidal-Naquet, P. *Torture: Cancer of Democracy – France and Algeria, 1954–1962*. London, Penguin, 1963.

'Views on National Security', *National Journal* (Washington, DC), 25 October 1986.

Wackerngel, Christoph. 'Transcript of a Talk by Christoph Wackerngel', 14 September 1995, unpublished.

Wald, Matthew L. 'Figuring What it Would Take to Take Down a Tower', *New York Times*, 21 March 1993.

Walker, Christopher. 'Arabs are Convinced Car Crash was a Murder Plot', *The Times* (London), 4 September 1997.

Walker, Christopher. 'Bahrain Arrests 29 in Move to foil "Iranian-backed Coup"', *The Times* (London), 4 June 1996.

Walker, Christopher. 'Hamas Calls for Uprising by Muslim Worshippers', *The Times* (London), 4 October 1996.

Walker, Christopher. 'Hamas Urges Suicide Attack', *The Times* (London), 11 January 1997.

Walker, Christopher. 'Handing Back of "Biblical Land" Angers Militants', *The Times* (London), 6 November 1995.

Walker, Christopher. 'Intelligence Experts See Hand of Tehran in Oslo Shooting', *The Times* (London), 13 October 1993.

Walker, Christopher. '£194m "Missing" as Arafat Seeks Aid from Britain', *The Times* (London), 14 July 1997.

Walker, Christopher. 'Palestinian "Was Duped into Being Suicide Bomber"', *The Times* (London), 27 March 1997.

Walker, Christopher. 'Rabin Killer "Trained by Shin Bet"', *The Times* (London), 21 November 1995.

Walker, Christopher. 'Rabin Killing "Part of Plot Backed by West Bank Rabbis"', *The Times* (London), 10 November 1995.

Walker, Tom. 'British Base is Attacked as Bosnia Serbs Vow Revenge', *The Times* (London), 18 July 1997.

Walsh, James. 'Shoko Asahara: The Making of a Messiah', *Time* (New York), 3 April 1995.

Walsh, Mary Williams. 'German Court Finds Iran's Leaders Ordered Slayings', *Los Angeles Times*, 11 April 1997.

Wardlaw, Grant. 'Linkages Between the Illegal Drugs Traffic and Terrorism', *Conflict Quarterly*, vol. 8, no. 3 (Summer 1988).

Wardlaw, Grant. *Political Terrorism: Theory, Tactics, and Counter-measures.* Cambridge, Cambridge University Press, 1990.

Watt, Nicholas. 'IRA's "Russian Roulette" Detonator', *The Times* (London), 16 March 1994.

'Wedded to Death in a Blaze of Glory – Profile: The Suicide Bomber', *Sunday Times* (London), 10 March 1996.

Welch, Craig. 'Three Guilty in Valley Bombings', *The Spokesman-Review* (Spokane, WA), 24 July 1997.

'What is Terrorism?', *The Economist* (London), 2 March 1996.

Wheeler-Bennett, John. *Munich: Prologue to Tragedy.* London, Macmillan, 1948.

White, Robert W. 'The Irish Republican Army: An Assessment of Sectarianism', *Terrorism and Political Violence*, vol. 9, no. 1 (Spring 1997).

Whymant, Robert. 'Cult Planned Gas Raids on America', *The Times* (London), 29 March 1997.

Wilkinson, Paul. 'Terrorism', in Michael Foley (ed.), *Ideas that Shape Politics.* Manchester, Manchester University Press, 1994.

Wilkinson, Paul. 'Terrorism and Propaganda', in Yonah Alexander and Richard Latter (eds), *Terrorism and the Media.* McLean, VA, Brassey's, 1990.

Wilkinson, Paul. *The New Fascists.* London, Grant McIntyre, 1981.

Williams, Phil and Woessner, Paul N. 'Nuclear Material Trafficking: An Interim Assessment', *Transnational Organized Crime*, vol. 1, no. 2 (Summer 1995).

Woessner, Paul N. 'Recent Developments: Chronology of Nuclear Smuggling Incidents, July 1991–May 1995', *Transnational Organized Crime*, vol. 1, no. 2 (Summer 1995).

Wolf, John B. 'The Palestine Resistance Movement', *Current History*, vol. 60 (1971).

Woodcock, George (ed.). *The Anarchist Reader.* Glasgow, Fontana, 1977.

Wright, Robin. 'Iran Supplies Lebanese Radicals Through Syria, US Aides Say', *International Herald Tribune* (Paris), 14–15 December 1996.

Wright, Robin and Ostrow, Ronald J. 'Pan Am 103 Clue Leads to Libyans', *Los Angeles Times*, 24 June 1991.

Wurth-Hough, Sandra. 'Network News Coverage of Terrorism: The Early Years', *Terrorism*, vol. 6, no. 3 (Summer 1983).

'Yeltsin Adds to Kremlin Power', *Foreign Report* (London), no. 2365, 24 August 1995.

Yisra'eli, Rafi. 'Islamikaze: Suicide Terrorism Examined', *Nativ* (Tel Aviv), January–April 1997.

Zaar, Isaac. *Rescue and Liberation: America's Part in the Birth of Israel.* New York, Bloch, 1954.

Zonis, Marvin and Brumberg, Daniel. 'Behind Beirut Terrorism', *New York Times*, 8 October 1984.

Zuckerman, Mortimer B. 'Playing the Terrorists' Game', *US News and World Report* (Washington, DC), 9 June 1986.

Index